The Harriman
Stock Market Almanac
2017

Stephen Eckett

HARRIMAN HOUSE LTD
18 College Street
Petersfield
Hampshire
GU31 4AD
GREAT BRITAIN
Tel: +44 (0)1730 233870
Email: enquiries@harriman-house.com
Website: www.harriman-house.com

First edition published in Great Britain in 2004
This 10th edition published in 2016
Copyright © Harriman House Ltd

The right of Stephen Eckett to be identified as the author has been asserted in accordance with the Copyright, Design and Patents Act 1988.

Print ISBN: 978-0-85719-565-4
eBook ISBN: 978-0-85719-566-1

British Library Cataloguing in Publication Data
A CIP catalogue record for this book can be obtained from the British Library.

CONTENTS

2. Statistics

3. Reference

INTRODUCTION

Welcome to the 2017 edition of the *Harriman Stock Market Almanac*, where we celebrate the Efficient Market Theory – that is, the failure of the theory. This book could alternatively be titled *The Inefficient Almanac*, as it revels in the trends and anomalies of the market that the Efficient Market Theory says shouldn't exist.

New in the 2017 Almanac

The *Almanac* comprises updates on strategies and studies covered in previous editions and also new research.

New research

New strategies and studies in this *Almanac* include:

- **World's Simplest Trading System** – a simple trading system based on moving averages with an impressive performance. [page 16]
- **Construction Sector 4M Strategy** – exploits a seasonality anomaly of the construction sector. [page 88]
- **Sell In May Sector Strategy** – how to exploit the Sell in May effect with sectors. [page 84]
- **Turn Of The Month Strategy** – all the market's gains occur in the six days around the turn of the month. [page 28]
- **January Barometer** – do the first five trading days of the year predict the full year? [page 106]
- **Odd/even weeks** – the market in odd weeks greatly outperforms that in even weeks. [page 36]
- **Santa Rally** – does a Santa Rally exist for shares and, if so, when does it start? [page 100]
- **Santa Rally Portfolio** – the ten stocks that have had positive returns over the two-week Santa Rally period for every year since 2007. [page 102]
- **Sell in May and come back... when?** – if you sell in May when should you come back into the market? [page 52]
- **Up/down ratio** – analysis of the correlation between the ratio of up/down days in a year and the overall annual return of the FTSE 100. [page 18]
- **Solar eclipse** – do solar eclipses affect stock markets? [page 70]
- **Dividend payment calendar** – analysis of when FTSE 100 companies pay dividends throughout the year. [page 42]
- **FOMC cycle** – the equity premium in the US and worldwide is earned entirely in weeks 0, 2, 4 and 6 of the FOMC cycle. [page 50]
- **The psychology of drawdowns** – why investors may almost always feel a prevailing sense of loss. [page 74]
- **Do European stocks follow the US on a daily basis?** – analysis of the correlation of the EuroSTOXX and S&P 500. [page 48]
- **Fed rate cycle** – analysis of the relationship between the Fed rate cycle and UK equities. [page 62]
- **UK bank rate since 1694** – analysis of Bank of England base rate changes over the last three centuries. [page 80]

Updated strategies and studies

The 2017 *Almanac* updates some of the studies of seasonality trends and anomalies that have featured in previous editions, including:

- **Bounceback Portfolio** – a strategy that buys the worst performing shares in a year, and then sells them after three months into the new year; the strategy had its best year ever, last year. [page 104]

- **Strong/weak shares by month** – analysis of FTSE 350 shares reveals those that have performed consistently strongly or weakly for each month for the past ten years. Some shares have risen (or fallen) in a specific month for every year since 2007. [page 10]

- **FTSE 100/S&P 500 Switching Strategy** – the strong/weak months for the FTSE 100 relative to the S&P 500 are identified; and a strategy of switching between the two markets is found that produces twice the returns of either market individually. [page 44]

- **Low-High Share Price Strategy** – a portfolio of the 20 lowest priced shares in the market has outperformed a portfolio of the 20 highest priced shares by an average 38.7 percentage points each year since 2002. [page 22]

- **Quarterly Sector Strategy** – the strongest/weakest sectors for each quarter are identified; and the Quarterly Sector Strategy continues to beat the market. [page 56]

- **Quarterly Sector Momentum Strategy** – a portfolio comprising the best FTSE 350 sector from the previous quarter, and rebalanced quarterly, outperforms the FTSE All-Share by an average of 2.0 percentage points per month. A variant – buying the worst sector of the previous quarter – has performed even better. [page 94]

- **FTSE 100/250 Monthly Switching Strategy** – on the back of research into the comparative monthly performance of the two indices, a strategy of switching between the two markets is found that greatly outperforms either index individually. [page 8]

- **Day of the Week Strategy** – a strategy exploiting the day of the week anomaly that outperforms the FTSE 100. [page 34]

- **Monthly Share Momentum Strategy** – a monthly rebalanced momentum portfolio of FTSE 100 stocks beats the market. [page 92]

- **Sell in May** – this extraordinary effect remains as strong as ever: since 1982 the market in the winter months has outperformed the market in the summer months by an average 8.8 percentage points annually; in the year since the last edition of the *Almanac* the outperformance was 4.2 percentage points. [page 40]

- **Sell Rosh Hashanah, Buy Yom Kippur** – the US equity market tends to be weak between these two Jewish holidays; is there a similar effect in the UK market? [page 78]

- **Market seasonality (day/week/month)** – December is still the strongest month in the year for the stock market, while September is the weakest. Analysis is also updated for the weekly and daily performance of the market (Sinclair Numbers). [page 176]

- **Day of the week performance** – Thursday is the new weakest day of the week (Monday used to be), and the strongest day is now Friday. [page 114]

- **Turn of the month** – the market tends to be strong a few days either side of the turn of the month, and especially strong on the first trading day of the new month (except December). [page 125]

- **FTSE 100 quarterly reviews** – share prices tend to rise immediately before a company joins the FTSE 100 and are then flat or fall back. Before a company leaves the index share prices tend to fall and then rise after the exit. [page 26 and page 86]

- **FTSE 100 and FTSE 250** – the trend continues for the FTSE 100 to greatly underperform the mid-cap index in January and February, and outperform it in September and October. [page 118]

- **FOMC announcements** – how do US and UK equities react in the days around the periodic announcements of the policy statement of the Federal Open Market Committee? [page 76]

- **Gold** – does the price of gold exhibit monthly seasonality? [page 24]

- **Holidays and the market** – in recent years the market has been significantly strong on the days immediately before and after holidays, and weak four days before and three days after holidays. [page 32]

- **Trading around Christmas** – how do share prices behave in the days around Christmas? [page 96]

- **The January Effect** – analysis suggests that performance in January is inversely proportional to company size (i.e. small companies like January). [page 6]

- **Very large one-day market falls** – analysis of the behaviour of the FTSE 100 for very large one-day falls. [page 116]

- **Lunar calendar and the stock market** – do the phases of the moon affect the stock market? [page 66]

- **Super Bowl** – does the Super Bowl Indicator accurately predict the market for the year? [page 14]

- **Market momentum grid** – a reference grid is presented giving the historic tendency of the market to rise (fall) following a series of consecutive daily/weekly/monthly/yearly rises (falls). As before, it is found that trends become more established the longer they last, and the market displays greater momentum for longer frequencies. [page 132]

- **UK and US markets** – the correlation between the UK and US markets has been increasing since the 1950s, and in the years since 2010 has been stronger than ever. [page 164]

- **Correlation of UK equity markets** – if you want to diversify away from FTSE 100, how effective will it be investing in the FTSE 250, FTSE Small Cap, FTSE Fledgling or FTSE AIM All-Share indices? [page 4]

- **Seasonality of GBPUSD** – what are the strong/weak months for GB sterling against the US dollar? [page 68]

- **The average market month** – by taking the average performance of the market on each day of a month it is possible to create a chart of the average performance of the market for that month, and then to combine the 12 charts to produce a chart of the average behaviour of the market in all months. [page 141]

- **The average market year** – the performance and volatility of the market for an average year. [page 140]

- **The market's decennial cycle** – can analysis of the market's performance in the equivalent years of decades reveal any pattern of behaviour? [page 167]

- **Ultimate Death Cross** – has the 50-month moving average crossed down through the 200-month moving average? [page 169]

- **The Long-Term Formula** – the formula that describes the long-term trend of the stock market and gives a forecast for the FTSE 100 in December 2040. [page 166]

In addition to the above, analysis is also updated for the standard *Almanac* features such as: comparative performance of UK equity indices, company ranking by financial and price behaviour criteria, price history profile of the FTSE All-Share, sector profiles of the FTSE 100 and FTSE 250 indices, and annual performance of sectors.

The Diary

The core of the *Almanac* is the 52-week diary. The diary lists financial and other events for each week in 2017 that are of interest to investors and traders. An explanation of the information on the diary pages can be found a few pages further on in the section 'Understanding the Diary Pages'.

Month summary pages

The diary section has a summary page for each month highlighting the major investment and seasonality characteristics of the month (e.g. the summary page for January is on page 2). Some features of these summary pages are:

1. There are two charts on each summary page: the left chart plots the performance of the FTSE 100 in the month for every year since 1980, and the right chart plots the average performance chart for the month. This latter chart is calculated by taking the average performance of the market on each day in the month since 1985. This is used to create a cumulative performance chart for the month to give an idea of the average behaviour of the market over the 22 or so trading days of that month.

2. In the summary table (in the lower half of the page), the first row gives the three main statistics that describe the historic performance of the market in that month: the average return, the percentage of months where the return is positive and the month's ranking among the 12 months.

3. In the summary table, the second row displays the FTSE 350 sectors that have been historically strong (and weak) that month.

4. In the summary table, the third row displays the FTSE 350 shares that have been historically strong (and weak) that month.

Quantitative analysis

It should be noted that the type of quantitative analysis contained in the *Almanac* in some cases is best exploited by an arbitraged or hedged strategy, not a simple long position. For example, to exploit the strong shares identified for January, it would be best to short the FTSE 100, or the weak shares, against a portfolio of long positions in the strong shares.

Outlook for 2017

What can we look forward to in 2017?

There are no big political or sporting events planned for 2017. And, while last year we had the excitement of the International Year of Pulses, the best the UN can come up with for 2017 is the International Year of Sustainable Tourism for Development – all very worthy. Cosmically, the big event of 2017 will be the solar eclipse in the US, the first such since 1979. Eclipses of the sun may become more frequent in future years due to the amount of space debris floating around up there; 2017 is set to see the launch of numerous space probes and satellites, such as the Transiting Exoplanet Survey Satellite.

In 2017 we'll be celebrating the 15th anniversary of the launch of the Euro (you can decide how loosely the term "celebrate" should be used), the 100th anniversary of the start of the Russian Revolution, and the 500th anniversary of European merchants arriving in Guangzhou to trade officially with Chinese merchants for the first time.

And the stock market in 2017?

The track record of the 7th year in the decennial cycle since 1800 is not great. However, since 1950 the 7th year of decades has been on quite a run: the average annual return has been 16% and the last time the market fell in a 7th year was 1957. The guidance from the centennial cycle is mixed; in 1717, 1817 and 1917 the respective annual returns for the UK market were +18%, +5% and -11%.

In the Chinese calendar it will be the year of the rooster. This is not a good sign for stocks. Since 1950, rooster years are the only Chinese zodiac years that have had a negative average annual return (of -4%). By contrast, the Long-Term Formula forecasts a long-term trend FTSE 100 level of 11,726 by December 2017.

So, "mixed" is probably the best that can be said regarding market forecasts for 2017.

Instead of quantitative analysis, perhaps we should turn to the arts for a lead on the year.

In 1987, the science fiction film *The Running Man* was released, with the storyline:

> "In the year 2017, the world economy has collapsed. The great freedoms of the United States are no longer, as the once great nation has sealed off its borders and become a militarized police state, censoring all film, art, literature, and communications."

But that's just a film obviously; nothing like real life.

Anyway, in the film a character (played by a future governor of California) says "I'll be back", which the *Almanac* will also be, in 2018.

Stephen Eckett

PREFACE

Definition

> *almanac (noun): an annual calendar containing dates and statistical information*

What the book covers

Topics in the *Almanac* cover a wide spectrum. The Diary includes essential information on upcoming company announcements and financial events such as exchange holidays and economic releases. There are also the results of a unique seasonality analysis of historic market performance for every day and week of the year – our Sinclair Numbers. Besides this, there is information of a lighter nature, such as important social and sporting occasions and notable events in history.

Accompanying the Diary is a series of articles about the stock market. Many of these focus on seasonality effects, such as the likely performance of the market in each month, momentum effects, and the difference in market performance between summer and winter.

In short, the *Almanac* is a unique work, providing everything from essential reference information to informative and entertaining articles on the stock market.

How the book is structured

The *Almanac* has three major parts:

1. **Diary**: A week-per-page format. (See the next page for a detailed explanation of the layout of each Diary page.) Opposite each Diary page is a short strategy-oriented article about the stock market – these articles reveal trading patterns and anomalies that investors and traders can exploit to make money.

2. **Statistics**: This section contains further seasonality and anomaly studies as well as background information on the profile characteristics of the market – the indices, sectors and companies.

3. **Reference**: This section includes background information about UK and international stock indices, and a look at the original constituents of the FT 30 of 1935 and the FTSE 100 of 1984.

Supporting website

The website supporting this book can be found at stockmarketalmanac.co.uk.

Follow the Almanac on Twitter

@UKAlmanac

Free eBook

Every owner of a physical copy of **The Harriman Stock Market Almanac 2017** can download the eBook edition for free direct from us at Harriman House, in a format that can be read on any eReader, tablet or smartphone.

Simply head to **ebooks.harriman-house.com/almanac2017** to get your copy now.

UNDERSTANDING THE DIARY PAGES

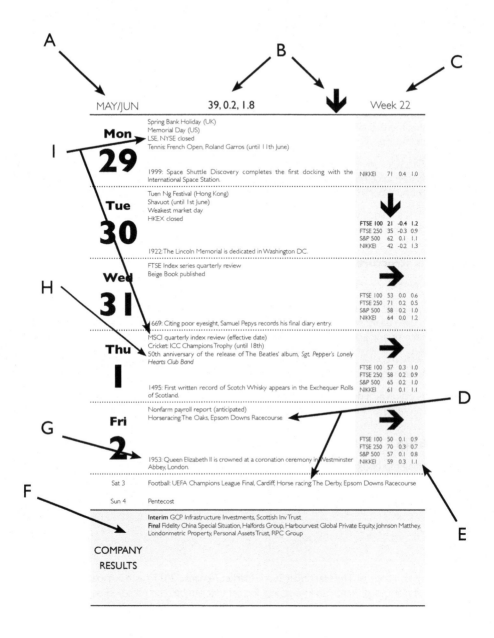

A

B

C

MAY/JUN   39, 0.2, 1.8   ⬇   Week 22

I

Mon
29

Spring Bank Holiday (UK)
Memorial Day (US)
LSE, NYSE closed
Tennis: French Open, Roland Garros (until 11th June)

1999: Space Shuttle Discovery completes the first docking with the International Space Station.

NIKKEI   71   0.4   1.0

Tue
30

Tuen Ng Festival (Hong Kong)
Shavuot (until 1st June)
Weakest market day
HKEX closed

⬇

FTSE 100   21   -0.4   1.2
FTSE 250   35   -0.3   0.9
S&P 500   62   0.1   1.1
NIKKEI   42   -0.2   1.3

1922: The Lincoln Memorial is dedicated in Washington DC.

H

Wed
31

FTSE Index series quarterly review
Beige Book published

➡

FTSE 100   53   0.0   0.6
FTSE 250   71   0.2   0.5
S&P 500   58   0.2   1.0
NIKKEI   64   0.0   1.2

1669: Citing poor eyesight, Samuel Pepys records his final diary entry.

Thu
1

MSCI quarterly index review (effective date)
Cricket: ICC Champions Trophy (until 18th)
50th anniversary of the release of The Beatles' album, *Sgt. Pepper's Lonely Hearts Club Band*

➡

FTSE 100   57   0.3   1.0
FTSE 250   58   0.2   0.9
S&P 500   65   0.2   1.0
NIKKEI   61   0.1   1.1

1495: First written record of Scotch Whisky appears in the Exchequer Rolls of Scotland.

D

G

Fri
2

Nonfarm payroll report (anticipated)
Horseracing: The Oaks, Epsom Downs Racecourse

➡

FTSE 100   50   0.1   0.9
FTSE 250   70   0.3   0.7
S&P 500   57   0.1   0.8
NIKKEI   59   0.3   1.1

1953: Queen Elizabeth II is crowned at a coronation ceremony in Westminster Abbey, London.

E

Sat 3   Football: UEFA Champions League Final, Cardiff; Horse racing: The Derby, Epsom Downs Racecourse

Sun 4   Pentecost

F

Interim GCP Infrastructure Investments, Scottish Inv Trust
Final Fidelity China Special Situation, Halfords Group, Harbourvest Global Private Equity, Johnson Matthey, Londonmetric Property, Personal Assets Trust, RPC Group

COMPANY
RESULTS

A – Diary page title

The Diary is a week-per-page format.

B – Weekly performance analysis (Sinclair Numbers)

These figures and arrow show the results of analysis of the historic performance of the FTSE 100 during this week. The ten best and ten worst performing weeks are marked by the figures being in bold. [See the next page for further explanation and the Statistics section (page 176) for more detail and full data tables of FTSE 100 daily, weekly and monthly Sinclair Numbers.]

C – Week number

The week number within the year.

D – Social and sporting events

Notable social and sporting events, including public holidays, are included each day.

E – Daily performance analysis (Sinclair Numbers)

These figures and arrow show the results of analysis of the historic performance of four world stock indices on this calendar day. The ten best and ten worst performing days for the FTSE 100 are marked by the figures being in bold. [See the next page for further explanation and the Statistics section (page 176) for more detail and full data tables of FTSE 100 daily, weekly and monthly Sinclair Numbers.]

F – Likely company announcements

A list of companies expected to announce interim or final results during the week. The list is provisional, using the date of announcements in previous years as a guide.

G – On this day

Events that happened on this calendar date in history.

H – Anniversaries

Significant anniversaries that occur on this day.

I – Financial events

Indicates days of financial and economic significance. For example, exchange holidays and important economic releases.

Abbreviations

FOMC – Federal Open Market Committee

MPC – Monetary Policy Committee

SINCLAIR NUMBERS – SEASONALITY ANALYSIS

Sinclair Numbers

Beginning on page 176 you will find an explanation of the *Almanac*'s unique analysis of the historic performance of four stock indices – the FTSE 100, FTSE 250, S&P 500 and Nikkei 225 – for each day, week and month of the year.

In order to understand the Diary pages, it will also be useful to read the following explanation of the Sinclair arrows.

Sinclair arrows

The figures for Positive (%) are displayed for the respective days and weeks on the Diary pages employing the following arrow symbols:

Daily arrows

↑ the Positive (%) is over 75%

↗ the Positive (%) is 64% to 75%

→ the Positive (%) is 43% to 63%

↘ the Positive (%) is 31% to 42%

↓ the Positive (%) is under 31%

Weekly arrows

↑ the Positive (%) is over 70%

↗ the Positive (%) is 60% to 69%

→ the Positive (%) is 50% to 59%

↘ the Positive (%) is 40% to 49%

↓ the Positive (%) is under 40%

The daily ranges were calculated on the following basis: the average Positive (%) for all days in the year is 53% and the standard deviation is 11. Adding two standard deviations to the average gives 75, adding one standard deviation gives 64, subtracting one standard deviation gives 42 and subtracting two standard deviations gives 31. The weekly ranges have been modified slightly from these figures so as to present the data with more variation.

The top ten days and weeks – with the highest Positive (%) – and the weakest ten days and weeks – with the lowest Positive (%) – are highlighted in bold.

See the Statistics section, beginning on page 176, for full data tables of FTSE 100 Sinclair Numbers.

I.
DIARY

JANUARY MARKET

Market performance this month

Since 1984, January has been a middle-ranking month for shares: the average monthly return has been 0.3% – ranking it eighth among months. However, as can be seen on the chart, much has changed since 2000. From that year, the January average return for the market has been -1.9% (placing it as the second worst month over the past 16 years).

Referring to the average month chart below, historically the euphoria of December (the strongest month of the year) carries over into the start of January as the market continues to climb for the first couple of days. But by around the fourth trading day the exhilaration is wearing off and the market then falls for the next two weeks – the second week of January has been the weakest week for the market in the whole year. Then, around the middle of the third week, the market has tended to rebound sharply.

The month is better for mid-cap and small-cap stocks. On average, since 2000, the FTSE 250 has outperformed the FTSE 100 by 1.7 percentage points in January – the best outperformance of all months. Small-caps do even better (known as the *January Effect* – see page 6), outperforming the FTSE 100 by an average 2.7 percentage points in the first month of the year.

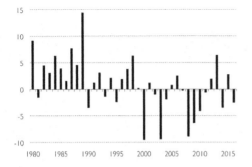
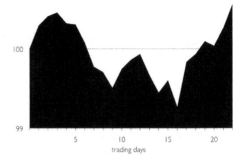

January summary

Market performance	Avg change (%): 0.3%		Positive (%): 56%	Ranking: 8th
Sector performance	*Strong* Construction & Materials, Electronic & Electrical Equipment, Equity Investment Instruments, Financial Services, General Industrials, Health Care Equipment & Services, Industrial Metals, Media, Software & Computer Services, Support Services		*Weak* Beverages, Food & Drug Retailers, Food Producers	
Share performance	*Strong* Paysafe Group [PAYS], JD Sports Fashion [JD.], Computacenter [CCC]		*Weak* FirstGroup [FGP], Vedanta Resources [VED], Antofagasta [ANTO]	
Main features	Small-cap stocks often outperform large-cap stocks in January (January Effect) The FTSE 250 is particularly strong relative to the FTSE 100 in this month FTSE 100 often underperforms the S&P 500 in January Strong month for silver First trading day average return: 0.29%; positive: 56% Last trading day average return: 0.21%; positive: 59% (year's 2nd strongest) 07 Jan: 10th weakest day of the year for shares 09 Jan: start of the weakest week of the year for shares 26 Jan: 4th strongest day of the year for shares			
Significant dates	01 Jan: LSE, NYSE, TSE, HKEX closed 06 Jan: US Nonfarm payroll report (anticipated) 16 Jan: Martin Luther King Day (US) – NYSE closed 18 Jan: Beige Book published 19 Jan: ECB Governing Council Meeting (monetary policy) 28 Feb: Chinese New Year (Year of the Rooster) 31 Jan: Two-day FOMC meeting starts Don't forget: the last date to file your 2015/16 tax return online is 31 January			

Mon
26

Boxing Day
LSE, NYSE, HKEX closed

1982: For the first time, *TIME* magazine's Man of the Year is given to a non-human: the personal computer.

NIKKEI	81	0.6	1.4

Tue
27

Christmas holiday
LSE, HKEX closed

1831: Charles Darwin embarks on his journey aboard the HMS Beagle, on which he will formulate the theory of evolution.

S&P 500	56	0.1	0.8
NIKKEI	59	0.2	0.8

Wed
28

1879: The central part of the Tay Rail Bridge in Dundee, Scotland, collapses, killing 75.

FTSE 100	62	0.2	0.5
FTSE 250	85	0.3	0.6
S&P 500	57	0.0	0.6
NIKKEI	55	-0.1	1.3

Thu
29

New Moon
9th strongest market day

1891: Thomas Edison patents the radio.

FTSE 100	77	0.5	1.1
FTSE 250	82	0.4	0.8
S&P 500	55	0.2	0.7
NIKKEI	68	0.2	0.5

Fri
30

1960: The farthing ceases to be legal tender in the UK.

FTSE 100	52	0.1	0.9
FTSE 250	64	0.2	0.6
S&P 500	61	0.2	0.7
NIKKEI	53	0.2	1.4

Sat 31   New Year's Eve

Sun 1   New Year's Day, 15th anniversary of the launch of the Euro

COMPANY
RESULTS

CORRELATION OF UK MARKETS

How much diversification away from the FTSE 100 do the other UK equity indices offer?

The charts on this page show the correlation of monthly returns between the FTSE 100 and five UK equity indices for the period 2000-2016.

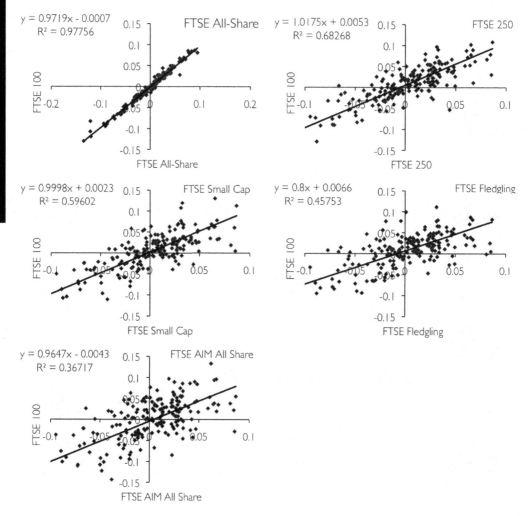

The table to the right summarises the R^2 values for the correlation between the FTSE 100 and five other UK equity indices. The higher the R^2 figure, the closer the correlation (R-Squared is a measure of correlation – visually, how close the points are to the line of best fit).

Firstly, and not surprisingly, we can observe that all the UK equity indices are correlated positively with the FTSE 100 (in other words, they all tend to rise and fall together). The FTSE All-Share has a very high correlation with the FTSE 100, which is because a very high proportion of the FTSE All-Share's capitalisation is composed of FTSE 100 stocks.

Index	R^2
FTSE All-Share	0.98
FTSE 250	0.68
FTSE Small Cap	0.60
FTSE Fledgling	0.46
FTSE AIM All-Share	0.37

The FTSE 250 of mid-cap stocks has a moderately high correlation with the FTSE 100.

Correlation begins to diminish significantly with the smaller cap indices; with the correlations of the FTSE Fledgling and FTSE AIM All-Share indices not particularly high. In other words, if you want to diversify the risk of the FTSE 100, these smaller indices are one place to look.

Mon

2

LSE, NYSE, TSE, HKEX closed

1882: The Standard Oil Trust agreement is completed, transferring 40 companies into the control of nine trustees led by John D. Rockefeller. This is the first example of a holding company.

Tue

3

TSE closed
Quadrantids Meteor Shower (until 4th)

FTSE 100	72	0.3	1.1
FTSE 250	71	0.4	1.0
S&P 500	49	0.2	1.1

1977: Apple Computer is incorporated.

Wed

4

50th anniversary of the release of The Doors' debut album, *The Doors*

FTSE 100	55	0.1	1.4
FTSE 250	70	0.4	1.0
S&P 500	54	0.0	1.2
NIKKEI	64	0.2	1.9

1999: The euro begins trading, at $1.1747. It hits a daily high of $1.1906.

Thu

5

FTSE 100	45	-0.1	1.0
FTSE 250	55	0.0	0.9
S&P 500	68	0.1	1.0
NIKKEI	41	-0.1	1.2

1914: The Ford Motor Company announces an eight-hour workday and a minimum wage of $5 a day.

Fri

6

Epiphany (Twelfth Night)
Nonfarm payroll report (anticipated)

FTSE 100	55	0.2	0.9
FTSE 250	78	0.3	0.6
S&P 500	58	0.1	0.8
NIKKEI	58	0.3	1.8

1914: Merrill Lynch is founded.

Sat 7

Sun 8

COMPANY
RESULTS

THE JANUARY EFFECT

In 1976, an academic paper[1] found that equally-weighted indices of all the stocks on the NYSE had significantly higher returns in January than in the other 11 months over the period 1904-1974. This indicated that small capitalisation stocks outperformed larger stocks in January. Over the following years many further papers were written confirming this finding. In 2006, a paper[2] tested this effect (now called the *January Effect*) on data from 1802 and found the effect was consistent up to the present time.

Does the January Effect work for UK stocks?

The following chart shows the cumulative performance from 1995 to 2016 of four stock indices in just the month of January. The four indices are:

1. FTSE 100

2. FTSE 250

3. FTSE Small Cap

4. FTSE Feldgling

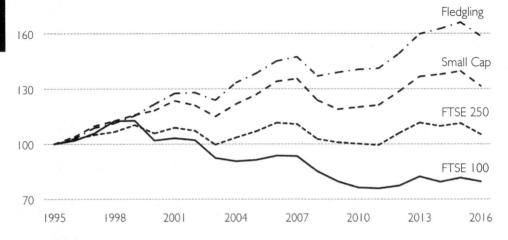

A portfolio investing in the FTSE 100 in just the Januaries since 1995 would have fallen 20.4% in value by 2016. By contrast, similar portfolios investing in the FTSE 250, Small Cap and Fledgling would have returned 5.2%, 31.4% and 58.5% respectively.

This suggests that not only does the January Effect hold for UK equities but also that, to a certain extent, performance in January is inversely proportional to company size (down to the level of FTSE Fledgling companies at least).

Other January Effects

In academic literature the term *January Effect* usually refers to the anomaly described above. It is occasionally used in another couple of cases as well:

1. The returns in January indicate the returns for the rest of the year. If January market returns are positive, then returns for the whole year will be positive (and vice versa). This is sometimes called the *January Predictor* or *January Barometer*. A variant of this effect has it that returns for the whole year can be predicted by the direction of the market in just the first five days of the year. [See page 106.]

2. In 1942, Sidney B. Wachtel wrote the paper 'Certain Observations on Seasonal Movements in Stock Prices', in which he proposed that stocks rose in January as investors began buying again after the year-end tax-induced sell-off.

1. Rozeff and Kinney, 'Capital market seasonality: The case of stock returns', *Journal of Financial Economics* 3 (1976), pp. 379-402.
2. M. Haug and M. Hirschey, 'The January effect', *Financial Analysts Journal* 62:5 (2006), pp. 78-88.

Mon

9

Coming of Age Day (Japan)
TSE closed

FTSE 100	41	-0.2	1.0
FTSE 250	45	-0.1	0.7
S&P 500	52	-0.1	1.0

1987: The Dow Jones closes above 2000 for the first time (2002.25).

Tue

10

FTSE 100	41	-0.1	0.8
FTSE 250	38	-0.1	0.7
S&P 500	56	0.1	0.8
NIKKEI	45	-0.6	1.4

1946: The first meeting of the United Nations, at Westminster Central Hall in London.

Wed

11

FTSE 100	36	-0.2	0.7
FTSE 250	62	0.0	0.6
S&P 500	60	0.0	0.8
NIKKEI	52	0.1	1.2

1569: The first recorded lottery is held in England.

Thu

12

Full Moon
MPC interest rate announcement at 12h00

FTSE 100	45	-0.3	0.7
FTSE 250	45	-0.1	0.7
S&P 500	52	-0.1	0.8
NIKKEI	47	-0.2	1.1

1967: Dr. James Bedford is the first person to be cryonically preserved with the intent of future resuscitation.

Fri

13

FTSE 100	43	-0.1	0.8
FTSE 250	57	0.0	0.7
S&P 500	42	-0.1	0.7
NIKKEI	50	-0.1	1.8

1928: RCA and General Electric install experimental televisions in three homes in New York. The sets display a 1.5 inch picture.

Sat 14

Sun 15

Interim Ashmore Group

COMPANY

RESULTS

THE FTSE 100/250 MONTHLY SWITCHING STRATEGY

Analysis of historic data shows that although the FTSE 250 has greatly outperformed the FTSE 100 in the medium and long term (since 2000 the FTSE 100 has fallen 2% compared with an increase of 175% for the FTSE 250), there are certain months for which the large-cap index on average outperforms the mid-cap index.

A previous edition of the *Almanac* presented a strategy that exploited this tendency; this page updates the performance of the strategy for the last year.

The following chart shows the average outperformance of the FTSE 100 over the FTSE 250 by month for the period 2000-2016. For example, on average the FTSE 100 has outperformed the FTSE 250 by -1.7. percentage points in January since year 2000.

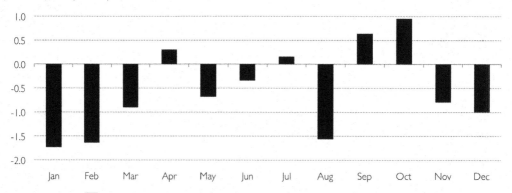

As can be seen, there are only two months, September and October, in which the FTSE 100 convincingly outperforms the FTSE 250.

The FTSE 100/FTSE 250 monthly switching strategy

The above results suggest a strategy of investing in the FTSE 250 for the year but switching into the FTSE 100 for just the two-month period September-October. In other words, the portfolio would be invested in the FTSE 250 from January to August, at the end of August it switches out of the FTSE 250 and into the FTSE 100 for two months, then back into the FTSE 250 until the end of August the following year.

The following chart shows the result of operating such a strategy from 2000. For comparison, the chart also includes the portfolio returns from continuous investments in the base FTSE 100 and FTSE 250. All the data series have been rebased to start at 100.

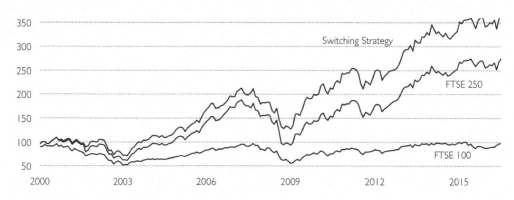

The result: from 2000 to 2016 the FTSE 100 portfolio would have grown -2%, the FTSE 250 portfolio would have risen 175%, and the FTSE 100/FTSE 250 monthly switching portfolio would have increased 267%.

Switching between the indices each year would have incurred transaction costs which have not been included here, but these would have been relatively negligible relative to the overall returns.

JANUARY

Mon
16

Martin Luther King, Jr. Day (US)
NYSE closed
Tennis: Australian Open, Melbourne (until 29th)

FTSE 100	57	0.2	0.9
FTSE 250	59	0.0	0.7
NIKKEI	43	0.0	2.1

1412: The Medici family is appointed official bankers of the Papacy.

Tue
17

World Economic Forum, Davos-Klosters (until 20th)

FTSE 100	59	0.2	0.8
FTSE 250	62	0.4	0.6
S&P 500	57	0.0	1.0
NIKKEI	52	0.2	1.4

1983: Britain's first breakfast news programme is launched on BBC1.

Wed
18

Beige Book published

FTSE 100	59	0.2	1.1
FTSE 250	67	0.2	0.7
S&P 500	59	0.1	0.6
NIKKEI	57	0.1	1.2

1644: Perplexed pilgrims in Boston report America's first UFO sighting.

Thu
19

ECB Governing Council meeting (monetary policy)

FTSE 100	45	-0.1	0.9
FTSE 250	59	0.3	1.0
S&P 500	52	0.0	0.6
NIKKEI	57	0.4	1.0

1906: William Kellogg founds his breakfast cereal company.

Fri
20

FTSE 100	35	-0.5	1.0
FTSE 250	39	-0.4	0.8
S&P 500	42	-0.3	1.0
NIKKEI	42	-0.5	1.4

1972: The UK Government has a majority of 21 in the House of Commons on signing of Treaty of Accession to the EEC.

Sat 21

Sun 22

Interim IG Group Holdings
Final Bankers Inv Trust, Unilever

COMPANY
RESULTS

MONTHLY SEASONALITY OF SHARES

Do individual shares display abnormal strength or weakness in particular months?

Shares that like February

The following table lists the five FTSE 350 shares with the best record of performance in February over the last ten years. For example, Hunting shares have seen an average return of 7.6% in the ten Februaries since 2007. And Weir Group shares have had positive returns in nine of the past ten Februaries.

Strong shares	TIDM	Avg Feb rtn (%)	Positive rtn
Hunting	HTG	7.6	10
Provident Financial	PFG	6.8	10
Anglo American	AAL	9.6	9
Croda International	CRDA	9.1	9
Weir Group	WEIR	7.4	9

An equally-weighted portfolio could be formed that comprised the above five shares. Such a portfolio would have outperformed the FTSE 350 every February over the past ten years. For example, in 2016 this *February Strong Portfolio* would have beaten the FTSE 350 by 18.9 percentage points in the month of February.

The following chart plots the cumulative performance of the February Strong Portfolio and the FTSE 350 for all Februaries since 2007 (with starting values rebased to 100).

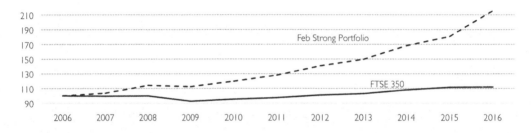

By 2016, a portfolio tracking the FTSE 350 would have had a value of 112, whereas the February Strong Portfolio would have had a value of 215. (Account has not been taken of dealing costs or cost of carry, but these would not have been significant relative to the scale of outperformance.)

Shares that dislike February

We can also identify those shares that have been historically weak in February (shown in the following table). For example, Vodafone shares have only seen positive returns in February in two of the past ten years.

Weak shares	TIDM	Avg Feb return (%)	Positive return
AstraZeneca	AZN	-4.1	2
Workspace Group	WKP	-3.8	3
Vectura Group	VEC	-3.4	2
Vodafone Group	VOD	-3.3	2
JPMorgan Indian Investment Trust	JII	-1.5	3

An interesting strategy might be to go long the February Strong Portfolio and go short the February Weak Portfolio (comprising the five shares in the above table).

Note: The results of such analysis of the strong/weak shares in respective months can be seen on the Month Summary pages throughout the Diary section of the *Almanac*.

Mon
23
1656: Blaise Pascal publishes the first of his Lettres provinciales.

FTSE 100	41	-0.3	0.8
FTSE 250	24	-0.3	0.6
S&P 500	63	0.1	0.7
NIKKEI	38	-0.3	1.7

Tue
24
1848: The New York Herald breaks news to the East Coast of the United States of the gold rush in California.

→

FTSE 100	59	0.4	1.2
FTSE 250	57	0.2	1.1
S&P 500	60	-0.1	1.0
NIKKEI	61	0.0	1.6

Burns Night

Wed
25
1879: The Bulgarian National Bank is founded.

FTSE 100	36	-0.2	0.7
FTSE 250	43	-0.1	0.6
S&P 500	57	0.0	0.7
NIKKEI	70	0.6	1.2

4th strongest market day

Thu
26
1995: Cadbury Schweppes takes over Dr. Pepper/Seven-Up.

↑

FTSE 100	**82**	**0.7**	**1.0**
FTSE 250	64	0.4	0.8
S&P 500	46	0.1	0.6
NIKKEI	48	0.2	1.2

Fri
27
1710: Czar Peter the Great sets the first Russian state budget.

→

FTSE 100	48	0.1	1.2
FTSE 250	52	0.1	1.0
S&P 500	51	0.1	0.9
NIKKEI	54	0.3	1.6

Sat 28 Chinese New Year (Year of the Rooster); New Moon

Sun 29

Interim NCC Group, PZ Cussons
Final Aberforth Smaller Companies Trust, Crest Nicholson Holdings, Safestore Holdings

COMPANY
RESULTS

FEBRUARY MARKET

Market performance this month

February is currently on something of a roll. Since 2009, the market has been up every year in February. This is a far better record than any other month of the year. And further, since 1994 the market has only seen significant negative returns in three years. Since 1984, the average return of the FTSE 100 in February has been 1.1%, with the month seeing positive returns in 63% of years. There's no obvious reason why the market has been so strong in recent years in this month; although one possible explanation might be that, also in recent years, shares have been weak in January and so they experience a bounceback rally in February.

With January, February is the best month for mid-cap stocks relative to large-caps. Since 2000, on average the FTSE 250 has outperformed the FTSE 100 by 1.6 percentage points in this month.

This is the busiest month for FTSE 100 results announcements – 36 companies announce their prelims in February (as do 55 FTSE 250 companies).

If you're running the Construction Sector 4M Strategy – see page 88 – it should be closed out at the end of this month.

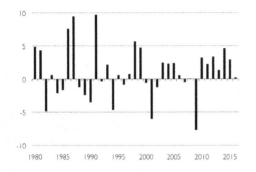
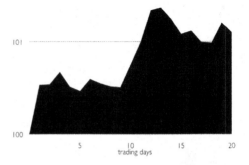

February summary

Market performance	Avg return: 1.1%		Positive: 63%	Ranking: 3rd
Sector performance	*Strong* Chemicals, Construction & Materials, General Retailers, Household Goods, Mining, Oil Equipment, Services & Distribution		*Weak* Electronic & Electrical Equipment, Financial Services, Fixed Line Telecommunications, Mobile Telecommunications, Technology Hardware & Equipment	
Share performance	*Strong* Hunting [HTG], Provident Financial [PFG], Anglo American [AAL]		*Weak* AstraZeneca [AZN], Workspace Group [WKP], Vectura Group [VEC]	
Main features	The FTSE 250 is particularly strong relative to the FTSE 100 in this month Busiest month for FTSE 250 preliminary results announcements GBPUSD historically weak this month Strong month for gold and silver First trading day average return: 0.53%; positive: 56% (year's 2nd strongest) Last trading day average return: -0.06%; positive: 44% (year's 2nd weakest) 13 Feb: start of the 5th strongest week of the year for shares 17 Feb: 6th strongest day of the year for shares Close out Construction Sector 4M Strategy			
Significant dates	02 Feb: MPC interest rate announcement at 12 noon 03 Feb: US Nonfarm payroll report (anticipated) 09 Feb: MSCI Quarterly Index Review announcement date 20 Feb: President's Day (US) – NYSE closed 28 Feb: Beige Book published			

Mon 30

Third day of Lunar New Year
HKEX closed

FTSE 100	52	0.2	1.0
FTSE 250	59	0.1	0.7
S&P 500	54	0.0	0.9
NIKKEI	54	-0.1	1.5

1934: In the US the Gold Reserve Act is passed, pegging the value of the dollar to gold.

Tue 31

Fourth day of Lunar New Year
HKEX closed; Two-day FOMC meeting starts
Deadline for online tax returns

FTSE 100	59	0.2	0.7
FTSE 250	57	0.2	0.6
S&P 500	62	0.3	0.8
NIKKEI	70	0.7	1.8

2010: *Avatar* becomes the first film to gross over $2 billion worldwide.

Wed 1

Imbolc
Vasant Panchami

FTSE 100	64	0.6	1.0
FTSE 250	86	0.8	0.9
S&P 500	60	0.1	0.8
NIKKEI	57	0.0	0.8

1849: Corn Laws are abolished in the United Kingdom.

Thu 2

MPC interest rate announcement at 12h00

FTSE 100	73	0.2	1.0
FTSE 250	77	0.2	1.0
S&P 500	63	0.1	0.8
NIKKEI	52	0.1	0.9

1998: The S&P 500 closes over 1000 for the first time.

Fri 3

Nonfarm payroll report (anticipated)

FTSE 100	48	0.3	1.2
FTSE 250	57	0.2	0.8
S&P 500	65	0.2	0.8
NIKKEI	33	-0.3	1.1

1959: Alaska becomes the 49th, and largest, American state.

Sat 4   Rugby: Six Nations (until 18th March)

Sun 5   American Football: Super Bowl LI, NRG Stadium, Houston

Interim Diageo, Rank Group, Renishaw, Sky
Final BP, Fisher (James) & Sons, GlaxoSmithKline, Ocado Group, St Modwen Properties

COMPANY
RESULTS

SUPER BOWL INDICATOR

On the Sunday just gone (5 February) was Super Bowl LI in Houston, Texas.

One of the most famous, and odd, market predictors in the US is the Super Bowl Indicator. This holds that if the Super Bowl is won by a team from the old National Football League the stock market will end the year higher than it began, and if a team from the old American Football League wins then the market will end lower.

Unlikely? Well, it certainly sounds far-fetched that a game of mutant rugby could affect the economy and stock market. However, in 1990 two academics published a paper[1] finding that the indicator was accurate 91% of the time.

And then in 2010 George Kester, a finance professor at Washington and Lee University, published a paper[2] with new research that found that the Super Bowl Indicator still worked (although its accuracy had fallen to 79%). Kester also calculated that a portfolio that switched between stocks and treasury bills governed by the Super Bowl Indicator would be worth twice that of a simple portfolio invested continuously in the S&P 500.

And the connection between American football and the UK stock market is…?

As the US and UK stock markets are so closely correlated, it might be interesting to see how the Super Bowl Indicator applies to the UK market.

The top chart to the right shows the annual percentage change of the FTSE All-Share since 1967 (when the Super Bowl started). For clarity, the Y-axis has been capped at +/- 40%, which truncates the bars for the years 1974 (-55%) and 1975 (+136%). The years for which the Super Bowl Indicator successfully predicted the direction of the market are indicated in the chart. Overall, the indicator was accurate in 74% of years (only slightly less than its accuracy rate in the US).

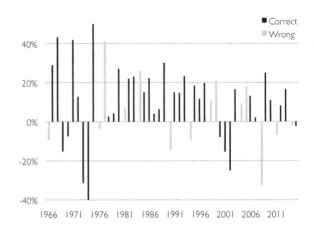

Market around the time of the Super Bowl

The bottom chart to the right shows market behaviour around the time of the Super Bowl; the bars represent the average daily change in the FTSE All-Share since 1967 for the three days before, and three days following, the Super Bowl.

The average change in the index for all days since 1967 is 0.03%; we can see therefore that the market is abnormally weak two days before a Super Bowl and abnormally strong one day before it.

Note: file the Super Bowl Indicator under "spurious stock market predictors" with the comment "correlation is not causation".

But you never know…

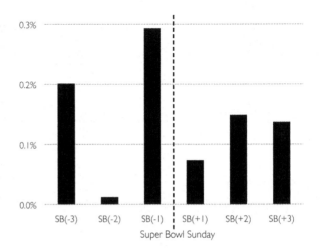

1. T. M. Krueger and W. F. Kennedy, 'An Examination of the Super Bowl Stock Market Predictor', *The Journal of Finance* 45:2 (1990), pp. 691-697.
2. G. W. Kester, 'What Happened to the Super Bowl Stock Market Predictor?', *The Journal of Investing* 19:1 (2010), pp. 82-87.

Mon
6

2005: Tony Blair marks 2838 days in his post at Number 10, making him Labour's longest-serving PM.

FTSE 100	61	0.0	0.9
FTSE 250	59	0.3	0.7
S&P 500	54	0.1	0.8
NIKKEI	63	0.1	1.4

Tue
7

1992: The European Union is formed.

FTSE 100	55	0.0	1.1
FTSE 250	57	0.1	0.8
S&P 500	50	0.1	0.6
NIKKEI	57	0.2	0.9

Wed
8

1971: The NASDAQ stock market index debuts.

FTSE 100	55	0.1	1.1
FTSE 250	62	-0.1	1.1
S&P 500	47	-0.1	0.8
NIKKEI	61	0.0	1.1

MSCI quarterly index review (announcement date)

Thu
9

1979: Britain's first £1m football transfer deal is signed when Trevor Francis joins Nottingham Forest.

FTSE 100	50	0.0	0.7
FTSE 250	55	0.1	0.8
S&P 500	40	-0.3	0.9
NIKKEI	35	-0.4	1.4

Fri
10

1987: The first trading day of the newly privatised British Airways.

FTSE 100	39	-0.2	0.8
FTSE 250	48	-0.1	0.8
S&P 500	51	0.0	1.0
NIKKEI	57	0.0	0.9

Sat 11   National Foundation Day (Japan); Full Moon; Penumbral Lunar Eclipse

Sun 12

Interim Dunelm Group, Redrow
Final ARM Holdings, AstraZeneca, Beazley, Randgold Resources, Royal Dutch Shell, Smith & Nephew, Smurfit Kappa Group, Tullow Oil

COMPANY
RESULTS

15

WORLD'S SIMPLEST TRADING SYSTEM

Here's the system. At the end of every month:

- If the index is *above* its 10-month simple moving average, the portfolio is 100% in the market for the following month.

- If the index is *below* its 10-month simple moving average, the portfolio is 100% in cash for the following month.

And that's it.

So, if we take the FTSE 100 as an example, if at the end of a month the FTSE 100 is above its 10-month simple moving average then either:

- The portfolio moves into the market, e.g. by buying FTSE 100 ETFs (these will be the easiest instrument for most investors, but equally futures, CFDs or spread bets could be used), or

- Nothing needs to be done if the portfolio is already in the market.

Conversely, if at the end of a month the FTSE 100 is below its 10-month simple moving average then the portfolio sells the ETFs and moves 100% to cash. If it is already in cash then nothing is done.

If this strategy had been applied to the FTSE 100, then starting with a value of 100 in 1995, it would have a value of 269 today (against a buy-and-hold the market value of 199).

But why the 10-month moving average? Perhaps the strategy would be even better with a different moving average parameter?

The following chart shows the result of back-testing the strategy with each month parameter from 4 to 16. The measure used here is the Sharpe Ratio, which combines returns with volatility to provide a comparative measure of profitability per unit of risk incurred. The ratio's purpose is to answer questions of the form: is the profitability of a strategy justified by the risk incurred, compared to another strategy? The higher the Sharpe Ratio the more attractive the strategy.

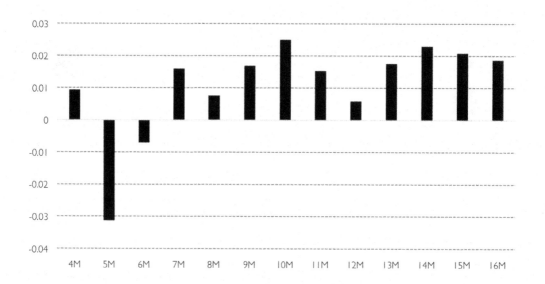

As can be seen, the 10-month moving average is indeed the best parameter over the test period.

NB. OK, it's possible that this isn't absolutely the simplest trading system imaginable, but apart from buy and hold it is unlikely there are many systems much simpler than this one!

Mon
13

1997: The DJIA closes above 7000 for the first time.

FTSE 100	65	0.2	0.5
FTSE 250	68	0.1	0.5
S&P 500	57	0.2	0.7
NIKKEI	42	-0.3	1.0

St Valentine's Day

Tue
14

1946: The world's first computer, ENIAC, is unveiled at the University of Philadelphia. It has 18,000 vacuum tubes and fills a room measuring 30ft by 60ft.

FTSE 100	45	0.0	0.7
FTSE 250	62	0.2	0.6
S&P 500	45	0.0	0.7
NIKKEI	70	0.2	1.4

Nirvana Day
150th anniversary of the first performance of Johann Strauss II's waltz *The Blue Danube*, in Vienna

Wed
15

1971: Decimal currency is launched in the UK.

FTSE 100	64	0.1	0.8
FTSE 250	62	0.1	0.7
S&P 500	54	0.1	0.6
NIKKEI	57	0.4	1.8

Thu
16

600: Pope Gregory the Great decrees saying "God bless You" is the correct response to a sneeze.

FTSE 100	45	0.2	1.0
FTSE 250	55	0.0	0.6
S&P 500	44	-0.1	0.8
NIKKEI	43	0.0	0.6

6th strongest market day
20th anniversary of the LSE flotation of Centrica

Fri
17

2003: The London Congestion Charge scheme begins.

FTSE 100	**78**	**0.5**	**1.0**
FTSE 250	83	0.4	1.0
S&P 500	45	-0.1	1.0
NIKKEI	71	0.4	1.1

Sat 18

Sun 19

Interim City of London Inv Trust, Hargreaves Lansdown
Final Acacia Mining, Anglo American, BGEO Group, Fidessa Group, Hammerson, Henderson Group, Informa, Pendragon, Reckitt Benckiser Group, Rio Tinto, Rolls-Royce Group, Shire, Spectris

COMPANY
RESULTS

FTSE 100 RATIO OF UP/DOWN DAYS

Is there necessarily a close correlation between the ratio of up/down days in a year and the overall annual return of the FTSE 100?

The following chart plots the ratio of up/down days for the FTSE 100 in each year and its annual returns since 1984.

For example, in 1985 (the second set of bars in the chart) there were 253 trading days. Of those the index was up on 136 days (53.7% of total trading days). This percentage figure is normalised by deducting 50% and plotted as 3.7% on the chart as a grey bar. In 1985 the index increased 15%, which is shown in the adjacent black bar.

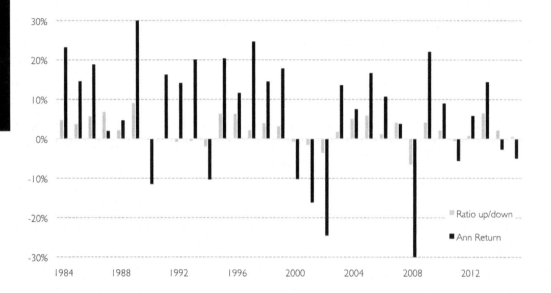

A quick glance indeed shows that positive return years are usually accompanied by a positive ratio of up/down days. In other words, when the index has risen on more days than it has fallen in a year, the index tends to be up overall in the year, and vice versa.

The largest annual return for the FTSE 100 (1989) was accompanied by the largest positive up/down ratio (9.3%); while the lowest annual return for the FTSE 100 (2008) was accompanied by the lowest up/down ratio (-6.5%). (NB. the Y-axis scale has been truncated in the chart to aid legibility; the annual returns in these two extreme years were: 1989: +35% and 2008: -31%.)

So far, so unsurprising, but there are some interesting features to note here:

- In the final run up to the dot-com crash (1995-1999), one can see that while the annual returns were, generally, increasing each year, the up-/down ratio was in fact decreasing. This divergence might have been an early indicator of trouble.

- There is a definite bias for the up/down ratio to be positive (i.e. for the market to be up on more days than it falls), and when the ratio is negative it is usually by quite a small amount (in only two years has the ratio been less than -2%: 2002, 2008).

- The greatest divergence in any year was in 1991, when the up/down ratio was marginally negative (the index fell on 127 of the 253 trading days), and yet the index ended the year up 16%. Oddly, the previous year, 1990, the up/down ratio was identical, but the index ended the year down 12%.

- The up/down ratio and annual returns for the FTSE 100 have only diverged (i.e. had opposite signs) in five years: a run of three years 1991-1993, then 2014 and 2015.

Mon

20

Washington's Birthday (US)
NYSE closed

→

FTSE 100	50	-0.2	1.0
FTSE 250	60	-0.1	0.6

1958: The UK Government announces the naval dockyards in Sheerness are
to be shut down.

NIKKEI	42	-0.2	1.2

Tue

21

→

FTSE 100	45	-0.1	0.8
FTSE 250	38	-0.2	0.6
S&P 500	32	-0.2	0.7
NIKKEI	43	0.3	1.8

1965: Black nationalist leader Malcolm X is assassinated.

Wed

22

→

FTSE 100	45	0.0	0.7
FTSE 250	62	0.0	0.6
S&P 500	47	0.0	1.0
NIKKEI	52	0.1	1.0

2002: Colt Telecom shares joined the 99% Club when they close at 37p (over
99% below their high in 2000).

Thu

23

↘

FTSE 100	41	-0.2	0.9
FTSE 250	50	-0.1	0.6
S&P 500	40	-0.2	0.7
NIKKEI	48	0.0	1.0

1955: First meeting of the Southeast Asia Treaty Organization (SEATO).

Fri

24

→

FTSE 100	43	-0.1	0.9
FTSE 250	57	0.0	0.6
S&P 500	57	0.2	1.0
NIKKEI	48	-0.4	1.1

1982: First trading day of the newly privatised Amersham.

Sat 25   Maha Shivaratri

Sun 26   Football: EFL Cup Final, Wembley; New Moon; Annular Solar Eclipse

COMPANY

RESULTS

Interim Barratt Developments, BHP Billiton, Dechra Pharmaceuticals, Genesis Emerging Markets Fund,
Genus, Go-Ahead Group, Hays
Final BAE Systems, Bovis Homes Group, Capital & Counties Properties, Centrica, Coca-Cola, Croda
International, Drax Group, Essentra, GKN, HSBC Holdings, Indivior, InterContinental Hotels Group,
International Personal Finance, Ladbrokes, Lancashire Holdings, Man Group, Meggitt, Millennium &
Copthorne Hotels, Morgan Advanced Materials, Persimmon, Petrofac, Provident Financial, Rathbone
Brothers, Segro, Standard Chartered, Standard Life, Temple Bar Inv Trust, The Renewables Infrastructure
Group, UNITE Group, Weir Group, Wood Group (John)

MARCH MARKET

Market performance this month

Since 1984, the market has had an average return of 0.5% in March, with returns positive in 56% of all years. This ranks March seventh among months for market performance.

As can be seen in the accompanying average month chart, the general trend for the market in March is to rise for the first three weeks and then fall back in the final week – the last week of March has historically been one of the weakest weeks for the market in the whole year.

The month tends to be good for medium-cap stocks – at least relative to large-caps. March marks the final month of the three-month period when the FTSE 250 strongly outperforms the FTSE 100 (in March on average the FTSE 250 has outperformed the FTSE 100 by 0.9 percentage points).

This is another busy month for company announcements: it is the busiest for FTSE 250 companies in the year with 71 companies announcing their prelims this month (along with 24 FTSE 100 companies).

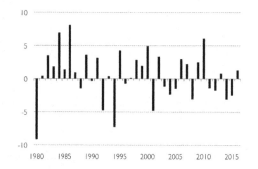
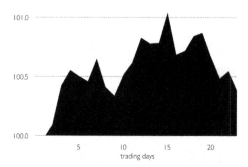

March summary

Market performance	Avg return: 0.5%		Positive: 56%	Ranking: 7th
Sector performance	*Strong* Aerospace & Defense, Financial Services, General Industrials, General Retailers, Industrial Engineering, Oil & Gas Producers, Oil Equipment, Services & Distribution		*Weak* Gas, Water & Multiutilities, Health Care Equipment & Services, Nonlife Insurance	
Share performance	*Strong* Clarkson [CKN], Petrofac Ltd [PFC], Intertek Group [ITRK]		*Weak* Vectura Group [VEC], Renishaw [RSW], Lancashire Holdings Ltd [LRE]	
Main features	The FTSE 250 is particularly strong relative to the FTSE 100 in this month Busiest month for FTSE 250 preliminary results announcements Busiest month for FTSE 100 dividend payments Weak month for gold, strong month for oil First trading day average return: -0.03%; positive: 56% (2nd weakest in year) Last trading day average return: 0.04%; positive: 47% Liquidate Bounceback Portfolio (if not done already)			
Significant dates	01 Mar: FTSE 100 review announced 01 Mar: MSCI Quarterly Index Review (effective date) 03 Mar: US Nonfarm payroll report (anticipated) 09 Mar: ECB Governing Council Meeting (monetary policy) 14 Mar: Two-day FOMC meeting starts 15 Mar: Chancellor's Budget (anticipated) 16 Mar: MPC interest rate announcement at 12 noon (anticipated) 17 Mar: Triple Witching 20 Mar: FTSE Index series quarterly changes effective today 26 Mar: Daylight Saving Time starts 31 Mar: US Nonfarm payroll report			

FEB/MAR

Mon
27

420: The University of Constantinople is founded by Emperor Theodosius II at the urging of his wife Aelia Eudocia.

FTSE 100	48	-0.1	0.8
FTSE 250	73	0.0	1.0
S&P 500	49	-0.2	0.9
NIKKEI	54	0.2	1.5

Tue
28

Shrove Tuesday (Pancake Day)
Beige Book published

FTSE 100	45	-0.2	1.1
FTSE 250	62	0.1	0.7
S&P 500	57	0.0	0.6
NIKKEI	61	0.1	1.3

1900: The British Labour Party is founded.

Wed
1

St David's Day
Ash Wednesday
FTSE Index series quarterly review
MSCI quarterly index review (effective date)
50th anniversary of the opening of Queen Elizabeth Hall in London

FTSE 100	68	0.3	1.0
FTSE 250	76	0.4	0.8
S&P 500	66	0.3	0.8
NIKKEI	52	-0.1	1.3

1946: The Bank of England is nationalised.

Thu
2

10th anniversary of the LSE flotation of Sports Direct International

FTSE 100	45	-0.1	1.3
FTSE 250	59	0.1	0.9
S&P 500	58	0.0	0.9
NIKKEI	61	0.0	1.9

1969: The supersonic airliner Concorde makes its maiden flight.

Fri
3

Nonfarm payroll report (anticipated)

FTSE 100	48	0.0	1.0
FTSE 250	61	0.1	0.7
S&P 500	68	0.1	0.7
NIKKEI	39	-0.2	1.3

1873: The Supreme Court grants Congress the power to authorise the printing of greenbacks, regardless of whether or not the nation is at war.

Sat 4

Sun 5

COMPANY RESULTS

Interim Galliford Try
Final Admiral Group, Aggreko, Barclays, BBA Aviation, Berendsen, Bodycote, British American Tobacco, Bunzl, Capita, Carillion, Cobham, Countrywide, CRH, Derwent London, Dignity, Direct Line Insurance Group, Domino's Pizza, Elementis, Fresnillo, Glencore, Greggs, Hiscox, Howden Joinery Group, IMI, Inmarsat, International Consolidated Airlines Group, Intertek Group, Intu Properties, IP Group, ITV, Jardine Lloyd Thompson Group, Jupiter Fund Management, Just Eat, KAZ Minerals, Keller Group, Kennedy Wilson Europe Real Estate, Laird, Lloyds Banking Group, Merlin Entertainments, Mondi, National Express Group, Pearson, Playtech, Regus, RELX, Rentokil Initial, Rightmove, Riverstone Energy, Rotork, Royal Bank of Scotland Group, RSA Insurance Group, Schroders, Senior, Serco Group, Shawbrook Group, Spirax-Sarco Engineering, St James's Place, Synthomer, Taylor Wimpey, Travis Perkins, Tullett Prebon, UBM, Ultra Electronics Holdings, Vesuvius, Virgin Money Holdings, William Hill

THE LOW-HIGH PRICE PORTFOLIO

Do investors like low share prices?

Investors liking low share prices is the reason often given for companies having share splits or bonus issues. But surely rational investors understand that price is independent of value? Apparently not.

Previous editions of the *Almanac* have compared the historic performance of low-priced shares against high-priced ones. This page updates the study to include last year's data.

To recap, an academic paper[1] in 2008 found that in the US equity market share returns are inversely proportional to share price (i.e. the lower the share price, the higher the future return). In addition, the paper found that a portfolio that was long of stocks under $5 and short of stocks over $20 and rebalanced annually generated average monthly returns of 0.53%. Lengthening the rebalancing period to two years increased the returns and reduced the costs.

To test whether this applies also to the UK market, the performance of two portfolios was compared. The two portfolios were:

1. **Low-price_20**: this portfolio buys equal amounts of the 20 lowest-priced shares in the FTSE All-Share at close on 31 December, holds the portfolio for one year, and then rebalances the next 31 December.

2. **High-price_20**: as above, but this portfolio buys the 20 highest priced shares.

The following chart plots the performance of the Low-price_20 portfolio and High-price_20 portfolio for the period 2004-2015. The portfolios were both rebased to start at 100.

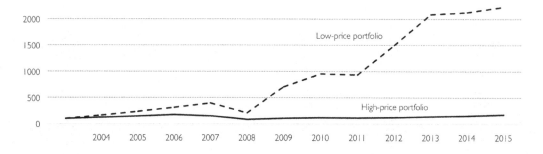

Since 2004, the average annual return of the Low-price portfolio has been 39.7%, against 5.4% for the High-price portfolio. And the former has outperformed the latter portfolio in nine of the past 12 years.

Share price frequency distribution

The bar chart shows the frequency distribution of share prices in the FTSE All-Share as at the end of 2015.

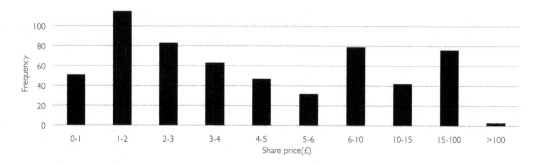

The chart shows that, for example, there are 51 companies with share prices below £1, 116 companies with share prices of £1-2, and 76 companies with share prices of £15-100.

1. Hwang, Soosung and Lu, Chensheng, 'Is Share Price Relevant?' (25 September 2008).

22

Mon
6
1957: Ghana becomes the first Sub-Saharan country to gain independence from Britain.

FTSE 100	52	0.2	0.9
FTSE 250	64	0.1	1.0
S&P 500	49	0.0	0.9
NIKKEI	63	0.4	1.4

100th anniversary of the release of 'Livery Stable Blues', the first commercially available jazz recording

Tue
7
1966: North Sea gas lands in the UK for the first time.

FTSE 100	43	-0.2	0.7
FTSE 250	55	-0.1	0.9
S&P 500	49	-0.2	0.7
NIKKEI	46	-0.4	1.2

100th anniversary of the start of the Russian Revolution

Wed
8
2000: Tech firms including Freeserve, Psion, Thus and Baltimore Technologies are promoted to FTSE 100.

FTSE 100	64	0.1	0.7
FTSE 250	52	0.0	0.8
S&P 500	60	0.0	0.9
NIKKEI	48	0.5	1.6

ECB Governing Council meeting (monetary policy)

Thu
9
1776: Adam Smith publishes *The Wealth of Nations*.

FTSE 100	45	0.0	0.7
FTSE 250	41	0.0	0.5
S&P 500	49	0.0	0.8
NIKKEI	57	0.2	1.0

Fri
10
2000: NASDAQ reaches a closing high of 5048.62 – the peak of the dot-com boom.

FTSE 100	61	0.1	1.4
FTSE 250	57	0.0	1.1
S&P 500	60	0.1	1.2
NIKKEI	52	-0.2	1.1

Sat 11

Sun 12   Full Moon

COMPANY RESULTS

Interim Close Brothers Group, JPMorgan Emerging Markets Inv Trust
Final Aldermore Group, Alliance Trust, Amec Foster Wheeler, Aviva, Cineworld Group, Clarkson, CLS Holdings, esure Group, Foreign & Colonial Inv Trust, G4S, Grafton Group, Hill & Smith Holdings, Hochschild Mining, Ibstock, John Laing Group, London Stock Exchange Group, Morrison (Wm) Supermarkets, Paddy Power Betfair, PageGroup, Prudential, Restaurant Group, Savills, SIG, Worldpay Group, WPP Group

GOLD

Does the price of gold exhibit a monthly seasonality?

49 years ago this week (on 17 March 1968), the system that fixed gold at USD35.00 collapsed and the price of gold was allowed to fluctuate.

The following chart on the left shows the average price returns for gold by month since 1986. The chart on the right shows the proportion of months that have seen positive returns.

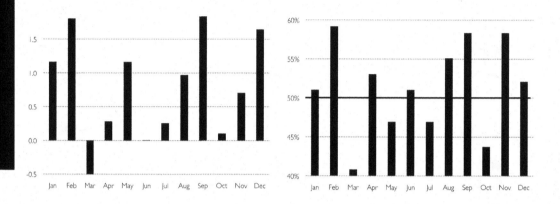

It can be seen that since 1968, gold has been strong in February, September and November, and weak in March and October. This profile of behaviour would seem to have some persistency as the same pattern can be seen for the more recent period 2000-2016, the main difference being that in recent years August has replaced September as one of the three strongest months.

Gold and equities

The following chart shows the ratio of the FTSE All-Share to gold (priced in sterling) since 1968. One can regard the chart as the UK equity market priced in gold.

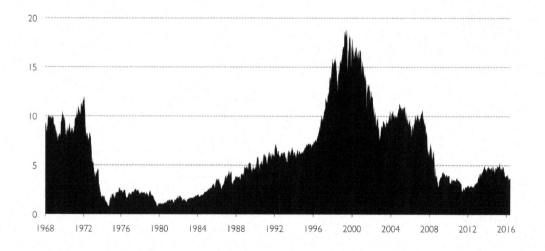

The ratio peaked at 18.8 in July 1999 and then fell to a low of 2.3 in September 2011. Since 1968 the ratio's average is 6.2.

Mon 13

Holi
10th anniversary of 3i Infrastructure listing on the LSE

FTSE 100	39	0.0	1.5
FTSE 250	55	0.0	1.0
S&P 500	60	0.0	0.9
NIKKEI	42	-0.2	1.9

2008: Gold prices on the New York Mercantile Exchange hit $1000 per ounce for the first time.

Tue 14

Two-day FOMC meeting starts
Pi day (3/14)
10th anniversary of BH Macro listing on the LSE

FTSE 100	61	0.3	1.2
FTSE 250	59	0.1	1.0
S&P 500	47	-0.1	0.9
NIKKEI	54	-0.2	1.9

2007: The first World Maths Day is celebrated.

Wed 15

UK Chancellor's Budget (anticipated)
Ides of March

FTSE 100	45	0.1	0.9
FTSE 250	52	0.0	0.9
S&P 500	66	0.2	0.7
NIKKEI	78	0.3	2.5

1906: Rolls-Royce Ltd is registered.

Thu 16

MPC interest rate announcement at 12h00

FTSE 100	50	0.1	1.2
FTSE 250	62	0.1	0.7
S&P 500	64	0.3	1.0
NIKKEI	43	0.1	1.6

2013: Banks in Cyprus are shut as politicians scramble to come up with a plan to raise enough funds for Cyprus to qualify for €10 billion of bailout loans for its stricken banking sector.

Fri 17

St Patrick's Day
Triple Witching

FTSE 100	61	0.0	1.2
FTSE 250	70	0.1	1.0
S&P 500	63	0.2	1.0
NIKKEI	61	0.3	1.4

2008: JPMorgan buys Bear Stearns for $240m – a $17.75bn discount on its value a year earlier – as the Wall Street bank comes close to imploding.

Sat 18   50th anniversary of the Torrey Canyon accident

Sun 19

COMPANY RESULTS

Interim JRP Group, Kier Group, Smiths Group, Softcat, Wetherspoon (J D)
Final Antofagasta, Ascential, Balfour Beatty, Cairn Energy, Circassia Pharmaceuticals, Computacenter, Evraz, Fidelity European Values, Hansteen Holdings, Hastings Group Holdings, Hikma Pharmaceuticals, Inchcape, John Laing Infrastructure Fund, Legal & General Group, Marshalls, Murray International Trust, NMC Health, Old Mutual, OneSavings Bank, Paysafe Group, Spire Healthcare Group, Ted Baker, Tritax Big Box REIT

FTSE 100 REVIEWS – COMPANIES JOINING THE INDEX

The charts below show the share prices of nine companies that have recently joined the FTSE 100. The time period for each chart is six months, starting from three months before the company joined the index. The vertical line in each chart indicates the announcement date of the company joining the index.

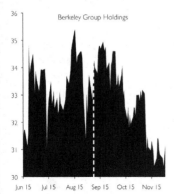

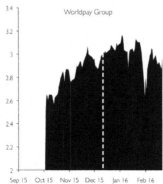

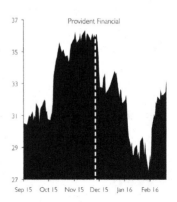

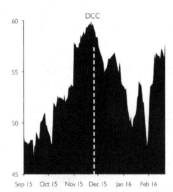

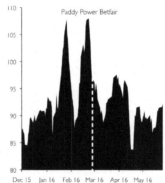

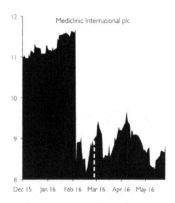

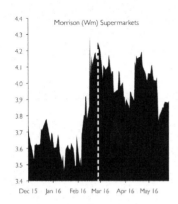

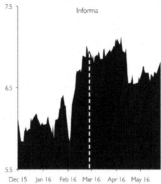

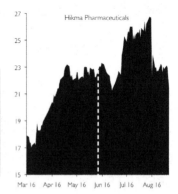

Observation

It can be seen that in most cases the share price rises for several weeks before the announcement of the company joining the FTSE 100. While afterwards the price is often flat or falls back again.

Mon 20

TSE closed
March Equinox
FTSE Index Series quarterly changes effective today

FTSE 100	48	0.1	1.0
FTSE 250	55	-0.1	0.7
S&P 500	50	0.0	0.8

1602: The Dutch East India Company is established.

Tue 21

FTSE 100	45	0.0	0.9
FTSE 250	52	0.1	0.8
S&P 500	38	-0.1	0.9
NIKKEI	78	1.5	2.3

1924: Mass Investors Trust becomes the first mutual fund in US.

Wed 22

FTSE 100	45	-0.4	1.1
FTSE 250	38	-0.3	0.8
S&P 500	47	0.0	0.6
NIKKEI	43	-0.2	1.6

1954: Closed since 1939, the London Bullion Market reopens.

Thu 23

FTSE 100	50	0.1	0.9
FTSE 250	59	0.0	0.6
S&P 500	57	0.3	1.3
NIKKEI	41	0.0	1.3

1888: In England, The Football League, the world's oldest professional Association Football league, meets for the first time.

Fri 24

FTSE 100	43	-0.3	1.3
FTSE 250	52	-0.1	0.9
S&P 500	47	-0.2	1.0
NIKKEI	43	0.0	1.5

1992: *Punch*, Britain's oldest satirical magazine, closes after suffering crippling losses of £1.5m a year.

Sat 25

Sun 26   Daylight Saving Time starts (clocks go forward)

Interim Bellway, DFS Furniture, Wolseley
Final BH Macro, Centamin, International Public Partnership, JPMorgan American Inv Trust, Kingfisher, Next, Phoenix Group Holdings, SVG Capital, Woodford Patient Capital Trust

COMPANY
RESULTS

TURN OF THE MONTH STRATEGY

A strategy that exploits the Turn of the Month anomaly.

The *Almanac* has previously investigated the Turn of the Month anomaly (whereby the market sees abnormally high returns around the turn of the month). An update of the analysis can be seen on page 125 of this edition.

A recent academic paper[1] addresses the same topic. The paper makes the rather remarkable claim that:

> "since July 1926, one could have held the US value-weighted stock index (CRSP) for only seven days a month and pocketed the entire market excess return with nearly fifty percent lower volatility compared to a buy and hold strategy."

These seven days straddle the turn of the month. What might cause this behaviour? The paper argues that it is the month-end liquidity needs of US institutions, pension funds and mutual funds. For example, the chart on the right taken from the paper shows the proportion of US pension payment dates around the turn of the month (day T denotes the last trading day of the month). And because settlement in the US is T+3, institutions have to sell at least three days in advance to ensure they have the necessary liquidity for the

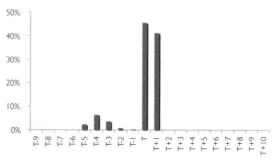

end of the month. Then, at the beginning of the month, institutions look to invest recently received dividends, which puts demand pressure on stocks over the first few days. (And, yes, some pension funds are now changing their distribution dates to get out of synchronisation with their peers!)

Generally, the paper has found that the turn of the month anomaly has become more pronounced as mutual funds' AUM as a proportion of the overall stock market has increased. The paper's authors also found that the anomaly exists in other developed markets and was more pronounced in countries with larger mutual fund sectors.

Is such behaviour seen in the UK?

As mentioned above, the *Almanac* has already previously documented the strength of the market around the turn of the month. The following chart replicates (for the UK market) one found in the Etula paper: it plots the cumulative returns of the FTSE All-Share for the six days around the turn of the month (TOM: T-3 to T+3) against the cumulative returns of the index for the rest of the month (X-TOM) for the period 1969-2016. Both series are rebased to start at 100.

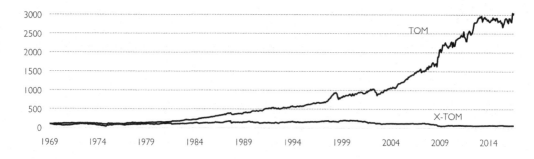

By 2016, a TOM portfolio would have had a value of 3039, and a X-TOM portfolio a value of 70. This does suggest that all the market's gains come in just a few days around the turn of the month. For comparison, a buy-and-hold FTSE All-Share portfolio would have had a value of 2129 by the end of the period, so the TOM portfolio would have outperformed the index by 40% (as the market actually fell during the X-TOM part of the month); in addition the TOM portfolio would have had 50% less volatility than the index.

1. E. Etula, K. Rinne, M. Suominen and L. Vaittinen, 'Dash for Cash: Month-End Liquidity Needs and the Predictability of Stock Returns' (May 2016).

Mon
27

ECB Governing Council meeting (monetary policy)

1980: Silver Thursday: A steep fall in silver prices, resulting from the Hunt Brothers attempting to corner the market in silver, led to panic on commodity and futures exchanges.

FTSE 100	45	0.0	1.0
FTSE 250	52	0.1	0.7
S&P 500	40	-0.1	0.9
NIKKEI	58	0.3	1.3

Tue
28

Ramayana (until 5th April)
New Moon

1871: The Paris Commune is formally established in Paris.

FTSE 100	42	-0.3	0.7
FTSE 250	50	0.0	0.5
S&P 500	52	-0.1	0.8
NIKKEI	61	0.3	1.2

Wed
29

1886: Dr John Pemberton brews the first batch of Coca-Cola in a backyard in Atlanta.

FTSE 100	53	0.2	0.7
FTSE 250	61	0.1	0.5
S&P 500	50	0.1	0.6
NIKKEI	43	-0.2	1.5

Thu
30

1949: A riot breaks out in Austurvöllur square in Reykjavík, as Iceland joins NATO.

FTSE 100	50	-0.3	1.2
FTSE 250	55	-0.1	0.7
S&P 500	36	-0.2	0.9
NIKKEI	43	-0.4	1.6

Fri
31

1980: The Chicago, Rock Island and Pacific railroad operates its final train after being ordered to liquidate its assets because of bankruptcy and debts owed to creditors.

FTSE 100	38	-0.1	1.3
FTSE 250	33	-0.1	0.8
S&P 500	41	0.0	0.7
NIKKEI	35	-0.5	1.5

Sat 1

Sun 2 · · · Rowing: The Mens and Womens Boat Races (Oxford v Cambridge)

Final Barr, Moneysupermarket.com Group, National Grid, Polymetal International, Polypipe Group, RIT Capital Partners, Witan Inv Trust

COMPANY
RESULTS

APRIL MARKET

Market performance this month

April is one of the most exciting months for investors! Five years ago, April was the strongest month for the stock market in the year, but it now ranks second behind December. The two months have been switching first and second places for quite a few years. For the last few years it has been December in top spot, but April is not far behind. Interestingly, this characteristic is not unique to the UK market; a study of 70 markets worldwide found that the strongest months for shares were (in descending order) December, January and April.

On average, the market rises 1.8% in this month; and the probability of a positive return in the month is 72%. Since 2003, the market has only fallen three times in April, although this doesn't match the earlier performance: from 1971 the market rose in April every year for 15 years – a recent record for any month.

The market often gets off to a strong start in the month – the first trading day of April is the third strongest first trading day of all months in the year. The market then tends to be fairly flat for the middle two weeks and then rises strongly in the final week.

The great seasonality significance of April is that it is the last month in the strong part of the six-month cycle (November-April) and therefore investors may be reducing their exposure to equities ahead of May.

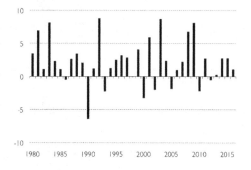

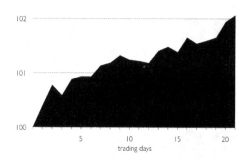

April summary

Market performance	Avg return: 1.8%		Positive: 72%	Ranking: 2nd
Sector performance	*Strong* Electronic & Electrical Equipment, Industrial Engineering, Personal Goods		*Weak* Household Goods, Mining, Mobile Telecommunications, Software & Computer Services	
Share performance	*Strong* JD Sports Fashion [JD.], Ashmore Group [ASHM], Aberdeen Asset Management [ADN]		*Weak* Balfour Beatty [BBY], RELX [REL], BAE Systems [BA.]	
Main features	Second strongest month of the year for shares FTSE 100 strong relative to S&P 500 this month Market abnormally strong on day before and day after Easter holiday GBPUSD historically strong this month Strong month for oil First trading day average return: 0.41%; positive: 69% (3rd strongest in year) Last trading day average return: 0.13%; positive: 55% 08 Apr: 3rd weakest day of the year for shares			
Significant dates	07 Apr: US Nonfarm payroll report 14 Apr: Good Friday, LSE, NYSE, HKEX closed 17 Apr: Easter Monday, LSE, HKEX closed 19 Apr: Beige Book published 27 Apr: ECB Governing Council Meeting			

Mon
3

FTSE 100	39	-0.3	1.0
FTSE 250	48	-0.1	1.0
S&P 500	51	0.0	0.9
NIKKEI	71	0.5	1.6

1986: IBM unveils its first laptop computer.

Tue
4

Ching Ming Festival
HKEX closed

FTSE 100	57	0.1	0.8
FTSE 250	60	-0.2	0.8
S&P 500	52	-0.1	0.6
NIKKEI	42	0.0	1.1

1984: Winston Smith in George Orwell's *1984* begins his secret diary.

Wed
5

Ram Navami
End of tax year 2016/17

FTSE 100	63	0.1	0.8
FTSE 250	56	-0.1	0.7
S&P 500	59	0.3	1.0
NIKKEI	52	0.2	1.0

1964: The first driverless trains run on the London Underground.

Thu
6

Golf: Masters, Augusta (until 9th)

FTSE 100	65	0.2	0.7
FTSE 250	78	0.4	0.8
S&P 500	57	0.1	0.8
NIKKEI	48	0.2	1.1

2012: Massachusetts becomes the first state in the US to set a minimum wage.

Fri
7

Nonfarm payroll report (anticipated)

FTSE 100	43	0.2	1.1
FTSE 250	43	0.0	1.0
S&P 500	51	-0.2	0.8
NIKKEI	70	0.2	1.2

1906: Mount Vesuvius erupts, destroying Naples.

Sat 8   Horse racing: Grand National, Aintree Racecourse

Sun 9   Palm Sunday

Final AA, Card Factory, F&C Commercial Property Trust, Mercantile Inv Trust

COMPANY
RESULTS

HOLIDAYS AND THE MARKET

How does the market behave around holidays?

In 1990, an academic paper[1] was published with the finding that the trading day prior to holidays in the US market had an average return 14 times greater than the average for the other days in the year. This, and other papers, found that the day immediately before holidays had the highest returns in the period around holidays, with the third day before the holidays having the next highest return, while the day following the holiday had negative returns.

Does such a holiday effect exist in the UK market?

The following charts show the results of research on the daily returns of the FTSE 100 around holidays. The three trading days immediately prior to holidays, H(-3) to H(-1), and the three trading days after holidays, H(+1) to H(+3), were analysed. A holiday was defined as a three-day (or longer) period with no trading. The bars in the chart show the average return for each of the six days around holidays. The chart on the left is for the period 1984-2016, the chart on the right for the period 2000-2016.

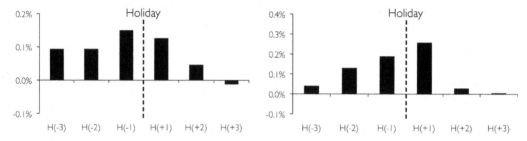

From the chart on the left we can see that, as with the US studies, H(-3) and H(-1) were strong during the holiday periods. Unlike the US studies, the day after a holiday, H(+1), was also found to be strong – this day has an average return of 0.13% (four times greater than the average return for all days in the year).

Looking at the chart on the right it can be seen that the UK holiday effect has changed slightly in recent years. In the last ten years or so the market has still been significantly strong on the days immediately before, and the day after, holidays, but weaker on the third day before holidays.

As Easter is upon us, let's look specifically at the market around the Easter holiday.

Easter

The following charts analyse the market behaviour around Easter.

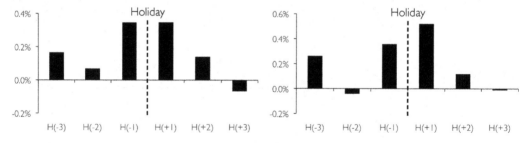

Looking at the chart on the left, the general profile of behaviour around Easter can be seen to be similar to that for all holidays. The main difference is that the average returns for the day immediately before, and after, Easter are significantly higher than for all holidays. For example, the average return for H(-1) is 0.35% (11 times greater than the average return for all days in the year).

The chart on the right shows that the behaviour of the market around Easter has not changed significantly in recent years.

1. R. A. Ariel, 'High stock returns before holidays: existence and evidence on possible causes', *Journal of Finance* (1990).

Mon
10

Passover (until 18th April)

2001: Tesco becomes the first UK supermarket to earn profits in excess of £1bn.

FTSE 100	59	0.4	1.6
FTSE 250	50	0.3	1.8
S&P 500	63	0.2	0.8
NIKKEI	46	0.3	1.9

Tue
11

Hanuman Jayanti
Theravadin (Buddhist New Year)
Full Moon

1957: The island of Singapore is granted self-government from Britain, coming into effect the next year.

FTSE 100	38	-0.2	0.9
FTSE 250	50	-0.1	0.7
S&P 500	48	-0.1	0.8
NIKKEI	46	0.2	1.5

Wed
12

1922: Coco Chanel introduces her new perfume, No. 5., created by a chemist on the French Riviera.

FTSE 100	57	0.1	0.7
FTSE 250	53	0.0	0.6
S&P 500	67	0.3	0.7
NIKKEI	57	-0.1	1.0

Thu
13

Maundy Thursday

2004: HSBC announces the launch of an Islamic law-compliant pension fund.

FTSE 100	61	0.2	0.7
FTSE 250	61	0.1	0.7
S&P 500	53	-0.1	0.7
NIKKEI	52	0.1	1.6

Fri
14

Good Friday
LSE, NYSE, HKEX closed

1927: The first Volvo car comes off the production line in Sweden.

NIKKEI	48	-0.1	1.3

Sat 15

Sun 16   Easter Sunday

Interim Debenhams, WH Smith
Final JD Sports Fashion, Tesco

COMPANY
RESULTS

DAY OF THE WEEK STRATEGY

Previous editions of the *Almanac* have looked at the performance of the Day of Week (DOTW) Strategy. This is an update on that strategy.

Since 2012, the FTSE 100 has had negative average returns on Monday and Wednesday, and positive average returns on Tuesday, Thursday and Friday. [See the Statistics section, page 114, for further analysis.]

This suggests a strategy of shorting the market for Monday (i.e. shorting at the close the previous Friday), switching to long on Tuesday, back to short on Wednesday, and then long on Thursday and Friday (and back to short at the close of Friday).

The following chart updates the results of implementing this strategy every week from January 2012 to mid-2016 (the time of writing). A spread cost of 1 point on each transaction is included in the performance figures. For comparison, a simple long-only FTSE 100 portfolio is also shown. The portfolios' values are rebased to start at 100.

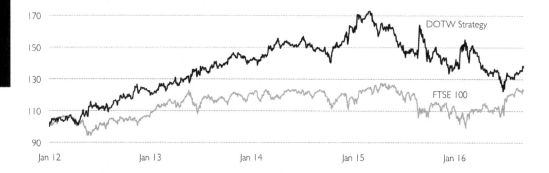

As can be seen this strategy was faring pretty well… but then something went wrong in 2015 when the strategy started underperforming the FTSE 100.

The reason, as can be seen in the Statistics section of this *Almanac*, is that since 2015 the market has considerably weakened on Thursday and strengthened on Wednesday. So, the strategy needs to be adjusted to be long on Tuesday, Wednesday and Friday, and short on Monday and Thursday.

The following chart shows the result of adjusted DTOW Strategy back-tested from January 2015. (Again, a 1-point transaction cost in included.)

This time the (adjusted) DOTW Strategy strongly outperforms the FTSE 100. Although note that this outperformance only really started from around September 2015.

It is clear that this strategy needs to be closely monitored and adjusted as the relative strengths of the days of the week change.

Mon
17

Easter Monday
LSE, HKEX closed

1956: The Chancellor's budget unveils inducements for private savings, including the introduction of Premium Bonds.

S&P 500	62	0.3	1.0
NIKKEI	46	-0.2	1.8

Tue
18

1955: Albert Einstein dies at the age of 76.

FTSE 100	50	0.0	0.9
FTSE 250	50	0.1	0.8
S&P 500	57	0.2	1.1
NIKKEI	58	0.2	1.7

Wed
19

Beige Book published

1770: Captain James Cook sights Australia.

FTSE 100	59	0.2	0.7
FTSE 250	67	0.3	0.6
S&P 500	50	-0.1	0.6
NIKKEI	48	0.1	1.3

Thu
20

Ridvan (until 2nd May)

1821: Edgar Allan Poe's *Murders In The Rue Morgue*, the world's first modern detective story, is published in America.

FTSE 100	65	0.0	1.1
FTSE 250	65	0.0	1.2
S&P 500	55	-0.1	1.0
NIKKEI	43	-0.1	1.0

Fri
21

1948: The first Polaroid camera is sold in the US.

FTSE 100	40	-0.1	0.5
FTSE 250	55	0.0	0.4
S&P 500	53	0.2	0.8
NIKKEI	48	0.1	1.4

Sat 22   Lyrids Meteor Shower (until 23rd)

Sun 23   St George's Day; Yom HaShoah (until 24th); London Marathon

Interim Associated British Foods, McCarthy & Stone
Final Brown (N) Group, NB Global Floating Rate Income Fund, Saga, UK Commercial Property Trust

COMPANY
RESULTS

MARKET RETURNS IN ODD AND EVEN WEEKS

This is a strange one. (Or odd may be the more appropriate description.)

The following chart shows the value of two portfolios:

- **Odd Week Portfolio**: this portfolio only invests in the FTSE 100 in odd-numbered weeks, and is in cash for the even-numbered weeks.

- **Even Week Portfolio**: this portfolio only invests in the FTSE 100 in even-numbered weeks, and is in cash for the odd-numbered weeks.

The portfolios started investing at the beginning of 2010 with values of 100.

Note: The weeks are numbered according to the ISO 8601 numbering system, whereby the week containing the first Thursday of the year is designated the first week of the year (this is also called European week numbering).

The divergence in performance of the two portfolios is quite striking. By September 2016, the Odd Week Portfolio would have had a value of 166, and the Even Week Portfolio a value of 77.

It may not be possible to exploit this phenomenon due to trading costs, but it is certainly rather bizarre.

Has this been a long-term phenomenon?

The following chart shows the FTSE 100 average returns for odd and even weeks for the past few decades. For example, from 1984-1989 the average return in odd weeks was 0.19% and for even weeks 0.41%.

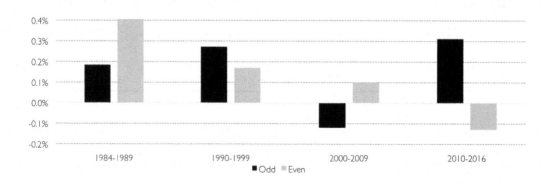

As can be seen, there has been no consistent relationship between odd and even week returns. In the decade 2000-2009, even weeks were on average stronger than odd weeks, whereas this decade the relationship has reversed.

While there is no obvious (or, for the moment, non-obvious) explanation for this weekly phenomenon, such odd/even weekly effects have been seen elsewhere – for example, the FOMC Cycle (see page 50).

Mon
24

2005: Snuppy becomes the world's first cloned dog.

FTSE 100	57	0.1	1.0
FTSE 250	52	0.1	0.8
S&P 500	48	-0.1	0.8
NIKKEI	33	-0.1	1.1

100th anniversary of the birth of Ella Fitzgerald

Tue
25

FTSE 100	57	0.0	0.5
FTSE 250	52	0.0	0.5
S&P 500	55	0.1	0.9
NIKKEI	58	0.1	1.0

2007: The DJIA closes above 13,000 (13,089.89) for the first time.

New Moon

Wed
26

FTSE 100	70	0.3	0.6
FTSE 250	67	0.1	0.4
S&P 500	55	0.1	0.6
NIKKEI	52	0.1	0.8

1928: Madame Tussaud's waxworks exhibition opens in London.

Thu
27

FTSE 100	55	-0.2	1.1
FTSE 250	55	-0.2	0.8
S&P 500	52	-0.1	0.8
NIKKEI	48	-0.1	1.2

1981: Xerox PARC introduces the computer mouse.

Fri
28

FTSE 100	52	0.1	1.0
FTSE 250	48	-0.1	0.8
S&P 500	56	0.0	0.7
NIKKEI	43	-0.4	1.3

2008: Mars announces it is buying the Wm. Wrigley Jr. Company, the world's largest chewing gum manufacturer, in a deal worth $23bn. The deal is partly financed by Warren Buffett's Berkshire Hathaway.

Sat 29   Showa Day (Japan)

Sun 30

Interim Redefine International
Final Allied Minds, Home Retail Group, P2P Global Investments, Whitbread

COMPANY
RESULTS

MAY MARKET

Market performance this month

One of the most famous sayings in the stock market is "Sell in May", so it is no surprise that May is one of the weakest months of the year for shares. There are only three months where, since 1970, the market has an average return of below zero in the month – May is one of them (the others are June and September). On average, the market falls -0.2% in the month. Since year 2000, performance has been even worse, with an average return of -0.5% for the month.

May is the start of the weaker half of the year (historically the market over November to April greatly outperforms the period May to October). Some investors therefore tend to reduce exposure to the stock market from May.

On average in May the market trades fairly flat for the first two weeks of the month, and then prices drift lower in the second half (as can be seen in the accompanying chart).

May is the weakest month of the year for the FTSE 100 relative to the S&P 500; on average the UK index underperforms the US index by 1.3 percentage points in May.

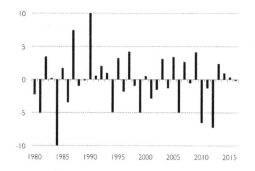
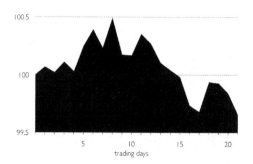

May summary

Market performance	Avg return: **-0.2%**		Positive: **48%**	Ranking: **10th**
Sector performance	*Strong* Aerospace & Defense, Electricity, Equity Investment Instruments, Food Producers, Gas, Water & Multiutilities		*Weak* General Industrials, Life Insurance	
Share performance	*Strong* 3i Group [III], Babcock International Group [BAB], Cranswick [CWK]		*Weak* Redefine International [RDI], Sainsbury (J) [SBRY], PageGroup [PAGE]	
Main features	Sell in May Effect: start of the weak six months of the year FTSE 100 often underperforms the S&P 500 in this month First trading day average return: 0.7%; positive: 55% Last trading day average return: -0.02%; positive: 45% (3rd weakest in year) 02 May: 8th strongest day of the year for shares 29 May: start of the 4th weakest week of the year for shares 30 May: weakest day of the year for shares			
Significant dates	01 May: May Day bank holiday, LSE closed, HKEX 02 May: Two-day FOMC meetings starts 05 May: US Nonfarm payroll report 11 May: MPC interest rate announcement at 12 noon (anticipated) 11 May: MSCI Semi-Annual Index Review announcement date 29 May: Spring bank holiday – LSE, NYSE, HKSE closed 31 May: FTSE 100 quarterly review			

Mon 1

May Day Bank Holiday (UK)
Labour Day (Hong Kong)
LSE, HKEX closed
Beltane
Yom Ha'atzmaut (until 2nd)

1840: The UK's Penny Black becomes the world's first adhesive postage stamp used in a public postal system.

S&P 500	56	0.3	0.7
NIKKEI	67	0.4	1.1

Tue 2

8th strongest market day
Two-day FOMC meeting starts

1997: The Labour Party's Tony Blair comes to power, ending 18 years of Conservative rule.

FTSE 100	78	0.5	0.8
FTSE 250	69	0.5	0.7
S&P 500	67	0.2	0.7
NIKKEI	57	0.3	1.1

Wed 3

Constitution Memorial Day (Japan)
The Birthday of the Buddha (Hong Kong)
TSE, HKEX closed

1973: The 38.4 million public flotation of Rolls-Royce Motors is announced.

FTSE 100	58	-0.2	1.0
FTSE 250	59	0.0	0.5
S&P 500	57	0.1	0.8

Thu 4

Greenery Day (Japan)
TSE closed

1776: Rhode Island is the first North American colony to renounce its loyalty and allegiance to King George III.

FTSE 100	50	-0.2	1.2
FTSE 250	59	-0.1	1.0
S&P 500	60	0.0	1.0

Fri 5

Children's Day (Japan)
TSE closed
Nonfarm payroll report (anticipated)

1930: Amy Johnson, the first woman to fly solo from England to Australia, takes off.

FTSE 100	50	0.0	1.0
FTSE 250	61	0.2	1.0
S&P 500	58	0.2	0.7

Sat 6   Horse racing: Kentucky Derby, Louisville; Eta Aquarids Meteor Shower (until 7th)

Sun 7

Interim Aberdeen Asset Management, Electra Private Equity, Finsbury Growth & Income Trust, Sage Group
Final BT Group, Sainsbury (J)

COMPANY
RESULTS

SELL IN MAY

An update on the strongest – and strangest – seasonality effect in the market.

When we look at historic time series of asset prices the frequency we use tends to be day, week, month or year. But new patterns of historic behaviour might be revealed using other time frames. In this case, we are going to split the year into two six-month periods:

1. *Winter period:* 1 November-30 April.

2. *Summer period:* 1 May-31 October.

(We will call them "winter" and "summer" for the sake of giving them names.)

The top chart to the right compares the performance from 1982 of the FTSE All-Share for the two periods; each bar represents the outperformance of the winter period over the following summer period. For example, in the winter period from 1 Nov 2014 to 30 Apr 2015 the index rose 7.3%, while during the following summer period 1 May 2015 to 31 Oct 2015 the index fell 7.3%. The difference in performance was therefore 14.7 percentage points, and that is the figure plotted on the chart for 2015.

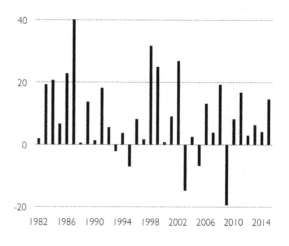

The chart shows a quite remarkable thing: namely that the market seems to perform much better in the winter period than the summer period. To quantify this outperformance:

- In the 34 years since 1982, the winter period has outperformed the summer period 29 times (85%).

- The average annual outperformance since 1982 has been 8.8 percentage points!

The behaviour is extraordinary and should not exist in a modern, efficient(ish) market. But exist it does. Indeed, a similar effect also exists in other markets such as the US.

How long has this effect been operating?

The bottom chart on the right is identical to that above except the data starts from 1922.

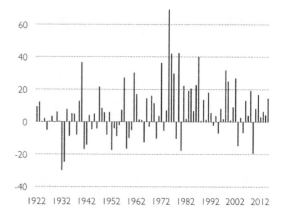

We can see from this chart that during the first half of the 20th century the market performance during the two periods was pretty equally balanced. Then the behaviour changed significantly around the beginning of the 1970s.

But it may be that the above study is woefully short-termist in its approach. An academic paper[1] of 2012 found evidence of the Sell in May effect (aka the Halloween effect in the US) starting from 1694 in the UK. The paper also found the effect was present in 36 of 37 developed and emerging markets.

1. B. Jacobsen and C.Y. Zhang, 'Are Monthly Seasonals Real? A Three Century Perspective' (15 February 2012).

Mon
8

FTSE 100	57	0.2	1.1
FTSE 250	62	0.2	1.2
S&P 500	57	0.2	0.8
NIKKEI	67	0.2	0.9

1963: *Dr No* premieres in the US, launching the James Bond film franchise.

Tue
9

FTSE 100	38	-0.1	0.6
FTSE 250	50	-0.1	0.4
S&P 500	49	-0.1	0.7
NIKKEI	33	-0.4	0.9

1904: The locomotive City of Truro becomes the first steam engine to exceed 100mph.

Full Moon

Wed
10

FTSE 100	48	0.3	1.4
FTSE 250	52	0.2	1.4
S&P 500	49	-0.1	1.1
NIKKEI	48	-0.1	1.5

1955: West Germany is accepted into NATO.

MPC interest rate announcement at 12h00
MSCI quarterly index review (announcement date)

Thu
11

FTSE 100	52	0.1	1.0
FTSE 250	41	-0.1	0.9
S&P 500	41	-0.2	0.9
NIKKEI	52	-0.2	1.3

1812: Spencer Perceval is assassinated while in office as UK Prime Minister.

Fri
12

FTSE 100	52	-0.1	0.9
FTSE 250	57	0.1	0.9
S&P 500	57	0.2	0.7
NIKKEI	48	0.1	1.1

1935: Bill Wilson and Dr Bob Smith (founders of Alcoholics Anonymous) meet for the first time in Akron, Ohio, at the home of Henrietta Siberling.

Sat 13

Sun 14   Lag BaOmer

Interim Compass Group, easyJet, Imperial Brands, TUI AG
Final 3i Infrastructure, Experian, TalkTalk Telecom Group, Vedanta Resources

COMPANY
RESULTS

THE DIVIDEND PAYMENT CALENDAR

May is the best month for FTSE 100 dividend payments.

It is easy to forget about the importance of dividends. After all, the prospect of a share price rising (or falling) by 50% seems a lot more exciting than a company paying a 3p dividend. But Jeremy Siegel (author of the famous book, *Stocks for the Long Run*) calculated that for US stocks roughly three-quarters of the real return came from dividends, with only one quarter from capital gains. The case for UK stocks would not be very different.

Dividends are also important for what they say about the fundamentals of a company. Making capital gains on a company that has paper profits may be nice, but profits that produce real cash dividends can be a lot more reassuring.

Of course, dividends can be especially important for some investors, such as retirees, who look to the regular dividend cheque as a vital source of income. The aggregate dividend yield on the FTSE 100 companies is currently around 4%, which is attractive, particularly when the base rate is 0.25%.

For income investors, it is not only the size of the dividend cheque that can matter, but also its timing.

The following chart plots the frequency distribution of dividend payment dates by month for FTSE 100 companies. For example, in January eight companies pay a final dividend and 28 companies pay an interim dividend.

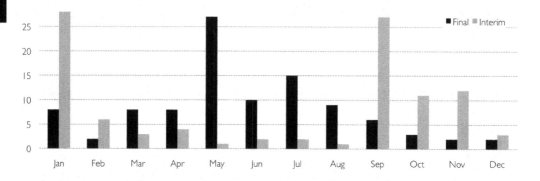

As can be seen, although dividend payments occur in all months of the year, the months with most dividend payments are January, May and September.

However, not all dividends are equal. Some companies pay a higher dividend (measured by the dividend yield) than others. This has been accounted for in the following chart, which plots aggregate dividends for all FTSE 100 companies in each month.

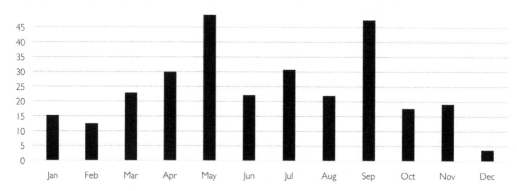

As can be seen, the best months for receiving FTSE 100 dividends are May and September. In this chart (compared to the first one above), January falls back because while number-wise many companies pay dividends in January, they are largely interim dividends which tend to be for smaller amounts than final dividends.

Mon
15

FTSE 100	50	0.1	0.8
FTSE 250	55	-0.1	0.9
S&P 500	54	0.0	0.9
NIKKEI	42	0.1	1.5

1940: McDonald's opens its first restaurant in San Bernardino, California.

Tue
16

FTSE 100	46	0.1	0.5
FTSE 250	48	0.0	0.7
S&P 500	48	0.0	0.7
NIKKEI	42	-0.3	1.0

1532: Sir Thomas More resigns as Lord Chancellor of England, citing ill health.

Wed
17

FTSE 100	52	-0.1	1.2
FTSE 250	62	-0.1	1.0
S&P 500	55	-0.1	0.8
NIKKEI	61	-0.2	1.3

1930: The Bank of International Settlements, the bank of central banks, is founded.

10th anniversary of the LSE flotation of Hargreaves Lansdown

Thu
18

FTSE 100	57	0.2	0.9
FTSE 250	73	0.2	0.6
S&P 500	46	0.0	0.9
NIKKEI	35	-0.4	1.3

1964: Mods and Rockers are jailed after riots in Brighton.

Fri
19

FTSE 100	52	-0.2	1.3
FTSE 250	61	0.0	1.1
S&P 500	52	-0.1	0.8
NIKKEI	57	0.2	1.2

1898: The Post Office authorises the use of postcards.

Sat 20

Sun 21

COMPANY RESULTS

Interim Brewin Dolphin Holdings, Britvic, Countryside Properties, Diploma, Euromoney Institutional Investor, Grainger, Greencore Group, Marston's, Mitchells & Butlers, SSP Group, Thomas Cook Group, UDG Healthcare, Victrex

Final 3i Group, Assura, Booker Group, British Land Co, BTG, Burberry Group, Caledonia Investments, Dairy Crest Group, DCC, Electrocomponents, HICL Infrastructure Company, ICAP, Investec, Land Securities Group, Royal Mail Group, SABMiller, Scottish Mortgage Inv Trust, SSE, Vodafone Group

THE FTSE 100/S&P 500 MONTHLY SWITCHING STRATEGY

An update on a strategy to exploit the monthly comparative returns of the FTSE 100 and S&P 500.

Although since 1984 the S&P 500 has greatly outperformed the FTSE 100 (+1216% against +578%), there are months in the year when the FTSE 100 fairly consistently outperforms the S&P 500.

The following chart shows the monthly outperformance of the FTSE 100 over the S&P 500 since 1984.

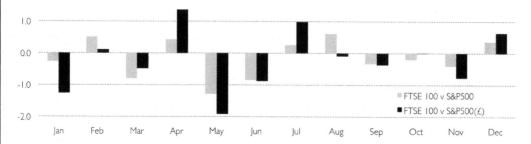

Looking first at the light grey bars in the chart, this shows, for example, that on average in January the FTSE 100 has outperformed the S&P 500 by -0.3 percentage points (i.e. the UK index has underperformed the US index). From the chart we can see that the five months that are relatively strong for the FTSE 100 are: February, April, July, August and December. For example, the FTSE 100 has outperformed the S&P 500 in February in 13 of the past 15 years.

Now, turning to the black bars, these display the same average monthly outperformance of the FTSE 100 over the S&P 500, except this time the S&P 500 has been sterling-adjusted. One effect of adjusting for currency moves is to amplify the outperformance of the FTSE 100 index in certain months (April, July and December). Conversely, the FTSE 100 underperformance is amplified in January, May and November.

Whereas, before, the relatively strong FTSE 100 months were February, April, July, August and December, we can see that the currency-adjusted strong months are just April, July and December.

The FTSE 100/S&P 500 monthly switching strategy (FSMSP)

The above results suggest a strategy of investing in the UK market (i.e. the FTSE 100) in the months April, July and December, and in the US market (i.e. the S&P 500) for the rest of the year. In other words, the portfolio would be invested in the S&P 500 from January to March, at the end of March it switches out of the S&P 500 into the FTSE 100 for one month, then back into the S&P 500 for two months, into the FTSE 100 for July, back into the S&P 500 for four months, then back into the FTSE 100 for December, and finally back into the S&P 500 to start the next year.

The following chart shows the result of operating such a strategy from 2000 to 2016. For comparison, the chart also includes the portfolio returns from continuous investments in the FTSE 100 and S&P 500 (in GB pounds).

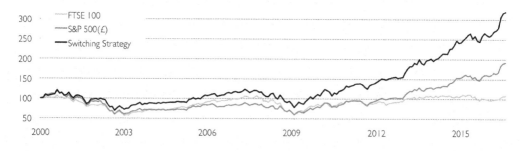

The final result: since 2000 the FTSE 100 portfolio would have grown 8% and the S&P 500(£) would have risen 91%, but the FTSE 100/S&P 500 monthly switching portfolio (FSMSP) would have increased 220%. Switching six times a year would have incurred some commission costs, but these would not have dented performance significantly.

Mon
22

1980: Namco releases the highly-influential video game Pac-Man.

FTSE 100	54	0.0	1.0
FTSE 250	64	0.0	1.1
S&P 500	53	0.0	0.7
NIKKEI	58	0.0	1.3

RHS Chelsea Flower Show (until 27th)

Tue
23

1933: World Trade Day is first celebrated.

FTSE 100	38	-0.4	1.1
FTSE 250	50	0.0	1.3
S&P 500	42	-0.2	0.8
NIKKEI	50	-0.3	1.8

Football: Europa League Final, Friends Arena, Solna

Wed
24

1993: Microsoft unveils Windows NT.

FTSE 100	43	-0.1	0.8
FTSE 250	48	-0.1	0.7
S&P 500	51	0.0	0.9
NIKKEI	59	0.1	0.9

New Moon

Thu
25

1967: Celtic win football's European Cup, defeating Internazionale Milano 2-1.

FTSE 100	56	-0.1	1.1
FTSE 250	47	-0.2	1.0
S&P 500	51	-0.1	0.8
NIKKEI	52	-0.1	1.3

Fri
26

1896: Charles Dow publishes the first edition of the DJIA.

FTSE 100	56	0.2	0.8
FTSE 250	44	0.3	1.0
S&P 500	50	0.1	0.8
NIKKEI	70	0.2	1.0

Sat 27   Ramadan (until 25th June); Football: FA Cup Final, Wembley

Sun 28   Motor racing: Indianapolis 500

COMPANY RESULTS

Interim British Empire Trust, CYBG, Paragon Group, Shaftesbury, Zoopla Property Group
Final Aveva Group, B&M European Value Retail, Babcock International Group, Big Yellow Group, Cranswick, Edinburgh Inv Trust, Entertainment One, Great Portland Estates, Homeserve, Intermediate Capital Group, Marks & Spencer Group, Mediclinic International, Mitie Group, PayPoint, Pennon Group, Pets at Home Group, QinetiQ Group, Severn Trent, Sophos Group, Tate & Lyle, TR Property Inv Trust, United Utilities Group, Vectura Group, Wizz Air Holding

JUNE MARKET

Market performance this month

A quick glance at the chart below shows that this is not a good month for shares. Historically, the May-June period has been the weakest two-month period in the year for the equity market. On average, the market has fallen 0.9% in June and the probability of a positive return in the month is a lowly 39% – which ranks it 11th of all months in the year.

Since year 2000, the situation has been even worse: the average return in the month has been -1.7%. And, as can be seen in the chart, the market falls in June can be quite large; the market has fallen over 3% in June in eight years since 1982.

In an average June the market starts strong, hitting its month high on the second or third trading day, but prices then drift down steadily for the rest of the month (the third week is the second weakest of all weeks in the year). The market does tend to end the month on a positive note – the last trading day is the third strongest in the year.

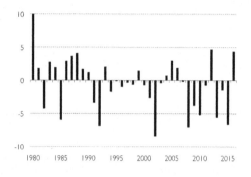
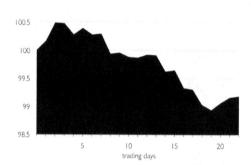

June summary

Market performance	Avg return: -0.9%		Positive: 39%	Ranking: 11th
Sector performance	*Strong* Beverages, Oil & Gas Producers, Pharmaceuticals & Biotechnology		*Weak* [None]	
Share performance	*Strong* RPC Group [RPC], NCC Group [NCC], BTG [BTG]		*Weak* Barclays [BARC], Travis Perkins [TPK], Marston's [MARS]	
Main features	Second weakest month of the year for shares Weak month for silver First trading day average return: 0.16%; positive: 52% Last trading day average return: 0.18%; positive: 64% (3rd strongest in year) 19 Jun: start of the 2nd weakest week of the year for shares			
Significant dates	01 Jun: MSCI quarterly index review (effective date) 02 Jun: US Nonfarm payroll report (anticipated) 08 Jun: ECB Governing Council Meeting (monetary policy) 13 Jun: Two-day FOMC meeting starts 15 Jun: MPC interest rate announcement at 12 noon (anticipated) 16 Jun: Triple Witching 19 Jun: FTSE Index series quarterly changes effective today			

Mon
29

Spring Bank Holiday (UK)
Memorial Day (US)
LSE, NYSE closed
Tennis: French Open, Roland Garros (until 11th June)

1999: Space Shuttle Discovery completes the first docking with the International Space Station.

NIKKEI	71	0.4	1.0

Tue
30

Tuen Ng Festival (Hong Kong)
Shavuot (until 1st June)
Weakest market day
HKEX closed

FTSE 100	21	-0.4	1.2
FTSE 250	35	-0.3	0.9
S&P 500	62	0.1	1.1
NIKKEI	42	-0.2	1.3

1922: The Lincoln Memorial is dedicated in Washington DC.

Wed
31

FTSE Index series quarterly review
Beige Book published

FTSE 100	53	0.0	0.6
FTSE 250	71	0.2	0.5
S&P 500	58	0.2	1.0
NIKKEI	64	0.0	1.2

1669: Citing poor eyesight, Samuel Pepys records his final diary entry.

Thu
1

MSCI quarterly index review (effective date)
Cricket: ICC Champions Trophy (until 18th)
50th anniversary of the release of The Beatles' album, *Sgt. Pepper's Lonely Hearts Club Band*

FTSE 100	57	0.3	1.0
FTSE 250	58	0.2	0.9
S&P 500	65	0.2	1.0
NIKKEI	61	0.1	1.1

1495: First written record of Scotch Whisky appears in the Exchequer Rolls of Scotland.

Fri
2

Nonfarm payroll report (anticipated)
Horseracing: The Oaks, Epsom Downs Racecourse

FTSE 100	50	0.1	0.9
FTSE 250	70	0.3	0.7
S&P 500	57	0.1	0.8
NIKKEI	59	0.3	1.1

1953: Queen Elizabeth II is crowned at a coronation ceremony in Westminster Abbey, London.

Sat 3
Football: UEFA Champions League Final, Cardiff; Horse racing: The Derby, Epsom Downs Racecourse

Sun 4
Pentecost

Interim GCP Infrastructure Investments, Scottish Inv Trust
Final Fidelity China Special Situation, Halfords Group, Harbourvest Global Private Equity, Johnson Matthey, Londonmetric Property, Personal Assets Trust, RPC Group

COMPANY
RESULTS

DO EUROPEAN STOCKS FOLLOW THE US DAY-BY-DAY?

Do European stocks follow the lead of the US market from the previous day? In other words if, say, the US market is down one day are European stocks more likely to fall in their trading session the following day?

To test this the following chart plots the daily returns of the S&P 500 against the corresponding daily return of the EuroSTOXX 50 for the following day.

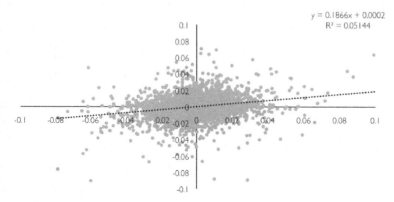

$$y = 0.1866x + 0.0002$$
$$R^2 = 0.05144$$

There is a positive correlation here, but as can be easily seen it is a very weak correlation (a very low R^2 of 0.05).

So the immediate answer to the question of whether European stocks follow the US is: only very slightly.

However, the following chart is interesting. It plots the daily returns for the two indices as above, but this time it is the daily returns for the same day. In other words, this time the US market movements come after those in Europe.

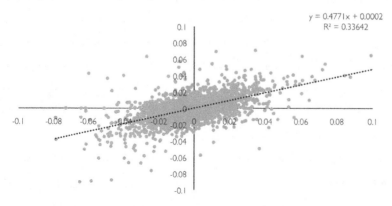

$$y = 0.4771x + 0.0002$$
$$R^2 = 0.33642$$

As can be seen, here the correlation is higher than in the above first case. The $R^2 = 0.3$, which while not statistically very significant is quite a bit higher than in the first case.

So, this might suggest that it is the US market that follows Europe.

Is this the case?

Probably not. Rather it is likely to be a feature of the trading hours of the respective markets.

Each day there is an overlap of a couple of hours between the Paris and New York exchanges, and longer for Frankfurt and New York. Each day European markets can be active at their open in the morning (reacting to overnight developments – including US stock movements), then often these markets can tread water for a while waiting for the US market to open in the afternoon. The European markets can then take their lead from the US for the rest of their trading day.

The higher correlation seen in the second chart above therefore most likely reflects this overlap period when European stocks are influenced by what is happening in the US that same day.

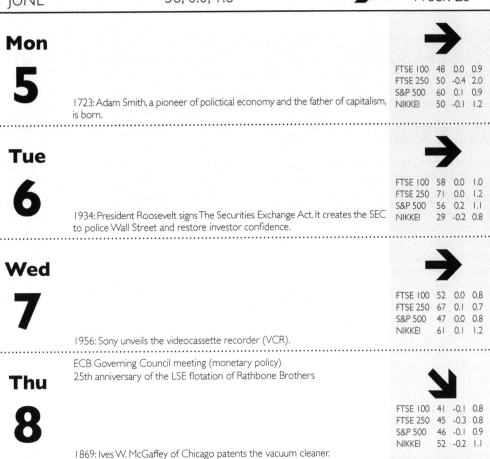

Mon
5

1723: Adam Smith, a pioneer of polictical economy and the father of capitalism, is born.

FTSE 100	48	0.0	0.9
FTSE 250	50	-0.4	2.0
S&P 500	60	0.1	0.9
NIKKEI	50	-0.1	1.2

Tue
6

1934: President Roosevelt signs The Securities Exchange Act. It creates the SEC to police Wall Street and restore investor confidence.

FTSE 100	58	0.0	1.0
FTSE 250	71	0.0	1.2
S&P 500	56	0.2	1.1
NIKKEI	29	-0.2	0.8

Wed
7

1956: Sony unveils the videocassette recorder (VCR).

FTSE 100	52	0.0	0.8
FTSE 250	67	0.1	0.7
S&P 500	47	0.0	0.8
NIKKEI	61	0.1	1.2

Thu
8

ECB Governing Council meeting (monetary policy)
25th anniversary of the LSE flotation of Rathbone Brothers

1869: Ives W. McGaffey of Chicago patents the vacuum cleaner.

FTSE 100	41	-0.1	0.8
FTSE 250	45	-0.3	0.8
S&P 500	46	-0.1	0.9
NIKKEI	52	-0.2	1.1

Fri
9

Full Moon

1975: The first live transmission from the House of Commons is broadcast by BBC Radio and commercial stations.

FTSE 100	43	0.1	0.8
FTSE 250	59	0.2	0.7
S&P 500	42	-0.2	0.6
NIKKEI	45	-0.3	1.1

Sat 10

Sun 11   Trinity Sunday

Final AO World, Auto Trader Group, CMC Markets, Monks Inv Trust, Perpetual Income & Growth Inv Trust, Templeton Emerging Markets Inv Trust, Workspace Group

COMPANY
RESULTS

FOMC CYCLE

An FOMC statement will be released this week following the FOMC's two-day meeting.

The Federal Open Market Committee (FOMC) is the monetary policy-making body of the US Federal Reserve System. Since 1981, the FOMC has had eight scheduled meetings per year. The timing of the meetings is quite irregular but the schedule of meetings for a particular year is announced ahead of time and can be found on the Federal Reserve website (www.federalreserve.gov/monetarypolicy/fomccalendars.htm).

A recent academic paper[1] came up with a remarkable finding regarding the influence of the FOMC meeting cycle on stock returns. To quote the paper:

> "since 1994 the equity premium in the US and worldwide is earned entirely in weeks 0, 2, 4 and 6 in FOMC cycle time, i.e. in even weeks starting from the last FOMC meeting."

The author of the paper explains this as a result of the Federal Reserve reacting to poor stock returns with more accommodation than expected (the infamous "Fed put"). The Fed's monetary-policy decision-making tends to take place in even weeks.

The effect on equities is quite striking. According to the paper, a strategy that bought the S&P 500 in the even weeks after FOMC announcements and sold in the odd weeks would have seen a 650% return since 1994, against a market return of 505% for the period. The opposite strategy (i.e. buying in odd weeks) would have had negative returns.

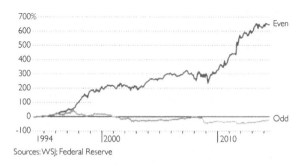

Sources: WSJ; Federal Reserve

The top chart on the right comes from a *Wall Street Journal* report on the findings in the paper. It shows the total return on the S&P 500 investing on odd and even weeks around the scheduled FOMC policy announcements. For example, the odd strategy holds stocks in the week before the announcement and the week following the one in which the announcement is made.

And this effect does not seem limited to the US market. The bottom chart on the right, taken from the original paper, shows the international returns over the FOMC cycle. Where: WI is the world index; DMxUS is the developed market index excluding US; and EM is the emerging market index. All indices are in USD. Although the lines are rather bunched together on the chart and difficult to read individually, we can clearly see that the effect has a very similar pattern throughout global markets.

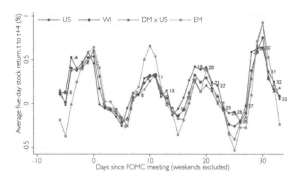

1. A. Cieslak, A. Morse and A. Vissing-Jorgensen, 'Stock Returns Over the FOMC Cycle', dx.doi.org/10.2139/ssrn.2687614 (12 June 2016).

Mon
12

200th anniversary of the Draisine – the earliest form of bicycle.

FTSE 100	42	-0.2	0.8
FTSE 250	36	-0.1	0.8
S&P 500	52	0.0	0.8
NIKKEI	42	-0.3	1.1

1987: At the Brandenburg Gate US President Ronald Reagan publicly challenges Mikhail Gorbachev to tear down the Berlin Wall.

Tue
13

Two-day FOMC meeting starts

FTSE 100	50	-0.2	0.8
FTSE 250	32	-0.3	0.9
S&P 500	63	0.1	0.8
NIKKEI	42	-0.6	1.7

2002: Royal Mail announce they are re-branding as, well, Royal Mail. The brand Consignia is consigned to the scrapheap.

Wed
14

50th anniversary of the LSE flotation of Electrocomponents

FTSE 100	43	-0.2	1.1
FTSE 250	52	0.0	1.1
S&P 500	51	-0.1	0.8
NIKKEI	57	0.1	1.0

2015: *Jurassic World* becomes the first film to make $500m worldwide in its opening weekend.

Thu
15

Corpus Christi
MPC interest rate announcement at 12h00
Golf: US Open, Erin Hills, Wisconsin (until 18th)

FTSE 100	48	-0.1	0.9
FTSE 250	48	-0.1	1.1
S&P 500	54	0.0	1.0
NIKKEI	43	-0.4	1.0

1215: King John stamps the Royal seal on the Magna Carta.

Fri
16

Triple Witching

FTSE 100	57	0.1	0.5
FTSE 250	50	0.3	1.8
S&P 500	65	0.2	0.8
NIKKEI	43	-0.1	1.5

1903: A one-year-old soft drinks company registers its trade name as Pepsi-Cola.

Sat 17   Motor racing: Le Mans 24 Hours (until 18th)

Sun 18

Interim Bankers Inv Trust, Crest Nicholson Holdings, Safestore Holdings
Final Ashtead Group, Atkins (W S), Berkeley Group Holdings, FirstGroup, Halma, Telecom plus, Worldwide Healthcare Trust

COMPANY
RESULTS

SELL IN MAY AND COME BACK...WHEN?

The old saying goes "Sell in May". But if you sell in May, when should you come back into the market?

In its original form the adage was, "Sell in May and go away, don't come back till St Leger Day". The St Leger is the last big event of the UK horse-racing calendar and usually takes place in mid-September.

A complementary anomaly (most likely originating in the US) is the Halloween Effect, which holds that stocks see the bulk of their gains in the six-month period 31 October to 1 May.

At some point it seems the sell in May saying and the Halloween Effect merged to become one, such that today the sell in May adage is usually taken to mean that the summer period of (relatively) poor returns ends on 31 October.

So, thus far we have possible entries back into the market of mid-September or the end of October.

What does the recent data say?

The following chart shows the annual trend of the FTSE 100 calculated on data from 1984. (More information on this chart can be found in the Average Year article, see page 140.)

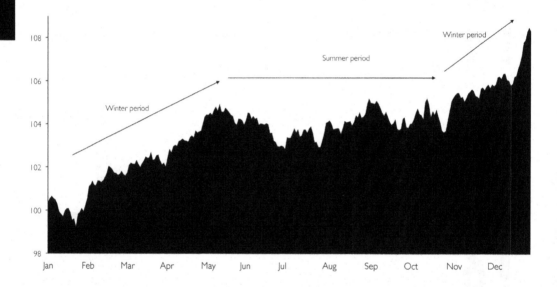

The chart illustrates fairly clearly the different nature of the two six-month periods:

- **1 May-31 October (Summer period)**: when the six-month return tends to be flat, and

- **1 November-30 April (Winter period)**: when the market tends to rise.

The data supports the claim that the greater part of the market's gains come in the Winter period.

Over the whole six-month Summer period the market doesn't necessarily fall, but it does tend to be flat, and certainly the returns are less than in the Winter period. However, it can be seen in the chart that the market is absolutely weak for the two-month period May to June.

So, according to the data since 1984, if you do sell in May **one time for coming back into the market would be the end of June**.

Mon
19

FTSE Index series quarterly changes effective today

1910: Father's Day is celebrated for the first time in Washington, after being suggested by Mrs John B. Dodd.

FTSE 100	50	0.0	0.9
FTSE 250	55	0.4	2.1
S&P 500	54	-0.1	0.8
NIKKEI	54	-0.1	1.4

Tue
20

60th anniversary of the LSE flotation of Bunzl

1789: James Madison proposes the Bill of Rights to the American House of Representatives.

FTSE 100	42	-0.3	1.2
FTSE 250	32	-0.4	1.8
S&P 500	48	-0.1	0.8
NIKKEI	58	0.1	1.0

Wed
21

June Solstice

2002: The weighting of IT companies in the FTSE All-Share shrinks to 1.1%, from its 7% high during the tech boom in February 2000.

FTSE 100	57	0.0	0.7
FTSE 250	52	-0.1	0.6
S&P 500	53	0.0	0.8
NIKKEI	65	0.4	1.4

Thu
22

Motor racing: Goodwood Festival of Speed (until 25th)

2009: Eastman Kodak Company announces that it will discontinue sales of colour film after 74 years.

FTSE 100	48	-0.2	0.9
FTSE 250	36	-0.1	0.7
S&P 500	49	-0.1	0.9
NIKKEI	39	-0.1	1.4

Fri
23

FTSE 100	39	-0.2	0.8
FTSE 250	35	-0.2	0.7
S&P 500	42	-0.1	0.8
NIKKEI	52	0.0	1.2

1972: UK Chancellor, Anthony Barber, announces his decision to float the pound.

Sat 24   New Moon; 600th anniversary of the Isle of Man's first known Tynwald Day

Sun 25

Final DS Smith

COMPANY
RESULTS

JULY MARKET

Market performance this month

The old stock market adage, "Sell in May and go away" continues, "don't come back till St Leger Day". However, analysis of the historic data shows that the worst returns over this period occur in May and June. After June, returns up to St Leger Day (in September) tend to be quite flat. In fact, after traditional weakness in June, prices quite often bounce back in July – making this month a small island of strength in an otherwise weak six-month period. Since 1984, the FTSE 100 has seen an average return of 1.0% in July, with 55% of years seeing positive returns in this month. This makes July the fifth strongest month of the year for shares.

As can be seen in the chart, in recent years shares have been particularly strong in this month. In the past seven years, the market's returns in July have been over 6% in three years. Currently, July is on quite a run!

On average, the start of the month tends to be strong – the first week of the month is among the top ten strongest weeks in the year. After that, the market has a propensity to drift lower for a couple of weeks before finishing strongly in the final week of the month.

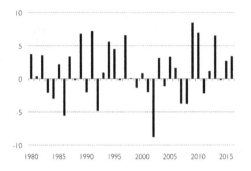

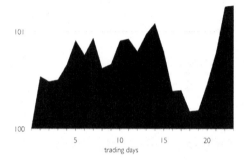

July summary

Market performance	Avg return: 1.0%		Positive: 55%	Ranking: 5th
Sector performance	*Strong* Chemicals, Personal Goods, Real Estate Investment Trusts, Technology Hardware & Equipment		*Weak* Beverages, Gas, Water & Multiutilities, Industrial Transportation, Support Services	
Share performance	*Strong* Elementis [ELM], Croda International [CRDA], Barclays [BARC]		*Weak* Halma [HLMA], Babcock International Group [BAB], Redefine International [RDI]	
Main features	FTSE 100 strong relative to S&P 500 this month 2nd busiest month for FTSE 100 interim results Strong month for silver First trading day average return: 0.54%; positive: 73% (strongest of the year) Last trading day average return: 0.14%; positive: 49% 08 Jul: 6th weakest day of the year for shares 10 Jul: start of the 5th weakest week of the year for shares 24 Jul: start of the 3rd weakest week of the year for shares 29 Jul: 7th strongest day of the year for shares 31 Jul: start of the strongest week of the year for shares			
Significant dates	04 Jul: Independence Day (US), NYSE closed 07 Jul: US Nonfarm payroll report (anticipated) 12 Jul: Beige Book published 20 Jul: ECB Governing Council Meeting 25 Jul: Two-day FOMC meeting starts			

Mon
26

Eid-Al-Fitr
Cricket: ICC Women's World Cup (until 23rd July)

FTSE 100	42	-0.4	1.0
FTSE 250	45	-0.3	0.9
S&P 500	40	-0.3	1.0
NIKKEI	50	-0.2	1.1

1906: The first Grand Prix motor race is held in Le Mans, France.

Tue
27

FTSE 100	58	0.1	0.9
FTSE 250	55	-0.3	1.6
S&P 500	54	0.0	0.7
NIKKEI	38	-0.1	1.6

1954: The world's first nuclear power station opens in Obninsk, near Moscow.

Wed
28

Rowing: Henley Royal Regatta (until 2nd July)

FTSE 100	65	0.3	1.0
FTSE 250	67	0.3	0.9
S&P 500	55	0.2	0.9
NIKKEI	65	0.4	1.3

1926: Mercedes-Benz is formed when Gottlieb Daimler and Karl Benz merge their companies.

Thu
29

FTSE 100	57	0.2	1.4
FTSE 250	68	0.3	1.2
S&P 500	51	0.0	1.1
NIKKEI	52	0.0	1.3

1966: The Barclaycard credit scheme is initiated.

Fri
30

FTSE 100	57	0.0	1.0
FTSE 250	65	0.3	0.6
S&P 500	51	0.1	0.7
NIKKEI	65	0.3	1.1

1987: The Royal Canadian Mint introduces the $1 coin, known as the Loonie.

Sat 1   Hong Kong Special Administrative Region Establishment Day; Cycling: Tour de France (until 23rd)

Sun 2

Interim Ascential, Carnival, Ocado Group
Final Dixons Carphone, Greene King, Stagecoach Group

COMPANY
RESULTS

QUARTERLY SECTOR STRATEGY

A previous edition of the Almanac proposed a simple quarterly trading strategy for FTSE 350 sectors. This page updates the results of the strategy's performance since the last edition.

To recap, in the Statistics section of this *Almanac* the performance of the FTSE 350 sectors in each quarter can be found (page 144). From this data can be identified the sectors that have been consistently strong in each quarter over the past ten years. The four strongest sectors for each quarter selected with this analysis can be seen in the table.

Quarter	Strong
1st	Industrial Engineering
2nd	Electricity
3rd	Software & Comp Srvs
4th	Beverages

The strategy cycles a portfolio through the four strong sectors throughout the year. In other words, the portfolio is 100% invested in the Industrial Engineering sector from 31 December to 31 March, then switches into Electricity to 31 June, then switches into Software and Computing Services to 30 September, then switches into Beverages to 31 December, and then switches back into Industrial Engineering and starts the cycle again.

Obviously, a more sophisticated strategy would be to run the analysis again each year to see if the strongest sectors in each quarter have changed. Another variation would be to hold the top three strongest sectors for each quarter – which would likely reduce the portfolio volatility. However, the purpose of this strategy is to keep things as simple as possible and to see how far such a simple strategy can go without any further analysis and modification.

The accompanying chart plots the performance of such a strategy for the period Q3 2007 to Q2 2016, with a comparison of the FTSE All-Share (both data series have been rebased to start at 100).

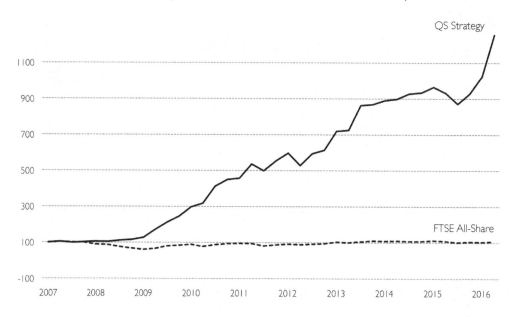

Over the nine years from 2007 the strategy would have grown £1000 into £12,550; while a £1000 investment in the FTSE All-Share would have become just £1070.

Elsewhere in this edition of the *Almanac* there is a moving average trading system that we have somewhat hyperbolically called the "World's Simplest Trading System" (page 16). It must be said that the trading system outlined above could also challenge for the title of simplest trading system.

Mon
3

NYSE closes early at 13h00
Tennis: Wimbledon (until 16th July)

1989: Leicester University announces it is setting up the first British degree course for space scientists.

→

FTSE 100	63	0.2	1.1
FTSE 250	59	0.2	0.7
S&P 500	73	0.3	0.6
NIKKEI	58	0.1	0.8

Tue
4

Independence Day (US)
NYSE closed

1884: The Statue of Liberty is presented to the US by France, commemorating the French and US Revolutions.

→

FTSE 100	54	0.3	1.0
FTSE 250	55	0.0	0.9
NIKKEI	48	-0.1	0.8

Wed
5

1979: The Queen presides over the 1000th annual open-air sitting of the Isle of Man's Parliament, Tynwald.

→

FTSE 100	43	0.1	1.0
FTSE 250	43	-0.1	0.8
S&P 500	61	0.2	1.1
NIKKEI	57	0.2	0.8

Thu
6

Cricket: England v South Africa, 1st Test, Lord's (until 10th)

1957: John Lennon meets Paul McCartney for the first time at a village festival.

→

FTSE 100	48	0.0	1.0
FTSE 250	55	0.1	0.8
S&P 500	53	0.1	0.9
NIKKEI	35	-0.4	1.2

Fri
7

Nonfarm payroll report (anticipated)

1993: In Snowdonia, a gold mine opens to the general public for a £9.50 entry fee. The three-hour trip includes a chance to dig for gold.

→

FTSE 100	55	0.3	1.0
FTSE 250	57	0.2	0.8
S&P 500	56	0.1	1.0
NIKKEI	35	0.3	1.5

Sat 8

Sun 9   Guru Purnima; Full Moon

Interim St Modwen Properties
Final Daejan Holdings, NCC Group, Polar Capital Technology Trust, Sports Direct International

COMPANY
RESULTS

HEDGED QUARTERLY SECTOR STRATEGY

On the previous page we saw the performance of a strategy cycling investment in historically strong sectors through the calendar quarters. On this page we look at enhancing that strategy by, in each quarter, going long of the strong sector and hedging that by shorting the quarter's weak sector.

First, the weak sectors for each quarter are shown in the table (with a recap of the strong sectors)

Quarter	Strong	Weak
1st	Industrial Engineering	Pharm & Biotech
2nd	Electricity	Construction & Materials
3rd	Software & Comp Srvs	Oil & Gas Producers
4th	Beverages	Banks

As before, the strategy trades just four times a year. For example, in Q1 the strategy would be long the Industrial Engineering sector and short the Pharmaceuticals & Biotech sector.

The following chart shows the outperformance of the strong sector over the weak sector for each respective quarter for the period 2007-2016.

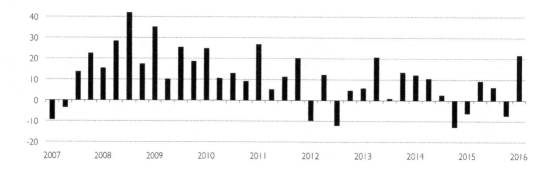

The following chart shows the cumulative performance of the Hedged Quarterly Sector (HQS) Strategy compared to the simple Quarterly Sector (QS) Strategy (from the previous page), and the FTSE All-Share – with all series rebased to start at 100.

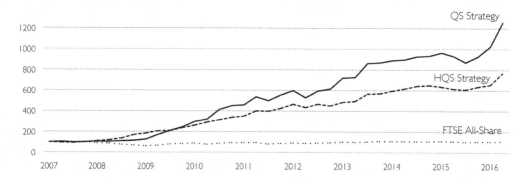

Although the hedge strategy underperforms the simple long strategy, the volatility of the former is less than that of the latter (the standard deviation of the hedge strategy is 0.10 compared to 0.15 for the simple long strategy).

Again, a more sophisticated variation would be to re-analyse the data annually to identify any changes in the strongest/weakest sectors; but this strategy keeps things simple and sticks with the same sectors each year.

Mon
10

30th anniversary of the LSE flotation of RPS Group

FTSE 100	38	-0.3	0.9
FTSE 250	45	-0.1	0.7
S&P 500	51	-0.1	0.8
NIKKEI	38	-0.1	1.0

2001: Lloyds TSB's £18bn takeover bid for Abbey National is blocked by trade and industry secretary Patricia Hewitt.

Tue
11

FTSE 100	57	-0.2	1.4
FTSE 250	55	-0.1	1.2
S&P 500	58	0.1	0.8
NIKKEI	42	-0.1	1.4

1859: The chimes of Big Ben sound for the first time.

Wed
12

Beige Book published

FTSE 100	36	-0.2	0.7
FTSE 250	55	0.1	0.5
S&P 500	49	0.1	1.0
NIKKEI	50	0.1	1.2

1932: Hedley Verity takes a cricket world record 10 wickets for 10 runs in a county match for Yorkshire.

Thu
13

Golf: US Women's Open, Trump National Golf Club, Bedminster, New Jersey (until 16th)

FTSE 100	73	0.3	0.9
FTSE 250	67	0.3	0.8
S&P 500	53	0.0	0.7
NIKKEI	50	0.0	1.1

1992: A 13-year-old boy became Britain's youngest ever Bachelor of Science, earning a first-class honours degree.

Fri
14

Bastille Day
Cricket: England v South Africa, 2nd Test, Trent Bridge (until 18th)

FTSE 100	64	0.3	0.9
FTSE 250	50	0.2	0.8
S&P 500	72	0.2	0.7
NIKKEI	64	0.4	1.2

1867: Alfred Nobel demonstrates dynamite for the first time at a quarry in England.

Sat 15   Asalha Puja Day

Sun 16

Interim NB Global Floating Rate Income Fund
Final Micro Focus International, SuperGroup

COMPANY
RESULTS

MONTHLY SEASONALITY OF THE FTSE 100

A table of all the monthly returns from 1984 for the FTSE 100 can be found in the Statistics section. The following charts show the average monthly returns for the index since 1984: the left chart shows the average monthly returns, while the right plots the proportion of years in which each month had a positive return.

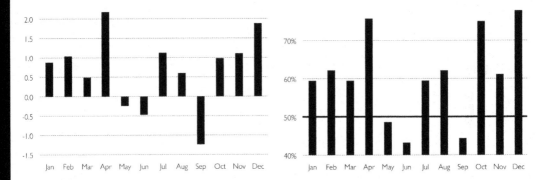

From these charts we can say that since 1984 the strong months for the FTSE 100 have been: April, October and December, and the weak months have been: May, June and September. There is some persistency in these observations as the same profile of behaviour can be seen for the recent period 2000-2016 (the only difference being that January joined the list of weak months in the recent period).

Cumulative performance by month

The following chart plots the cumulative returns of the FTSE 100 for each of the 12 months from 1979 (e.g. the January line plots the returns a portfolio would see if it only invested in the FTSE 100 in January each year).

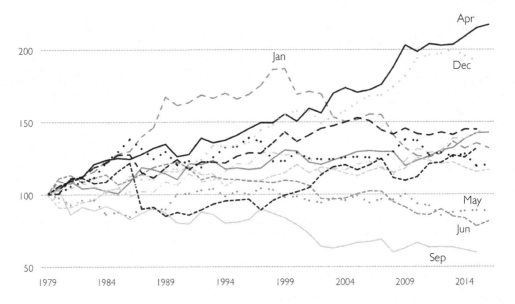

The two consistently strong months are April and December; while it can be seen that September has been consistently a poor performer since 1980. Up till year 2000, the strongest month had been January, but since then it has suffered a steady decline in performance. Conversely, since 1989 October has been one of the stronger months.

See also: Statistics/Monthly Performance of FTSE 100 (page 121).

Mon

17

Marine Day (Japan)
TSE closed
25th anniversary of the LSE flotation of Howden Joinery Group

FTSE 100	58	0.2	1.2
FTSE 250	59	0.1	1.0
S&P 500	60	0.1	0.8

122: Building begins on Hadrian's Wall.

Tue

18

FTSE 100	43	-0.1	1.0
FTSE 250	48	0.0	0.9
S&P 500	36	-0.1	0.8
NIKKEI	29	-0.5	1.1

1968: N.M. Electronics is incorporated – later to be renamed Intel.

Wed

19

FTSE 100	50	-0.1	1.2
FTSE 250	60	0.3	0.8
S&P 500	51	0.0	0.9
NIKKEI	50	-0.3	1.0

2007: The DJIA closes above the 14,000 mark (14,000.41) for the first time.

Thu

20

ECB Governing Council meeting (monetary policy)
Golf: Open Championship, Royal Birkdale, Southport

FTSE 100	45	-0.1	0.8
FTSE 250	48	0.0	0.7
S&P 500	47	-0.1	0.8
NIKKEI	50	-0.5	1.7

1999: Gold trades at $252.85, its lowest price since the 1970s.

Fri

21

FTSE 100	41	-0.2	0.8
FTSE 250	41	0.0	0.7
S&P 500	39	-0.2	0.7
NIKKEI	50	0.1	1.1

1969: American Neil Armstrong becomes the first man to walk on the moon.

Sat 22

Sun 23   New Moon

Interim Howden Joinery Group, Unilever
Final IG Group Holdings

COMPANY
RESULTS

FED RATE CYCLE AND THE UK EQUITY MARKET

The FOMC meets this week to decide its policy on interest rates. If it raises rates what are the likely short-term consequences for UK equities?

The federal funds rate is the interest rate at which depository institutions trade federal funds. So balances held overnight at the Federal Reserve Banks are traded between depository institutions (i.e. a bank with a surplus may lend to a bank needing to increase its liquidity). The rate that the borrowing institution pays to the lending institution is determined between the two banks. The weighted average of all these deals is called the *effective federal funds rate*. This rate is determined by the market but is influenced by the Federal Reserve through open market operations to reach the *federal funds rate target* (which is set by the FOMC).

The following chart plots the FTSE All-Share against the effective federal funds rate for the period 1954-2016. The FTSE All-Share is plotted with a log scale (more appropriate for long periods such as this). The vertical grey bars highlight nine times when interest rates were increased after periods of monetary loosening.

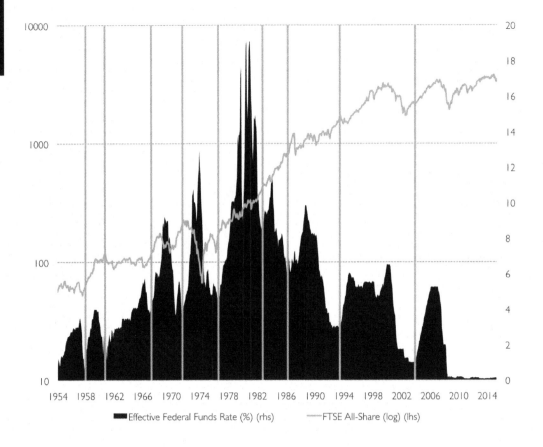

From the chart it can be seen that in six cases the UK market rose following a turn in the monetary policy cycle when rates were first increased; and in three cases the UK market fell afterwards.

Mon
24

20th anniversary of the LSE flotation of Ted Baker

2000: BP reverts to its old name (after two years as BP Amoco) and unveils a new green brand image in an attempt to win over environmentally aware consumers.

FTSE 100	46	-0.4	1.0
FTSE 250	45	-0.4	1.0
S&P 500	44	0.0	1.1
NIKKEI	58	0.2	1.6

Tue
25

Two-day FOMC meeting starts
Horse racing: Glorious Goodwood (until 29th)

1603: James VI of Scotland is crowned as king of England (James I of England), bringing the Kingdom of England and Kingdom of Scotland into personal union. Political union would occur in 1707.

FTSE 100	39	0.1	1.1
FTSE 250	38	-0.2	0.7
S&P 500	57	0.1	0.8
NIKKEI	48	-0.2	1.0

Wed
26

1908: The Federal Bureau of Investigation is established in Washington DC.

FTSE 100	55	0.1	1.0
FTSE 250	55	-0.1	0.9
S&P 500	63	0.1	0.8
NIKKEI	50	-0.1	1.2

Thu
27

Cricket: England v South Africa, 3rd Test, The Oval (until 31st)

1967: Britain's pirate radio stations are declared illegal as BBC Radio One is launched.

FTSE 100	55	0.1	0.9
FTSE 250	33	-0.1	0.7
S&P 500	48	0.0	0.8
NIKKEI	45	-0.1	1.3

Fri
28

Delta Aquarids Meteor Shower (until 29th)
20th anniversary of the LSE flotation of BHP Billiton

FTSE 100	73	0.2	0.6
FTSE 250	59	-0.1	0.7
S&P 500	55	-0.1	0.9
NIKKEI	68	0.4	1.0

1586: Sir Thomas Harriot introduces potatoes to Europe.

Sat 29   20th anniversary of the LSE flotation of Aggreko

Sun 30

COMPANY RESULTS

Interim Aberforth Smaller Companies Trust, Acacia Mining, Alliance Trust, Anglo American, ARM Holdings, BAE Systems, Barclays, Beazley, Berendsen, Bodycote, BP, British American Tobacco, Capita, Capital & Counties Properties, Centrica, Circassia Pharmaceuticals, Countrywide, Croda International, Dignity, Domino's Pizza, Drax Group, Elementis, Essentra, GKN, GlaxoSmithKline, Hammerson, Hastings Group, Henderson Group, Hiscox, IMI, Inchcape, Indivior, Informa, International Consolidated Airlines, International Personal Finance, Intu Properties, ITV, Jardine Lloyd Thompson Group, Jupiter Fund Management, Just Eat, Laird, Lancashire Holdings, Lloyds Banking, Man Group, Merlin Entertainments, Metro Bank, Morgan Advanced Materials, National Express, Pearson, Provident Financial, Rathbone Brothers, Reckitt Benckiser, RELX, Rentokil Initial, Rightmove, Riverstone Energy, Rolls-Royce, Royal Dutch Shell, Schroders, Segro, Shawbrook Group, Shire, Smith & Nephew, Smurfit Kappa Group, Spectris, St James's Place, Temple Bar Inv Trust, Tullow Oil, UBM, UNITE Group, Vesuvius, Virgin Money Holdings, Weir Group
Final Diageo, PZ Cussons, Renishaw, Sky

AUGUST MARKET

Market performance this month

August used to be a good month for the stock market, but this has changed in recent years. Indeed, as can be seen in the accompanying chart, the market has fallen by over 6% in this month in two of the last six years. As it's a month for holidays, trading volumes tend to be low for stocks, which in some years can lead to some increased volatility. The average return for the market in the month is 0.3%, while the probability of a positive return in August is 56%. Internationally, August is not a good month for equities; August has the second lowest average monthly returns for 70 world equity markets.

In an average month for August the market tends to drift lower for the first couple of weeks and then increase for the final two weeks of the month. The final trading day of the month has historically been strong.

Finally, August is the busiest month for interim results announcements for both the FTSE 100 (30 companies reporting) and the FTSE 250 (80 companies).

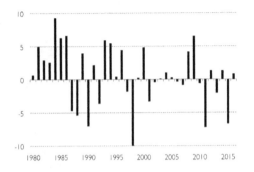
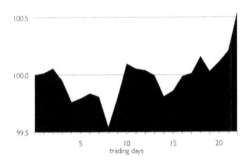

August summary

Market performance	Avg return: 0.3%		Positive: 56%		Ranking: 9th
Sector performance	*Strong* Food & Drug Retailers, Gas, Water & Multiutilities, Health Care Equipment & Services, Household Goods, Software & Computer Services		*Weak* Chemicals		
Share performance	*Strong* Fisher (James) & Sons [FSJ], Petrofac Ltd [PFC], Synthomer [SYNT]		*Weak* Standard Chartered [STAN], Rio Tinto [RIO], Vedanta Resources [VED]		
Main features	Busiest month for FTSE 100 and FTSE 250 interim results announcements GBPUSD historically weak this month Weak month for silver First trading day average return: 0.01%; positive: 58% (3rd weakest of the year) Last trading day average return: 0.11%; positive: 61% 04 Aug: 2nd weakest day of the year for shares 10 Aug: 8th weakest day of the year for shares 21 Aug: start of the 4th strongest week of the year for shares				
Significant dates	03 Aug: MPC interest rate announcement at 12 noon 04 Aug: US Nonfarm payroll report (anticipated) 10 Aug: MSCI Quarterly Index Review announcement date 21 Aug: Total Solar Eclipse (in US) 28 Aug: Summer bank holiday, LSE closed 30 Aug: FTSE 100 quarterly review				

Mon
31

Tisha B'av (until 1st August)
10th anniversary of the LSE flotation of Moneysupermarket.com Group

FTSE 100	46	0.2	0.9
FTSE 250	55	0.6	1.8
S&P 500	62	0.1	0.8
NIKKEI	54	0.3	1.1

1912: Economist and Nobel laureate Milton Friedman is born.

Tue
1

Lammas; Lughnasadh

FTSE 100	57	-0.2	1.3
FTSE 250	43	-0.4	1.4
S&P 500	47	0.0	0.9
NIKKEI	39	-0.1	1.4

1981: 'Video Killed the Radio Star' by The Buggles is the first video played on the new channel MTV.

Wed
2

FTSE 100	73	0.5	1.0
FTSE 250	65	0.1	1.0
S&P 500	57	0.2	1.0
NIKKEI	55	0.4	1.3

1939: Albert Einstein and Leó Szilárd write to Franklin D. Roosevelt, urging him to begin the Manhattan project to develop a nuclear weapon.

Thu
3

MPC interest rate announcement at 12h00
Golf: Women's British Open, Kingsbarns Golf Links (until 6th)

FTSE 100	41	-0.1	1.1
FTSE 250	48	-0.1	0.9
S&P 500	52	0.0	0.9
NIKKEI	32	-0.4	1.1

1978: The British government pumps £54m into John DeLorean's car company, based in Northern Ireland. By 1982 the company is insolvent.

Fri
4

2nd weakest market day
Nonfarm payroll report (anticipated)
Cricket: England v South Africa, 4th Test, Old Trafford (until 8th)

FTSE 100	27	-0.3	0.9
FTSE 250	52	-0.1	1.0
S&P 500	45	-0.3	1.1
NIKKEI	23	-0.6	0.7

1693: The date traditionally ascribed to Dom Perignon's invention of Champagne.

Sat 5 50th anniversary of the release of Pink Floyd's debut album, *The Piper at the Gates of Dawn*

Sun 6 100th anniversary of the birth of Robert Mitchum

COMPANY RESULTS

Interim Aggreko, AstraZeneca, Aviva, BBA Aviation, Direct Line Insurance Group, esure Group, Fidelity European Values, Fidessa Group, Fisher (James) & Sons, Foreign & Colonial Inv Trust, Fresnillo, Greggs, Hill & Smith Holdings, HSBC Holdings, Ibstock, Inmarsat, InterContinental Hotels Group, Intertek Group, Keller Group, Kennedy Wilson Europe Real Estate, Ladbrokes, London Stock Exchange Group, Meggitt, Millennium & Copthorne Hotels, Mondi, Moneysupermarket.com Group, Murray International Trust, Pendragon, Randgold Resources, Rotork, Royal Bank of Scotland Group, RSA Insurance Group, Senior, Serco Group, Standard Chartered, Taylor Wimpey, Travis Perkins, Tullett Prebon, Ultra Electronics Holdings, William Hill

LUNAR CALENDAR AND THE STOCK MARKET

Do the phases of the moon affect the stock market?

Lunar calendars are based on the phases of the moon. Most lunar calendars used today (e.g. the Chinese calendar, Hebrew calendar and Hindu calendar) are in fact *lunisolar*, which means they reconcile a lunar calendar with the solar year. The only widely used calendar that is purely lunar is the Islamic calendar.

One half of the moon is always illuminated by the sun, but its visibility from the earth varies from zero (new moon) to 100% (full moon). The time between new moons is approximately 29.5 days.

In folklore (and sometimes scientific studies), full moons have been said to affect human behaviour. Of course, it is ridiculous to ask, but can full moons affect the behaviour of investors and thereby influence the stock market?

The table below shows the result of an analysis of this (on FTSE 100 daily data since January 2000). "All days" refers to all market days since Jan 2000. FM(0) refers to the day of the full moon and the other columns to the one and two days before and after the full moon.

	All days	FM(-2)	FM(-1)	FM(0)	FM(+1)	FM(+2)
Number of days	4212	206	206	206	206	206
Positive days (%)	51.4	44.7	55.3	52.4	54.9	50.5
Average daily return (%)	0.008	-0.168	0.082	0.055	0.023	0.013
Standard deviation	0.012	1.417	1.361	1.051	1.267	1.169

It was found that on days with a full moon the FTSE 100 rose on average 0.055% (seven times the average increase of 0.008% for all days). The market had a tendency to rise the day after a full moon as well. By contrast, two days before a full moon the market tended to be weak.

Lunar eclipses

Lunar eclipses occur when the earth passes between the sun and the moon – they can only happen at full moons. The chart below shows the FTSE 100 since 2004 and the incidence of lunar eclipses (the vertical bars).

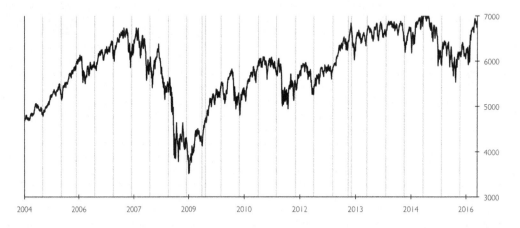

A quick look at the above chart shows that there is no close correlation between lunar eclipses and the behaviour of the stock market. However... if one was so minded, it is possible to see some correlation on occasions. Occasionally the eclipses do accompany strong moves in the market, including significant turning points. An interesting time can be when two eclipses unusually occur in consecutive months (this happened in July 2009 when the market rose 12% in 22 days between the two eclipses, and again in 2013 when the market increased sharply between the two eclipses in April and May). No doubt a coincidence...

There will be two lunar eclipses in 2017: 11 February and 7 August.

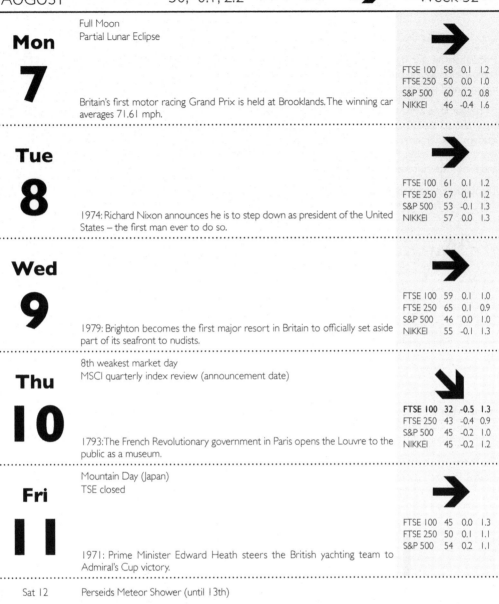

Mon 7

Full Moon
Partial Lunar Eclipse

Britain's first motor racing Grand Prix is held at Brooklands. The winning car averages 71.61 mph.

FTSE 100	58	0.1	1.2
FTSE 250	50	0.0	1.0
S&P 500	60	0.2	0.8
NIKKEI	46	-0.4	1.6

Tue 8

1974: Richard Nixon announces he is to step down as president of the United States – the first man ever to do so.

FTSE 100	61	0.1	1.2
FTSE 250	67	0.1	1.2
S&P 500	53	-0.1	1.3
NIKKEI	57	0.0	1.3

Wed 9

1979: Brighton becomes the first major resort in Britain to officially set aside part of its seafront to nudists.

FTSE 100	59	0.1	1.0
FTSE 250	65	0.1	0.9
S&P 500	46	0.0	1.0
NIKKEI	55	-0.1	1.3

Thu 10

8th weakest market day
MSCI quarterly index review (announcement date)

1793: The French Revolutionary government in Paris opens the Louvre to the public as a museum.

FTSE 100	32	-0.5	1.3
FTSE 250	43	-0.4	0.9
S&P 500	45	-0.2	1.0
NIKKEI	45	-0.2	1.2

Fri 11

Mountain Day (Japan)
TSE closed

1971: Prime Minister Edward Heath steers the British yachting team to Admiral's Cup victory.

FTSE 100	45	0.0	1.3
FTSE 250	50	0.1	1.1
S&P 500	54	0.2	1.1

Sat 12   Perseids Meteor Shower (until 13th)

Sun 13   Tisha B'av (until 14th)

COMPANY RESULTS

Interim Aldermore Group, Amec Foster Wheeler, Balfour Beatty, Centamin, Cineworld Group, Cobham, Coca-Cola, Derwent London, G4S, IP Group, JPMorgan American Inv Trust, Legal & General Group, Old Mutual, PageGroup, Paysafe Group, Prudential, Regus, Rio Tinto, Savills, SIG, Spirax-Sarco Engineering, Standard Life, Synthomer, Tritax Big Box REIT, Woodford Patient Capital Trust, Worldpay Group

Final Associated British Foods

SEASONALITY OF GBPUSD

Does the GB pound/US dollar exchange rate exhibit a monthly seasonality?

Fluctuations in sterling are very important to equity investors. Over half of all aggregate revenues of FTSE 100 companies originate outside of the UK, and any overseas investors in the UK equity market, and UK investors in international markets, are affected by the sterling exchange rate.

Of course, for a while after World War II nobody needed to worry about currency fluctuations because currencies were tied to the US dollar under the Bretton Woods system. Exchange controls were in place and some older readers may remember being restricted to taking no more than £50 out of the UK. But on 15 August 1971 (45 years ago this week), President Nixon announced the US was ending the convertibility of the US dollar to gold and fixed-rate currencies, such as sterling, became free-floating.

The following chart shows the fluctuations of GBPUSD since it became free-floating in 1971.

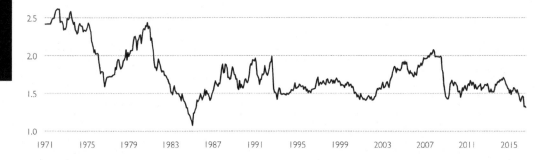

For just over a decade following 1971, sterling fell against the dollar (almost reaching parity in February 1985). Afterwards it traded sideways in the approximate range 1.4-2.0 for almost 30 years. Following the EU referendum in the UK in June 2016, the rate fell out of this established range and at the time of writing is trading at 1.32.

The following charts show the monthly changes in GBPUSD since 1971. The chart on the left shows the average returns for each month; for example, on average GBPUSD has fallen 0.74% in January. The chart on the right shows the proportion of years the rate has risen that month; for example, GBPUSD has risen in January in 44% of years since 1971.

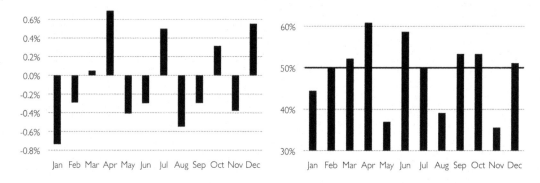

Notes

- Weak months for GBPUSD have been: January, May, August and November.

- Strong months for GBPUSD have been: April, October and December.

These observations would seem to have some persistency as they are also valid for the period 2000-2016.

Mon
14

FTSE 100	67	0.2	0.9
FTSE 250	77	0.3	0.6
S&P 500	57	0.0	0.9
NIKKEI	71	0.7	1.1

1885: Japan's first patent is issued to the inventor of a rust-proof paint.

Tue
15

FTSE 100	57	0.0	1.1
FTSE 250	71	0.1	0.9
S&P 500	53	0.0	0.8
NIKKEI	57	0.3	1.6

2001: Enron employee Sherron Watkins sent a letter to Chief Executive Kenneth Lay warning of accounting irregularities that could pose a threat to the company.

Wed
16

FTSE 100	59	-0.1	1.1
FTSE 250	65	-0.1	1.0
S&P 500	59	0.1	0.8
NIKKEI	50	0.2	1.4

1620: The Mayflower ship departs from Southampton for North America.

Cricket: England v West Indies, 1st Test, Edgbaston (until 21st)
Golf: US PGA, Quail Hollow Club, North Carolina

Thu
17

FTSE 100	59	0.1	1.2
FTSE 250	57	0.0	1.1
S&P 500	77	0.3	1.0
NIKKEI	41	-0.6	1.5

2008: American swimmer Michael Phelps becomes the first person to win eight gold medals in one Olympic Games.

Fri
18

FTSE 100	55	0.0	1.4
FTSE 250	64	-0.1	1.2
S&P 500	45	-0.2	1.0
NIKKEI	59	0.0	1.2

1868: French astronomer Pierre Janssen discovers helium.

Sat 19

Sun 20

Interim Admiral Group, Antofagasta, Bovis Homes Group, Cairn Energy, Clarkson, CLS Holdings, Evraz, Hochschild Mining, KAZ Minerals, Polypipe Group, Spire Healthcare Group, The Renewables Infrastructure Group, Wood Group (John)
Final BHP Billiton, Rank Group

COMPANY
RESULTS

SOLAR ECLIPSE

Do solar eclipses affect stock markets?

A solar eclipse occurs when the moon passes between the earth and the sun. A total eclipse occurs when the moon fully blocks the sun; these are quite rare as they only take place along a narrow path on the surface of the Earth. Other types of eclipses are annular and partial, when only part of the sun is obscured.

On 21 August 2017, the US will experience a total eclipse. This is a big event as the last total eclipse observable in the continental US was in 1979 (when, in fact, the weather was not the best). And the last solar eclipse whose path of totality moved from coast to coast (as it will in 2017) was back in 1918. Of course, this being the United States, the Americans will no doubt play the whole thing down and it may pass many by without being noticed at all.

It can be a scary thing when the sun suddenly disappears in the middle of the day and in olden times people would become fearful at the time of eclipses. Various stories were told to explain the terrible event. Many of these myths involved the sun being eaten by a large animal, for example in Vietnam people believed that a giant frog was devouring the sun (has this actually been properly disproved yet?). Customs developed to chase away whatever was eating the sun by banging pots and pans – so far this has proved a remarkably successful strategy and has worked every time.

Eclipse Date	DJIA
28 May 1900	
08 Jun 1918	
10 Sep 1923	
24 Jan 1925	
28 Apr 1930	
31 Aug 1932	
04 Feb 1943	
09 Jul 1945	
30 Jun 1954	
02 Oct 1959	
20 Jul 1963	
07 Mar 1970	
26 Feb 1979	
11 Jul 1991	
26 Feb 1998	

Scientists (slayers of myths, and general killjoys) claim that there is no evidence that solar eclipses affect human behaviour, health or the environment. But is this true?

The above table lists all the total solar eclipses seen in the US since 1900, with in each case a sparkline showing the Dow Jones Industrial Average for the four days around the eclipse (the eclipse is on the third day).

And the following two charts plot the returns of the Dow Jones Industrial Average on the days around the 15 total solar eclipses that have been visible from the United States since 1900. S(-1) is the day before the eclipse, S(0) the day of the eclipse, and S(+1) the day after. The chart on the left plots the average return for the three days; the right chart plots the proportion of days that had positive returns.

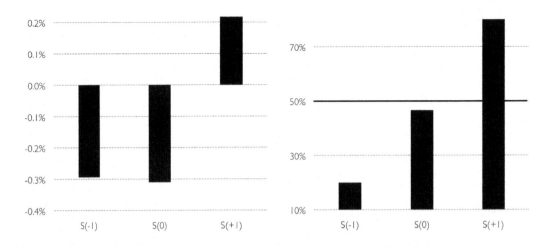

It can be observed in both the sparklines and the bar charts that on the day before the eclipse, and on the day itself, the market tends to be weak (investors are fearful of the big frog). But on the day after the eclipse the market bounces back – the frog has gone and the sun is back.

Mon
21

New Moon
Total Solar Eclipse

FTSE 100	63	0.0	1.3
FTSE 250	64	0.1	1.0
S&P 500	47	-0.1	1.1
NIKKEI	54	0.1	1.6

1972: The first hot air balloon flight over the Alps takes place.

Tue
22

100th anniversary of the birth of John Lee Hooker

FTSE 100	52	0.2	0.9
FTSE 250	57	0.3	0.9
S&P 500	60	0.0	0.7
NIKKEI	45	0.0	1.5

1770: James Cook formally claims eastern Australia for Great Britain, naming it New South Wales.

Wed
23

FTSE 100	55	0.0	0.8
FTSE 250	68	0.0	0.7
S&P 500	41	0.1	1.1
NIKKEI	41	-0.3	1.7

1971: The UK Pound is allowed to float for the first time since the Bretton Woods Agreement in 1944.

Thu
24

FTSE 100	71	0.0	1.3
FTSE 250	71	0.0	1.1
S&P 500	49	0.0	1.1
NIKKEI	55	0.0	1.6

1995: Microsoft's Windows 95 computer operating system is released, with much fanfare.

Fri
25

Cricket: England v West Indies, 2nd Test, Headingley (until 29th)

FTSE 100	71	0.2	1.2
FTSE 250	59	0.2	1.1
S&P 500	47	-0.1	0.8
NIKKEI	41	-0.3	1.3

1530: Ivan the Terrible, future Russian ruler, is born.

Sat 26

Sun 27

Interim Allied Minds, BGEO Group, BH Macro, Carillion, Computacenter, CRH, Glencore, Hansteen Holdings, Hikma Pharmaceuticals, John Laing Group, Marshalls, NMC Health, OneSavings Bank, Paddy Power Betfair, Persimmon, Phoenix Group Holdings, Playtech, Polymetal International, Restaurant Group, UK Commercial Property Trust, WPP Group

COMPANY
RESULTS

SEPTEMBER MARKET

Market performance this month

After summer the stock market tends to burst back into life in September. Unfortunately, the renewed activity in shares tends to be on the downside. Since 1984, the FTSE 100 has an average return of -1.1% in this month, which gives September the worst record for shares of any month in the year. And things haven't improved recently – since year 2000 the average return in September has been -1.9%.

However, although the average return is bad for the month, about half of all Septembers actually have positive returns. The problem is that when the market does fall in this month, the falls can be very large. For example, as can be seen in the accompanying chart, the market has fallen over 8% in three years since 2000.

In an average month for September, the market tends to gently drift lower for the first three weeks before rebounding slightly in the final week – although the final trading day (FTD) of the month has historically been one of the weakest FTDs of all months in the year.

This is the month to consider the Sell Rosh Hashanah, buy Yom Kippur trade (see page 78), and also at the end of the month the Construction Sector 4M Strategy (see page 88).

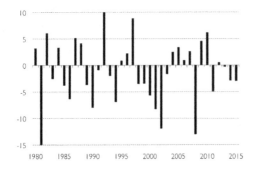
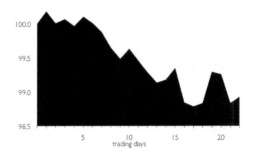

September summary

Market performance	Avg return: -1.1%		Positive: 44%	Ranking: 12th
Sector performance	*Strong* Electricity, Food & Drug Retailers, Mobile Telecommunications, Pharmaceuticals & Biotechnology		*Weak* Aerospace & Defense, Chemicals, Electronic & Electrical Equipment, General Retailers, Media, Real Estate Investment Trusts, Technology Hardware & Equipment	
Share performance	*Strong* JD Sports Fashion [JD.], Lancashire Holdings Ltd [LRE], Beazley [BEZ]		*Weak* Cairn Energy [CNE], PayPoint [PAY], Essentra [ESNT]	
Main features	Weakest month of the year for shares The FTSE 250 is particularly weak relative to the FTSE 100 in this month Strong month for gold Strong month for silver First trading day average return: 0.16%; positive: 64% Last trading day average return: 0.00%; positive: 44% 09 Sep: 5th weakest day of the year for shares 11 Sep: 7th weakest day of the year for shares Consider implementing Construction Sector 4M Strategy Sell Rosh Hashanah, buy Yom Kippur strategy			
Significant dates	01 Sep: MSCI quarterly index review (effective date) 01 Sep: US Nonfarm payroll report (anticipated) 04 Sep: Labor Day (US), NYSE closed 06 Sep: Beige Book published 07 Sep: ECB Governing Council Meeting (monetary policy) 14 Sep: MPC interest rate announcement at 12 noon 15 Sep: Triple Witching 18 Sep: FTSE Index series quarterly changes effective today 19 Sep: Two-day FOMC meeting starts			

Mon
28

Summer Bank Holiday (UK)
LSE closed
Tennis: US Open, Flushing Meadows (until 4th September)

S&P 500	49	-0.1	0.8
NIKKEI	46	-0.1	1.4

1937: Toyota Motors becomes an independent company.

Tue
29

FTSE 100	53	0.0	0.8
FTSE 250	53	0.1	0.6
S&P 500	59	0.1	0.8
NIKKEI	57	0.0	1.4

1786: Shays' Rebellion, an armed uprising of Massachusetts farmers, begins in response to high debt and tax burdens.

Wed
30

FTSE Index series quarterly review
Warren Buffett's birthday

FTSE 100	67	0.3	1.0
FTSE 250	56	0.2	1.0
S&P 500	49	-0.1	0.9
NIKKEI	45	0.2	1.1

1464: Pope Paul II succeeds Pope Pius II as the 211th pope.

Thu
31

Eid-Al-Adha (until 1st September)

FTSE 100	59	0.2	0.9
FTSE 250	81	0.5	0.8
S&P 500	63	0.1	1.2
NIKKEI	45	-0.2	1.4

1955: The first sun-powered automobile is demonstrated in Chicago.

Fri
1

MSCI quarterly index review (effective date)
Nonfarm payroll report (anticipated)

FTSE 100	64	0.1	1.3
FTSE 250	68	0.0	1.2
S&P 500	69	0.1	1.2
NIKKEI	57	0.0	1.5

1901: Construction begins on the New York Stock Exchange.

Sat 2

Sun 3

Interim Bunzl, F&C Commercial Property Trust, Grafton Group, International Public Partnership, P2P Global Investments, Petrofac, RIT Capital Partners, Witan Inv Trust
Final Hays

COMPANY
RESULTS

THE PSYCHOLOGY OF DRAWDOWNS

September has a reputation for market volatility, so let's look at losses.

How do investors measure unrealised losses? One way, of course, is to compare the current price with the price paid for an investment. So, for example, if you pay 100 for an investment and its current market price is 90, then you are sitting on a (unrealised) loss of 10%. But if, after buying the investment at 100, the price had risen to 120 before then falling back to 90, then there is the temptation to anchor the price at 120 and regard the current price of 90 as a 25% loss.

This 25% loss is referred to as the *drawdown*, which is defined as the percentage loss from a previous peak. The concept is common in trading but can also be useful for investors.

The following chart shows the drawdowns for the FTSE All-Share for the period 1969-2016.

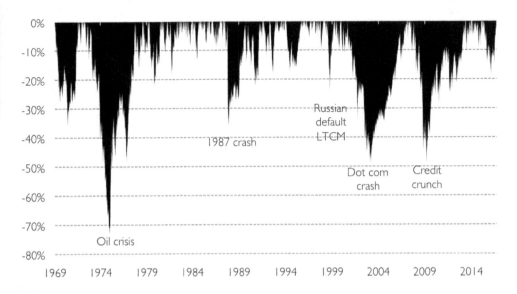

The first thing to notice about the chart is that there are an awful lot of drawdowns! In fact, because the market doesn't make new highs every day, it is usually in a drawdown state. And this can have a psychological effect on investors.

If you look at a typical long-term chart of the stock market, and many individual shares, you will usually see a line that starts at the bottom left and increases (moderately steadily) to the top right. This is a good thing – stocks go up in the long term! However, this chart does not necessarily reflect the actual experience of being invested in the market over this period. For this, the drawdown chart above may more accurately represent the feelings of investors. This is because investors' portfolios are underwater for most of the time, i.e. the portfolio value is below its peak value (which will likely be a recent and strong memory for the investor).

The table to the right breaks down how long the market spends at various drawdown levels. So, for 16% of the time from 1969, the market had a drawdown of 5%-10%, and it was in a drawdown state of over 20% for 27% of the time. And, while a drawdown of just up to 5% may not seem very much, in practice it is 31% of the time that investors are likely feeling slightly disgruntled, having "lost" money.

Drawdown	Time spent
0% to 5%	31%
5% to 10%	16%
10% to 20%	21%
Greater than 20%	27%

So, while the data shows us that stock markets increase over the long term, the direct personal experience of investing may be for investors largely that of a prevailing sense of loss. This sense of loss is something that investors have to learn to live with.

Mon

4

Labor Day (US)
NYSE closed

| FTSE 100 | 58 | -0.1 | 1.0 |
| FTSE 250 | 64 | 0.0 | 0.9 |

1998: Google is incorporated and takes up residence in a Menlo Park, California, garage with four employees.

| NIKKEI | 33 | -0.3 | 1.2 |

Tue

5

FTSE 100	48	-0.3	1.0
FTSE 250	57	-0.3	1.0
S&P 500	39	-0.1	0.8
NIKKEI	48	-0.4	1.2

1698: A tax on beards is imposed by Russian Czar Peter the Great.

Wed

6

Beige Book published
Full Moon

FTSE 100	68	0.1	1.1
FTSE 250	55	0.1	0.8
S&P 500	65	0.1	0.9
NIKKEI	32	-0.2	1.0

1899: Carnation processes its first can of evaporated milk.

Thu

7

ECB Governing Council meeting (monetary policy)
Cricket: England v West Indies, 3rd Test, Lord's (until 11th)
30th anniversary of the LSE flotation of Edinburgh Dragon Trust

FTSE 100	55	0.1	1.4
FTSE 250	52	0.2	1.1
S&P 500	51	-0.1	0.8
NIKKEI	50	0.1	1.6

70: A Roman army under Titus occupies and plunders Jerusalem.

Fri

8

FTSE 100	41	0.0	1.1
FTSE 250	55	0.2	1.0
S&P 500	53	0.1	1.1
NIKKEI	50	0.2	1.4

1966: The first *Star Trek* series premieres on NBC.

Sat 9   Horse racing: St Leger, Doncaster racecourse

Sun 10

Interim John Laing Infrastructure Fund
Final Ashmore Group, Barratt Developments, Dechra Pharmaceuticals, Genus, Go-Ahead Group, Hargreaves Lansdown, Redrow, Wetherspoon (J D)

COMPANY
RESULTS

FOMC ANNOUNCEMENTS

An FOMC statement will be released next week following the committee's meeting.

The Federal Open Market Committee (FOMC) is the monetary policy-making body of the US Federal Reserve System. Since 1981, the FOMC has had eight scheduled meetings[1] per year, the timing of which is quite irregular. The schedule of meetings for a particular year is announced ahead of time.

Starting in 1994, the FOMC began to issue a policy statement (the FOMC statement) after the meetings that summarised the Committee's economic outlook and the policy decision at that meeting. The FOMC statements are released around 14h15 Eastern Time.

Before 1994, monetary policy decisions were not announced; investors therefore had to guess policy actions from the size and type of open market operations in the days following each meeting. But since 1994 there has been far greater transparency over both the timing and the motivation for monetary policy actions.

This has led to a number of academic papers investigating the influence of these FOMC statements on financial markets. One such recent paper[2] found large average excess returns in US equities in the 24-hour period immediately before the announcements (an effect the paper called the "Pre-FOMC Announcement Drift"). In other words, equities tended to be strong just before the FOMC statement. Further, these excess returns have increased over time and they account for sizable fractions of total annual realised stock returns. Quantifying this, the paper says:

> "[since 1994] the S&P 500 index has on average increased 49 basis points in the 24 hours before scheduled FOMC announcements. These returns do not revert in subsequent trading days and are orders of magnitude larger than those outside the 24-hour pre-FOMC window. As a result, about 80% of annual realized excess stock returns since 1994 are accounted for by the pre-FOMC announcement drift."

A quite extraordinary finding!

And the relevance to UK equities is…?

The above quoted paper found that such pre-FOMC excess returns occurred also in major international equity indices.

Let's see if that is the case.

The following chart shows the average daily returns for the FTSE 100 for the seven days around the FOMC statements for the period 1994-2016. The seven days cover the three days leading up to the statement, the day of the statement itself A(0), and then the three days after the statement. Given that the FOMC statement is usually released around 18h15 GMT (i.e. after the UK market has closed), A(0) can be taken as occurring in the 24 hours before the statement.

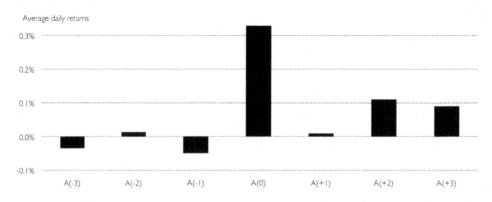

Average daily returns

The result is quite clear: the average daily return for A(0) is 0.33%, over ten times greater than the average daily return on all other days. This does support the claim in the above referenced paper. It is also interesting to note the weakness in equities on the day prior to the FOMC statement.

1. FOMC meeting calendars, statements, and minutes (www.federalreserve.gov/monetarypolicy/fomccalendars.htm).
2. D. O. Lucca and E. Moench, 'The Pre-FOMC Announcement Drift' (2013).

Mon
11

7th weakest market day

FTSE 100	30	-0.1	0.8
FTSE 250	23	-0.3	0.9
S&P 500	57	0.0	1.1
NIKKEI	46	-0.8	1.7

1997: After a nationwide referendum, Scotland votes to establish a devolved parliament within the United Kingdom.

Tue
12

20th anniversary of the LSE flotation of JPMorgan Asian Investment Trust

FTSE 100	48	-0.2	1.1
FTSE 250	52	-0.2	0.9
S&P 500	50	0.0	0.9
NIKKEI	52	-0.2	1.8

2005: Hong Kong Disneyland opens in Penny's Bay, Lantau Island, Hong Kong.

Wed
13

FTSE 100	50	0.1	0.8
FTSE 250	55	0.0	0.6
S&P 500	69	0.2	0.9
NIKKEI	82	0.5	0.9

1503: Michelangelo begins work on his statue of David.

Thu
14

MPC interest rate announcement at 12h00
150th anniversary of the publication of the first volume of Karl Marx's *Das Kapital*

FTSE 100	55	0.0	1.4
FTSE 250	43	-0.1	1.0
S&P 500	54	0.1	0.8
NIKKEI	59	0.3	1.4

1960: The Organisation of the Petroleum Exporting Countries (OPEC) is founded.

Fri
15

Triple Witching

FTSE 100	50	-0.1	1.3
FTSE 250	59	-0.1	1.0
S&P 500	53	-0.1	1.0
NIKKEI	75	0.7	1.2

2008: Investment bank Lehman Brothers files for Chapter 11 bankruptcy having posted a $3.9bn quarterly loss a few days earlier.

Sat 16

Sun 17

Interim JD Sports Fashion, Morrison (Wm) Supermarkets, Next
Final Dunelm Group, Galliford Try, JRP Group

COMPANY
RESULTS

SELL ROSH HASHANAH, BUY YOM KIPPUR

The Jewish holiday Rosh Hashanah will start at sundown on Wednesday of this week. In 1935, the *Pennsylvania Mirror* referred to a Wall Street adage, "Sell before Rosh Hashanah; buy before Yom Kippur". Recently an academic paper[1] quoted this article and set out to establish if the adage was true and still valid today.

The theory is that the market is weak during the approximately seven trading-day gap between the Jewish New Year (Rosh Hashanah) and the Day of Atonement (Yom Kippur). To test this theory, the authors studied the results of short-selling the Dow Jones Industrial Average on one of the three days before Rosh Hashanah and buying back on one of the three days following Yom Kippur. They analysed the nine different combinations of trade dates, i.e. selling on the third day before Rosh Hashanah (R-3) and buying back on the day after Yom Kippur (Y+1), R-3 and Y+2, R-3 and Y+3, R-2 and Y+1, etc. The period tested was 1907 to 2008.

The paper found that the mean returns for the DJIA for the nine trade dates considered ranged from -0.47% for R-3 and Y+2 (i.e. shorting three days before Rosh Hashanah and covering two days after Yom Kippur), to -1.01 for R-2 and Y+1.

In other words, they found that the market had indeed been weak between the two Jewish holidays, and that five of the nine scenarios yielded statistically significant results. They checked to see if this *Jewish Holiday Effect* might have diminished in recent years and found that the effect over 1998-2008 was actually stronger for six of the nine trade scenarios than for the prior period 1907-1998.

So, what's the reason for this?

The authors of the paper found that this was not a result of the influence of other anomalies (e.g. the weekend effect), nor was it the result of data outliers. One Wall Street trader gave the traditional explanation that people of the Jewish religion "wished to be free (as much as possible) of the distraction of worldly goods during a period of reflection and self-appraisal." Of course, Jewish traders are only a small part of the market, but at the margin their withdrawal from the market over this period may increase volatility and risk, and thus discourage others from trading, and then the arbitrage traders exploiting the effect can make it self-fulfilling.

Is this a peculiarity of just the US market, or is the effect present in other markets?

The above cited paper starts by quoting a 9 September 1915 *New York Times* article titled 'The London Market Quiet – Jewish Holiday Causes Small Attendance on the Exchange'. The newspaper reported that money and discount rates on the London Stock Exchange were "easy today" and attendance at the exchange was low due to the Jewish holiday of Rosh Hashanah.

So, might this effect still be in force in the London market today?

The following chart shows the mean returns for the FTSE 100 for the nine combinations of trade dates (as above) for the period 1984-2013.

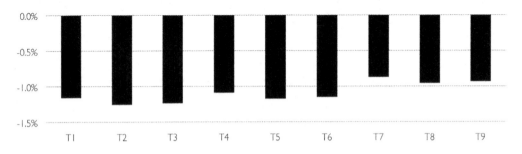

As can be seen, the market was weak for all nine combinations of trade dates over the Rosh Hashanah to Yom Kippur period. The weakest combination was for selling on the third day before Rosh Hashanah and buying back on the second day after Yom Kippur, when the mean return has been -1.3%.

The Jewish Holiday Effect would therefore seem to be as strong in the London market as it is in New York.

1. P. Yaktrakis and A. Williams, 'The Jewish Holiday Effect: Sell Rosh Hashanah, Buy Yom Kippur', *Advances in Business Research* 1:1 (2010).

Mon 18

Respect for the Aged Day (Japan)
TSE closed
FTSE Index series quarterly changes effective today

FTSE 100	46	-0.2	1.3
FTSE 250	45	-0.2	1.2
S&P 500	49	0.1	1.0

1970: Rock guitarist Jimi Hendrix dies after collapsing at a party in London.

Tue 19

Two-day FOMC meeting starts

FTSE 100	57	0.3	2.1
FTSE 250	33	0.2	2.0
S&P 500	46	0.0	1.2
NIKKEI	76	0.8	1.3

1931: The UK comes off the gold standard.

Wed 20

Rosh Hashanah (at sundown, until 22nd)
New Moon
50th anniversary of the LSE flotation of Ladbrokes

FTSE 100	45	-0.1	1.3
FTSE 250	45	-0.3	1.1
S&P 500	46	-0.1	0.8
NIKKEI	32	-0.3	1.2

1999: From today the London Stock Exchange opens one hour earlier at 8h00 to bring trading hours into line with those in Frankfurt.

Thu 21

Al Hijra (until 19th October)
Navratri (until 29th)

FTSE 100	36	-0.4	0.9
FTSE 250	43	-0.3	1.1
S&P 500	38	-0.2	0.9
NIKKEI	55	-0.1	1.1

1937: J. R. R. Tolkien's *The Hobbit* is published.

Fri 22

September Equinox

FTSE 100	45	-0.4	1.4
FTSE 250	23	-0.6	1.0
S&P 500	46	-0.1	1.0
NIKKEI	30	-0.7	1.6

2011: CERN scientists announce their discovery of neutrinos breaking the speed of light.

Sat 23

Sun 24

Interim AA, Barr, Kingfisher, Mercantile Inv Trust, Saga, SVG Capital
Final City of London Inv Trust, Kier Group

COMPANY
RESULTS

UK BANK RATE SINCE 1694

There are many different interest rates in the UK but one of the most important is the *official bank rate* (sometimes also referred to as the *Bank of England base rate*). This is the rate at which the Bank of England lends to banks. It has a direct influence on interest rates in the domestic banking system and as such the bank rate is a reference level for the rates which the London clearing banks pay on deposits and charge on loans.

Changes to the bank rate are recommended by the Monetary Policy Committee (MPC), which meets once a month to consider changes to the bank rate. Further information on the official bank rate can be found at the BoE website.[1]

Over the years, this interest rate has been referred to variously as the Bank Rate, Minimum Lending Rate, Minimum Band 1 Dealing Rate, Repo Rate and, today, the Official Bank Rate. But we can regard them all as essentially the same thing. And we can concatenate these rates over the years to create a continuous record of base rates from 1694.

The following chart plots this continuous times series of base rate levels from 1694. [NB. The X-axis is not a uniform scale.]

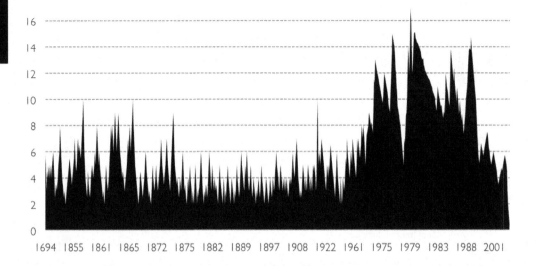

The following table gives some statistics by century on this bank rate data from 1694.

	1700s	1800s	1900s	2000s	All
Count	2	408	383	31	828
Mean	4.5	4.3	8.0	4.3	6.0
Standard deviation	0.7	1.6	3.6	1.4	3.3
Median	4.5	4.0	7.5	4.8	5.0
Maximum	5.0	10.0	17.0	6.0	17.0
Minimum	4.0	2.0	2.0	0.5	0.5

The Count row gives the number of times the bank rate was changed in each respective century.

Until 1973, the average bank rate had been around 4%, but then shot up to levels not seen before – reaching a maximum of 17% in 1980. Volatility (measured by standard deviation) of the bank rate also increased at the same time to levels not seen before.

The low bank rate we have today is clearly unprecedented. Previously, the lowest rates seen had been 2% in the 18th and 19th centuries.

1. www.bankofengland.co.uk/statistics/pages/iadb/notesiadb/wholesale_baserate.aspx

Mon
25

FTSE 100	46	0.0	1.1
FTSE 250	50	0.1	0.9
S&P 500	43	-0.2	0.9
NIKKEI	50	-0.2	1.3

1997: Travelers Group acquires Salomon Brothers for $9 billion.

Tue
26

FTSE 100	57	0.2	1.4
FTSE 250	57	-0.1	0.9
S&P 500	57	-0.2	1.3
NIKKEI	43	-0.2	1.5

1580: Sir Francis Drake finishes his circumnavigation of the earth.

Wed
27

FTSE 100	73	0.6	1.1
FTSE 250	63	0.3	0.8
S&P 500	53	0.0	0.9
NIKKEI	55	0.3	1.4

1998: The Google internet search engine retrospectively claims this as its birthday.

Thu
28

FTSE 100	50	0.0	1.2
FTSE 250	52	0.1	0.7
S&P 500	63	0.2	1.0
NIKKEI	55	-0.1	1.6

1066: William the Conqueror invades England, landing at Pevensey Bay, Sussex

Yom Kippur (until 30th)

Fri
29

FTSE 100	41	-0.3	1.3
FTSE 250	59	-0.3	1.3
S&P 500	45	-0.3	1.4
NIKKEI	45	-0.1	1.1

2008: Following the bankruptcies of Lehman Brothers and Washington Mutual, the DJIA falls 777.68 points, the largest single-day point loss in its history.

Sat 30

Sun 1

Interim Card Factory, Harbourvest Global Private Equity
Final Close Brothers Group, Genesis Emerging Markets Fund, JPMorgan Emerging Markets Inv Trust, Smiths Group, Softcat, Wolseley

COMPANY
RESULTS

OCTOBER MARKET

Market performance this month

October can be a volatile month for equities. Since 1984, seven of the ten largest one-day falls in the market have occurred in October. The largest fall occurred on 20 October 1987 when the FTSE 100 fell 12.2%. So, this would appear to bode ill for investors in October. However, if you look at the accompanying chart you will see why averages don't tell the whole story and how things have changed in recent years. For example, since 1992 the market has only fallen in five years (and two of those of years were the exceptional years of 2008 and 2009). And since 2000, the average stock market return for month has been 1.7%, making it the second best month for equities after April in that period.

The strength of equities in October may not be unconnected with the fact that the strong six-month period of the year starts at the end of October (part of the Sell in May effect) and investors may be anticipating this by increasing their weighting in equities during October. But while October, therefore, should be regarded as a good month for shares, any occasional weakness in the month can be severe.

In an average month for October, the market tends to rise in the first two weeks then fall back, before a surge in prices in the last few days of the month (Sell in May Effect – aka Halloween Effect – again!)

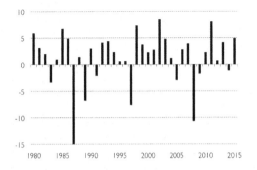
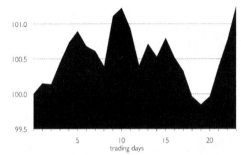

October summary

Market performance	Avg return: 0.9%		Positive: 75%	Ranking: 4th
Sector performance	*Strong* [None]		*Weak* Automobiles & Parts, Construction & Materials, Equity Investment Instruments, Food & Drug Retailers, Health Care Equipment & Services, Household Goods, Life Insurance, Pharmaceuticals & Biotechnology	
Share performance	*Strong* Diageo [DGE], Tate & Lyle [TATE], Whitbread [WTB]		*Weak* Marshalls [MSLH], William Hill [WMH], UDG Healthcare [UDG]	
Main features	Sell in May Effect: end of the weak six months of the year The FTSE 100 is particularly strong relative to the FTSE 250 in this month Weak month for gold, silver and oil GBPUSD historically strong this month First trading day average return: 0.15%; positive: 59% Last trading day average return: 0.49%; positive: 69% (year's strongest) 05 Oct: 10th strongest day of the year for shares			
Significant dates	06 Oct: US Nonfarm payroll report (anticipated) 18 Oct: Beige Book published 26 Oct: ECB Governing Council Meeting 29 Oct: Daylight Saving Time starts 31 Oct: Two-day FOMC meeting starts			

Mon
2

Day following National Day (Hong Kong)
HKEX closed

1900: In Britain, Keir Hardy becomes the Labour Party's first Member of Parliament.

FTSE 100	38	-0.1	1.2
FTSE 250	48	0.0	0.7
S&P 500	68	0.2	1.0
NIKKEI	46	0.1	3.1

Tue
3

1990: The official re-unification of East and West Germany, with Berlin named as the country's capital.

FTSE 100	61	0.3	1.0
FTSE 250	48	0.0	0.7
S&P 500	46	-0.1	1.0
NIKKEI	43	-0.1	1.1

Wed
4

1957: A Russian satellite is launched into space, becoming the first man-made object ever to leave the Earth's atmosphere.

FTSE 100	64	0.1	1.0
FTSE 250	60	0.0	1.1
S&P 500	61	0.1	0.8
NIKKEI	50	0.1	1.2

Thu
5

Day following Mid-Autumn Festival (Hong Kong)
10th strongest market day
HKEX closed
Full Moon

2001: *Pop Idol* debuts on British TV.

FTSE 100	77	0.4	1.7
FTSE 250	67	0.2	1.0
S&P 500	62	0.2	0.8
NIKKEI	64	0.3	1.1

Fri
6

Nonfarm payroll report (anticipated)

2007: Jason Lewis completes the first human-powered circumnavigation of the globe.

FTSE 100	59	0.3	2.2
FTSE 250	64	0.1	1.8
S&P 500	53	0.2	1.1
NIKKEI	68	0.2	1.4

Sat 7   Draconids Meteor Shower

Sun 8

Interim Tesco
Final DFS Furniture

COMPANY

RESULTS

SELL IN MAY SECTOR STRATEGY (SIMSS)

The Sell in May Effect is one of the best known and strongest market anomalies, but exploiting it can be tricky. Here's one way.

The idea is to stay in the market throughout the year but to rebalance a stock portfolio according to which sectors perform the best in the two six-month periods as defined by the Sell in May Effect.

First, the performance of the respective FTSE 350 sectors is analysed for the two periods in recent years. Then some filters are applied:

1. Sectors with less than four component stocks are not considered.

2. Sectors must have a minimum 13-year track record.

3. Standard deviation (i.e. volatility) of a sector's returns must be below the average standard deviation.

4. Positive returns must be over 50%.

From this, the sector portfolios selected were:

Summer Portfolio	Winter Portfolio
Gas, Water & Multiutilities	Construction & Materials
Beverages	Industrial Engineering
Health Care Equipment & Services	Chemicals

The Sell in May Sector Strategy (SIMSS) is therefore:

*   In the **summer period**: long sectors Gas, Water & Multiutilities, Beverages, and Health Care Equipment & Services, and then switch to...

*   In the **winter period**: long sectors Construction & Materials, Industrial Engineering, and Chemicals.

Performance of SIMSS

The following chart shows the simulated performance of the Sell in May Sector Strategy (SIMSS) backdated to 1999 compared to the FTSE 350.

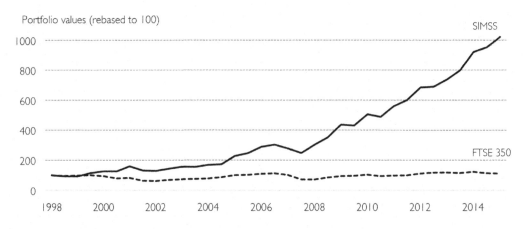

After 17 years the SIMSS portfolio would have grown in value to 1021 (from a starting value of 100), while the FTSE 350 (buy and hold) portfolio would have grown to 111.

This simulation does not include transaction costs, but as the strategy only trades twice a year these would not significantly affect the above results.

Mon
9

Health and Sports Day (Japan)
TSE closed

FTSE 100	42	-0.2	1.1
FTSE 250	45	-0.2	0.9
S&P 500	45	-0.3	1.6

1974: Austrian economist Friedrich Hayek wins the Nobel Prize in Economics.

Tue
10

100th anniversary of the birth of Thelonious Monk

FTSE 100	43	-0.3	2.1
FTSE 250	55	-0.3	1.6
S&P 500	45	0.1	1.3
NIKKEI	40	-1.2	3.1

1986: The first trading day of the newly-privatised TSB.

Wed
11

Shemini Atzeret (until 12th)

FTSE 100	67	0.4	1.2
FTSE 250	65	0.4	0.9
S&P 500	54	0.2	1.0
NIKKEI	56	0.2	1.7

2001: The Polaroid Corporation files for federal bankruptcy protection.

Thu
12

Simchat Torah (until 13th)

FTSE 100	45	0.2	1.2
FTSE 250	43	0.1	0.8
S&P 500	43	0.0	0.9
NIKKEI	35	0.1	1.6

1983: Tanaka Kakuei, former Japanese Prime Minister, is found guilty of taking a $2m bribe from Lockheed and sentenced to four years in jail.

Fri
13

FTSE 100	59	0.6	1.9
FTSE 250	55	0.1	1.1
S&P 500	48	0.3	2.1
NIKKEI	42	-0.3	1.0

1987: The first military use of trained dolphins (by the US Navy in the Persian Gulf).

Sat 14

Sun 15

Interim Brown (N) Group, Ted Baker
Final WH Smith

COMPANY
RESULTS

FTSE 100 REVIEWS – COMPANIES LEAVING THE INDEX

The charts below show the share price of nine companies that have recently left the FTSE 100. The time period for each chart is six months, starting from three months before the company left the index. The vertical line in each chart indicates the announcement date of the company leaving the index.

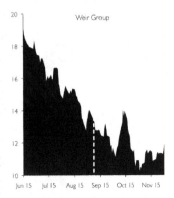

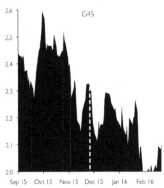

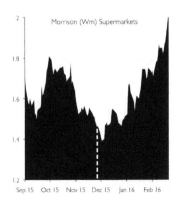

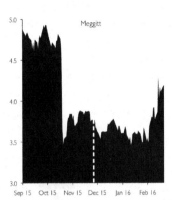

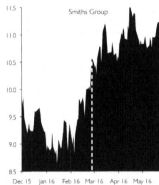

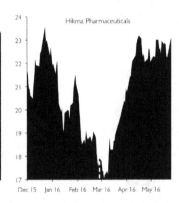

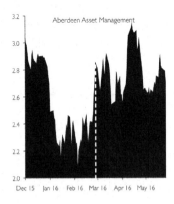

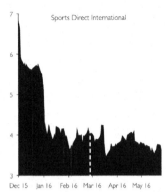

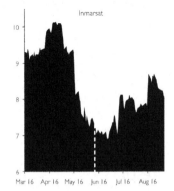

Observation

It can be seen that in most cases the share price falls in the period before the company leaves the FTSE 100. In many cases, after the review announcement the shares rise.

Mon

16

FTSE 100	46	-0.6	1.8
FTSE 250	50	-0.3	1.8
S&P 500	51	-0.1	1.3
NIKKEI	58	-0.2	2.6

1987: Hurricane-force winds batter southern England.

Tue

17

FTSE 100	70	0.5	1.5
FTSE 250	57	0.2	0.8
S&P 500	45	-0.1	0.9
NIKKEI	48	0.2	1.0

2006: The United States population reaches 300m, based on a United States Census Bureau projection.

Wed

18

Beige Book published

FTSE 100	55	-0.1	0.8
FTSE 250	60	0.0	0.8
S&P 500	65	0.3	0.9
NIKKEI	45	-0.1	1.3

1922: The British Broadcasting Corporation (BBC) is established.

Thu

19

Diwali
New Moon
30th anniversary of the LSE flotation of Jardine Lloyd Thompson Group

FTSE 100	45	-0.2	1.6
FTSE 250	52	-0.4	2.0
S&P 500	47	-0.6	3.1
NIKKEI	50	-0.2	1.1

1985: The first Blockbuster video store opens in Dallas, Texas.

Fri

20

30th anniversary of the LSE flotation of Shaftesbury

FTSE 100	45	-0.3	3.0
FTSE 250	59	-0.3	2.5
S&P 500	62	0.4	1.3
NIKKEI	73	0.0	3.6

1997: The Stock Exchange Electronic Trading System (SETS) is launched, introducing electronic order-driven trading for the FTSE 100.

Sat 21   Orionids Meteor Shower (until 22nd)

Sun 22

Interim Booker Group, Home Retail Group, Whitbread
Final Bellway

COMPANY
RESULTS

CONSTRUCTION SECTOR 4M STRATEGY

Elsewhere in the *Almanac* we look at seasonality of various cycle lengths, for example, month, quarter or annual. Here we look at an interesting seasonality effect over a period of four months.

The following two charts analyse the monthly seasonality of the outperformance of the FTSE 350 Construction & Material sector over the FTSE 100.

The chart on the left plots the average outperformance for each month since 1999. For example, the construction sector has outperformed the FTSE 100 in January by an average of 2.6 percentage points over the 17 years since 1999. The value for April is negative (-0.9), indicating that on average the construction sector has underperformed the market in that month.

The chart on the right plots the proportion of years that have seen a positive outperformance by the construction sector. For example, the sector has outperformed the market in January in 13 of the last 17 years (i.e. 76%).

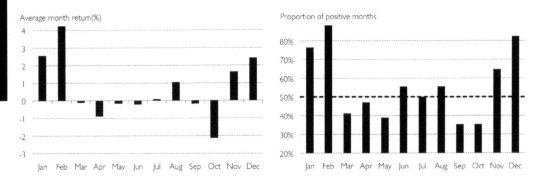

The feature that jumps out from this analysis is the relative strength of the construction sector in four months: January, February, November and December. In fact, the sector has been so strong in February that it has only underperformed the market in one year since 2001.

Strategy

The above analysis suggests a simple strategy (*Construction Sector 4M Strategy*) that invests in the Construction sector continuously in the four months from November through to February of the following year, and is in cash for the rest of the year (i.e. the remaining eight months). The following chart plots the value of this strategy if it had been set up in 1999 and run through to today. For comparison, also plotted is the value of a buy-and-hold FTSE 100 portfolio (both series are rebased to start with values of 100).

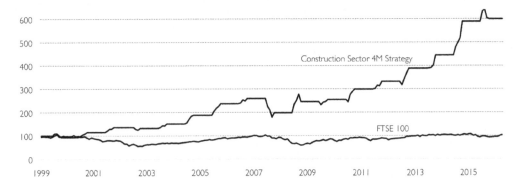

By mid-2016, the FTSE 100 portfolio would have had a value of 103, while the Construction Sector 4M Strategy portfolio would have a value of 600. A good way to build value!

Mon
23

10th anniversary of the LSE flotation of Reckitt Benckiser Group

2007: Nike's purchase of United Kingdom sportswear firm Umbro for £285m is announced.

FTSE 100	58	-0.1	1.3
FTSE 250	41	-0.3	1.1
S&P 500	52	0.0	1.1
NIKKEI	46	-0.4	2.0

Tue
24

1979: Exchange control restrictions are removed in the UK. Sterling and foreign currency can now be used for any purpose.

FTSE 100	48	-0.2	1.4
FTSE 250	43	-0.2	1.4
S&P 500	49	-0.1	1.0
NIKKEI	39	-0.4	2.1

Wed
25

1861: The Toronto Stock Exchange is formed.

FTSE 100	41	-0.3	0.7
FTSE 250	47	0.1	0.6
S&P 500	37	-0.2	0.9
NIKKEI	36	-0.2	1.2

Thu
26

ECB Governing Council meeting (monetary policy)

1529: Sir Thomas More is appointed Lord Chancellor of England.

FTSE 100	41	-0.3	1.5
FTSE 250	43	-0.5	2.1
S&P 500	49	-0.2	1.5
NIKKEI	55	-0.3	1.2

Fri
27

1987: Andrew Krieger, a currency trader at Bankers Trust, allegedly sells short more kiwis than the entire money supply of New Zealand.

FTSE 100	50	0.0	1.2
FTSE 250	45	-0.2	1.1
S&P 500	52	-0.1	1.4
NIKKEI	45	-0.5	1.8

Sat 28

Sun 29   Daylight Saving Time ends (clocks go back)

Final Debenhams, McCarthy & Stone, Redefine International

COMPANY
RESULTS

NOVEMBER MARKET

Market performance this month

Since 1984, the FTSE 100 has risen in 56% of years in November, with an average return of 0.7%. This gives it a rank of 6th place for monthly performance. From 1980, its relative performance had been steadily improving, but that trend has reversed since 2006 – the market has risen only three times in November in the last nine years.

Although the longer-term performance of November is only average, the significant feature of November is that it marks the start of the strong six-month period of the year (November to April). In other words, investors should be increasing exposure to the market this month (if they haven't already done so in October).

On average the market tends to rise for the first three days of the month, then give up those gains over the following few days, then rise again and fall back, before finally increasing quite strongly over the final seven trading days of the month.

Elsewhere, November is a strong month for gold and weak for GBPUSD.

This is a busy month for interim results: 64 companies from the FTSE 350 make their announcements this month.

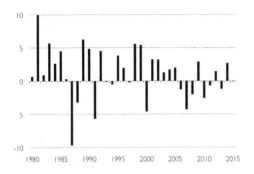
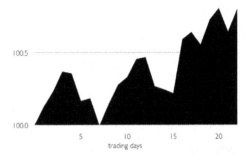

November summary

Market performance	Avg return: 0.7%		Positive: 56%	Ranking: 6th	
Sector performance	*Strong* Beverages, Electronic & Electrical Equipment, Fixed Line Telecommunications, Food Producers, Life Insurance, Media, Mining, Technology Hardware & Equipment, Travel & Leisure			*Weak* Aerospace & Defense, Banks, General Industrials, Oil & Gas Producers, Real Estate Investment Trusts	
Share performance	*Strong* Babcock International Group [BAB], Compass Group [CPG], CRH [CRH]			*Weak* Vedanta Resources [VED], Royal Bank of Scotland Group (The) [RBS], Tullett Prebon [TLPR]	
Main features of the month	Busy month for FTSE 350 interim results Strong month for gold Weak month for oil GBPUSD historically weak this month First trading day average return: 0.13%; positive: 66% Last trading day average return: -0.12%; positive: 41% (year's weakest) 19 Nov: 9th weakest day of the year for shares				
Significant dates	02 Nov: MPC interest rate announcement at 12 noon 03 Nov: US Nonfarm payroll report (anticipated) 09 Nov: MSCI semi-annual index review (announcement date) 23 Nov: Thanksgiving Day (US), NYSE closed 29 Nov: FTSE 100 quarterly review 29 Nov: Beige Book published				

Mon
30

25th anniversary of the LSE flotation of JD Wetherspoon

FTSE 100	67	0.3	1.3
FTSE 250	68	0.4	1.2
S&P 500	56	0.2	1.1
NIKKEI	38	0.4	2.4

1920: The Communist Party of Australia is founded in Sydney.

Tue
31

Halloween
Reformation Day
Samhain
Two-day FOMC meeting starts

FTSE 100	74	0.4	1.0
FTSE 250	81	0.4	1.0
S&P 500	51	0.1	0.9
NIKKEI	61	0.1	1.7

1924: World Savings Day is announced in Milan at the 1st International Savings Bank Congress.

Wed
1

FTSE 100	59	-0.1	0.9
FTSE 250	55	0.0	0.9
S&P 500	59	0.2	1.2
NIKKEI	41	-0.3	1.2

1982: Honda becomes the first Asian automobile company to produce cars in the United States with the opening of their factory in Marysville, Ohio. The Honda Accord is the first car produced there.

Thu
2

All Souls Day
MPC interest rate announcement at 12h00

FTSE 100	59	0.2	0.8
FTSE 250	62	0.3	0.6
S&P 500	67	0.4	0.7
NIKKEI	45	0.1	1.5

2000: The first crew arrives at the International Space Station.

Fri
3

Culture Day (Japan)
TSE closed
Nonfarm payroll report (anticipated)

FTSE 100	55	0.1	1.2
FTSE 250	64	0.2	0.6
S&P 500	68	0.4	1.1

2008: UK Financial Investments Ltd (UKFI) is set up by the government to manage its shareholding in banks subscribing to its recapitalisation fund.

Sat 4   Full Moon; Taurids Meteor Shower (until 5th)

Sun 5

Interim BT Group, Burberry Group, Tate & Lyle

COMPANY
RESULTS

MONTHLY SHARE MOMENTUM

Do shares exhibit a momentum effect from one month to the next?

If we select the best performing shares in one month and create an equally-weighted portfolio of those shares to hold for the following month and then repeat this every month, would that portfolio outperform the market index?

Previous editions of the *Almanac* analysed this for the companies in the FTSE 100; here that study is updated, comparing momentum portfolios comprising each month five and ten of the best performing shares from the previous month.

The following chart shows the results of operating such momentum portfolios from 2011-2016 and, for comparison, the FTSE 100 (all three series have been rebased to start at 100). So, to summarise, the two portfolios in the chart are:

1. **MSMP(5)**: a portfolio rebalanced at the end of each month comprising the *five* best performing FTSE 100 shares of the previous month.

2. **MSMP(10)**: as above, but this portfolio contains the *ten* best performing FTSE 100 shares of the previous month.

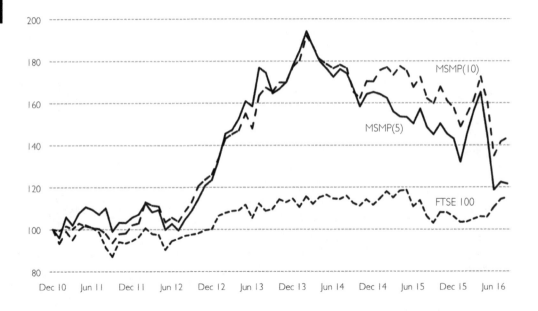

As can be seen in the chart, the ten-stock portfolio only marginally outperforms the five-stock portfolio, suggesting the latter may be adequate for this strategy. But the big story is the decline in momentum profitability from 2014. Profitability may well return, so this is a situation that should be monitored closely.

Reversal portfolio

Previous editions of the *Almanac* have studied reverse momentum portfolios, i.e. portfolios that held the worst performing shares of the previous month.

To summarise quickly here: some form of reversal effect was found (the Reversal Portfolio has outperformed the FTSE 100), but for the moment the extent of the outperformance is not significant and would be unlikely to cover the trading costs required to exploit it.

NOVEMBER

Mon

6

FTSE 100	58	-0.1	1.3
FTSE 250	77	0.2	0.9
S&P 500	56	-0.1	1.1
NIKKEI	54	-0.2	1.8

1972: The British Government imposes controversial measures, freezing pay and halting prices, to try to halt spiralling inflation.

Tue

7

FTSE 100	48	-0.2	0.9
FTSE 250	43	-0.1	0.7
S&P 500	49	-0.2	1.0
NIKKEI	17	-0.8	1.3

2002: Iran bans advertising of United States products.

Wed

8

FTSE 100	59	0.1	0.6
FTSE 250	45	0.1	0.8
S&P 500	51	0.1	0.7
NIKKEI	38	-0.3	1.2

1895: Wilhelm Röntgen discovers the X-ray.

MSCI quarterly index review (announcement date)

Thu

9

FTSE 100	41	-0.3	1.1
FTSE 250	38	-0.2	0.9
S&P 500	53	0.0	1.1
NIKKEI	41	-0.4	1.2

1998: US brokerage houses are ordered to pay $1.03 billion to cheated NASDAQ investors, to compensate for price-fixing.

Fri

10

FTSE 100	50	0.0	0.5
FTSE 250	59	-0.1	0.7
S&P 500	60	0.0	0.8
NIKKEI	50	0.0	1.7

1871: Henry Morton Stanley locates missing explorer and missionary, Dr. David Livingstone in Ujiji, near Lake Tanganyika, famously greeting him with the words, "Dr. Livingstone, I presume?"

Sat 11

Sun 12

Interim 3i Infrastructure, Auto Trader Group, Aveva Group, Dairy Crest Group, Experian, Halfords Group, ICAP, Marks & Spencer Group, Mediclinic International, National Grid, SABMiller, Sainsbury (J), Scottish Mortgage Inv Trust, Sophos Group, SSE, Vedanta Resources, Wizz Air Holding, Workspace Group **Final** British Empire Trust, Imperial Brands

COMPANY
RESULTS

QUARTERLY SECTOR MOMENTUM STRATEGY

Do FTSE 350 sectors display a quarterly momentum behaviour that can be exploited?

This analysis updates the performance of two strategies, defined as:

1. **Strong quarterly sector momentum strategy (Strong QSMS).** The portfolio comprises just one FTSE 350 sector, that being the sector with the strongest performance in the previous quarter. So at the end of each quarter, the portfolio is liquidated and a 100% holding established in the strongest sector of the quarter just finished. This is held for three months, when the portfolio is liquidated and re-invested in the newly strong sector. Therefore the strategy will trade four times a year.

2. **Weak quarterly sector momentum strategy (Weak QSMS).** As above, but in this case it is the weakest sector of the previous quarter that is held by the portfolio. (This could be called a *bounceback*, or *reversal*, strategy.)

Only FTSE 350 sectors with at least three component companies are considered. The period studied was from 2005 to the second quarter 2016.

The accompanying chart compares the performance of the two strategies, and adds the FTSE All-Share as a benchmark. All series are rebased to start at 100.

Notes:

1. As can be seen, both the QSMS strategies outperformed the index over the period of the study. However, they did so with greater volatility (the standard deviation of the Strong QSMS quarterly returns was 0.11, against comparable figures of 0.13 for the Weak QSMS and 0.07 for the FTSE All-Share).

2. From 2012, the reversal portfolio (Weak QSMS) started strongly outperforming the Strong QSMS.

3. A refinement of the strategy would be to hold the two or three best/worst performing sectors from the previous quarter instead of just one (which would likely have the effect of reducing volatility).

4. Costs were not taken into account in the study, but given that the portfolio was only traded four times a year costs would not have had a significant impact on the overall performance.

Mon
13

1998: TheGlobe.com, a little-known Web portal (remember those?) breaks IPO records with a 606% first-day rise.

FTSE 100	46	-0.2	1.0
FTSE 250	27	-0.3	0.8
S&P 500	46	0.1	1.3
NIKKEI	29	0.0	1.8

Tue
14

1972: The DJIA closes above 1000 for the first time.

FTSE 100	57	0.2	0.7
FTSE 250	57	0.1	0.6
S&P 500	51	0.0	1.1
NIKKEI	57	0.2	1.2

Wed
15

1923: The Rentenmark is introduced in Germany to counter inflation in the Weimar Republic.

FTSE 100	59	0.1	0.7
FTSE 250	65	0.2	0.7
S&P 500	46	-0.1	0.9
NIKKEI	50	0.5	1.5

Thu
16

1914: The Federal Reserve Bank of the United States officially opens.

FTSE 100	64	0.1	0.9
FTSE 250	67	0.1	0.8
S&P 500	55	0.0	0.9
NIKKEI	45	0.0	1.0

Leonids Meteor Shower (until 18th)

Fri
17

1967: Beatles Ltd and Apple Music Ltd swap names.

FTSE 100	45	-0.1	1.1
FTSE 250	50	-0.2	0.9
S&P 500	63	0.0	0.8
NIKKEI	50	0.1	2.1

Sat 18   New Moon

Sun 19

COMPANY RESULTS

Interim 3i Group, Atkins (W S), B&M European Value Retail, British Land Co, BTG, DCC, Edinburgh Inv Trust, Entertainment One, Fidelity China Special Situation, Great Portland Estates, HICL Infrastructure Company, Intermediate Capital Group, Investec, Johnson Matthey, Land Securities Group, Royal Mail Group, TalkTalk Telecom Group, Vectura Group, Vodafone Group

Final easyJet, Electra Private Equity

TRADING AROUND CHRISTMAS AND NEW YEAR

This page updates the analysis of the historical behaviour of the FTSE 100 in the nine days around Christmas and New Year since 1984. The days studied were:

1. **Days 1-3**: the three trading days leading up to Christmas.

2. **Days 4-6**: the three trading days between Christmas and New Year.

3. **Days 7-9**: the first three trading days of the year.

The following chart plots the average daily returns for these nine days for two time ranges: 1984-2016 and 2000-2016.

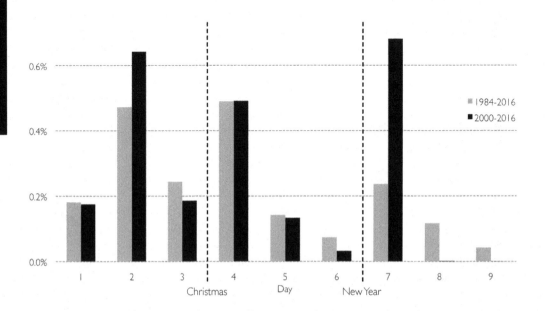

Analysis

1. The market strength increases to the fourth day (the trading day immediately after Christmas). Since 1984, this has been the strongest day of the whole period, with an average daily return of 0.49% (albeit the volatility of returns on this day is high).

2. Generally the profile of returns for the shorter time range (2000-2016) is similar to that for the whole period from 1984. The one significant difference is that since 2000 the strongest day of the period has been the first trading day of the new year. The new year generally starts strongly on the first day, with performance trailing off in the following two days.

3. The weakest day in the period is the third day of the new year, followed by the last trading day of the year.

50, 0.0, 3.1

Mon
20

FTSE 100	50	0.0	1.1
FTSE 250	55	-0.2	0.8
S&P 500	57	-0.1	1.3
NIKKEI	54	0.0	1.9

1969: Native American activists seize control of Alcatraz Island, San Francisco.

Tue
21

FTSE 100	57	0.0	1.2
FTSE 250	33	-0.3	1.0
S&P 500	57	0.2	1.2
NIKKEI	59	03	1.2

1905: Albert Einstein's paper, 'Does the Inertia of a Body Depend Upon Its Energy Content?', is published. The paper reveals the relationship between energy and mass, leading to the formula $E = mc^2$.

Wed
22

FTSE 100	45	-0.1	0.9
FTSE 250	60	-0.1	0.6
S&P 500	56	0.0	0.9
NIKKEI	64	0.1	1.2

1977: British Airways inaugurates a regular London to New York City supersonic Concorde service.

Thu
23

Thanksgiving (US)
Labor Thanksgiving Day (Japan)
NYSE, TSE closed

FTSE 100	55	0.3	1.2
FTSE 250	67	0.2	1.0

1644: John Milton publishes Areopagitica, a pamphlet decrying censorship.

Fri
24

NYSE closes early at 13h00

FTSE 100	50	0.5	2.2
FTSE 250	55	0.3	1.3
S&P 500	79	0.5	1.2
NIKKEI	53	-0.2	1.0

1997: In response to a 554 point fall in the market, NYSE officials invoke the 'circuit breaker' rule for the first time and put a halt to trading.

Sat 25

Sun 26

COMPANY RESULTS

Interim AO World, Assura, Babcock International Group, Caledonia Investments, Daejan Holdings, Electrocomponents, Halma, Homeserve, Mitie Group, Perpetual Income & Growth Inv Trust, Personal Assets Trust, Pets at Home Group, QinetiQ Group, Severn Trent, Telecom plus, Templeton Emerging Markets Inv Trust, TR Property Inv Trust, United Utilities Group

Final Compass Group, CYBG, Diploma, Euromoney Institutional Investor, Grainger, Mitchells & Butlers, Paragon Group, Shaftesbury, Thomas Cook Group, UDG Healthcare

DECEMBER MARKET

Market performance this month

Towards the end of the year shares tend to rise strongly – a characteristic sometimes called the end of the year rally, or the Christmas rally. It makes December the best month of the year for investors. Since 1984, the FTSE 100 has risen in 81% of all years with an average monthly return of 2.2%. Incredibly, the index has only fallen three times in December since 1995, although two of those times were in 2014 and 2015 – so things may be changing.

As can be seen in the accompanying chart, the market tends to increase gently in the first two weeks of the month, but then goes into overdrive and rises strongly in the final two weeks. Indeed, this is the strongest two-week period in the whole year, with the three strongest days of the year all occurring in this two-week period.

In this month investors may like to look at the Santa Rally Portfolio (see page 102), and also consider implementing the Bounceback Portfolio (see page 104) at the end of the month.

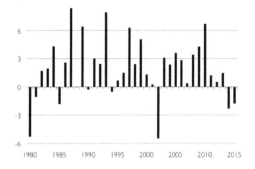

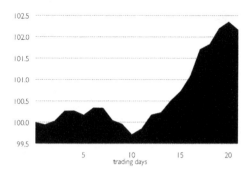

December summary

Market performance	Avg return: 2.2%		Positive: 81%	Ranking: 1st
Sector performance	*Strong* Construction & Materials, Life Insurance, Support Services, Travel & Leisure		*Weak* Banks, General Retailers, Pharmaceuticals & Biotechnology	
Share performance	*Strong* Ashtead Group [AHT], Balfour Beatty [BBY], William Hill [WMH]		*Weak* Debenhams [DEB], Marks & Spencer Group [MKS], Rank Group (The) [RNK]	
Main features	FTSE 100 often outperforms the S&P 500 in December Worst month for FTSE 100 dividend payments First trading day average return: -0.05%; positive: 47% (year's weakest) Last trading day average return: 0.04%; positive: 50% 04 Dec: 4th weakest day of the year for shares 16 Dec: 5th strongest day of the year for shares 18 Dec: start of the 2nd strongest week of the year for shares 23 Dec: 3rd strongest day of the year for shares 24 Dec: 2nd strongest day of the year for shares 25 Dec: start of the strongest week of the year for shares 27 Dec: strongest day of the year for shares Consider Bounceback Portfolio Santa Rally starts on 10th trading day			
Significant dates	01 Dec: MSCI quarterly index review (effective date) 01 Dec: US Nonfarm payroll report (anticipated) 12 Dec: Two-day FOMC meeting starts 14 Dec: MPC interest rate announcement at 12 noon 14: ECB Governing Council Meeting (monetary policy) 15 Dec: Triple Witching 18 Dec: FTSE Index series quarterly changes effective today 25 Dec: Christmas Day – LSE, NYSE, HKSE closed 26 Dec: Boxing day – LSE, HKSE closed 30 Dec: LSE closed			

Mon
27

FTSE 100	58	0.2	0.7
FTSE 250	64	0.3	1.0
S&P 500	66	0.2	0.9
NIKKEI	50	0.3	1.3

1095: Pope Urban II declares the First Crusade at the Council of Clermont.

Tue
28

FTSE 100	48	0.1	1.1
FTSE 250	57	0.3	1.1
S&P 500	53	0.1	1.1
NIKKEI	55	0.1	1.5

1948: Edwin Land's first polaroid cameras go on sale in Boston.

FTSE Index series quarterly review
Beige Book published

Wed
29

FTSE 100	68	0.1	0.7
FTSE 250	58	0.1	0.7
S&P 500	48	0.0	0.6
NIKKEI	59	0.2	1.3

1994: Chancellor Kenneth Clarke announces 17.5% VAT on domestic fuel.

St Andrew's Day

Thu
30

FTSE 100	41	-0.2	1.4
FTSE 250	67	0.0	1.2
S&P 500	47	0.0	1.3
NIKKEI	59	0.2	1.3

1998: The London International Financial Futures and Options Exchange (LIFFE) launches an electronic trading system, Liffe Connect.

MSCI quarterly index review (effective date)
Nonfarm payroll report (anticipated)

Fri
1

FTSE 100	57	0.1	1.8
FTSE 250	68	0.0	1.2
S&P 500	60	0.1	1.6
NIKKEI	64	0.7	1.5

1998: Exxon announces a $73.7bn deal to buy Mobil, creating Exxon-Mobil, the world's largest company.

Sat 2

Sun 3   Full Moon (Supermoon), 50th anniversary of the world's first heart transplant

Interim Berkeley Group Holdings, Big Yellow Group, CMC Markets, Cranswick, FirstGroup, Greene King, Londonmetric Property, Monks Inv Trust, PayPoint, Pennon Group, RPC Group, Worldwide Healthcare Trust

Final Aberdeen Asset Management, Brewin Dolphin Holdings, Britvic, Countryside Properties, Greencore Group, Marston's, Sage Group, Scottish Inv Trust, SSP Group, Zoopla Property Group

COMPANY
RESULTS

SANTA RALLY

Does a Santa Rally exist for shares and, if so, when does it start?

The UK market is often strong from the start of November (this is a feature of the Sell in May Effect). But we can also see an acceleration of the market at the very end of the year. To analyse this further, the following chart plots the cumulative average daily return of the FTSE 100 for December. (NB. The X-axis represents trading – not calendar – days.)

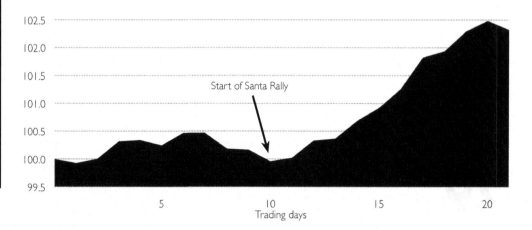

From this we can see that, on average, the market is flat for the first ten trading days of December, after which it rises strongly. So, we can say that the Santa Rally starts on the tenth trading day of December.

How has this played out in recent years?

The following chart shows the performance of the FTSE 100 in the Decembers of 2014 and 2015.

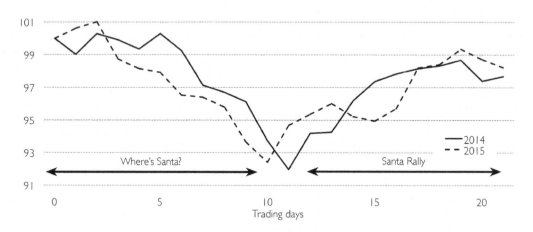

In both cases the index fell for the first ten days of December – during which time people may have asked "Where's Santa?" and "Is the Santa Rally no more?" Then from the tenth day (11th in the case of 2014) the market rallied to the end of the year.

There is no definitive explanation for this Santa effect, but various causes have been suggested. These include: fund managers window dressing their portfolios; positive sentiment in the market caused by the festive season being accentuated by low trading volumes; anticipation of the January Effect; and tax reasons. (NB. Tax reasons are often cited in the absence of any definitive explanation.)

In 2017 the tenth trading day of the month is 14 December.

Mon
4th weakest market day

4

1791: The first issue of *The Observer*, the world's first Sunday newspaper, is published.

FTSE 100	29	-0.2	0.7
FTSE 250	50	-0.2	0.7
S&P 500	64	0.2	1.0
NIKKEI	54	-0.3	1.3

Tue

5

1996: Alan Greenspan makes his famous "irrational exuberance" speech, causing fluctuations in markets around the world.

FTSE 100	57	0.3	1.1
FTSE 250	67	0.3	1.0
S&P 500	49	0.2	1.1
NIKKEI	61	0.2	1.0

Wed
St Nicholas' Day

6

1897: London becomes the world's first city to host motorised taxi cabs.

FTSE 100	55	0.0	0.7
FTSE 250	50	0.1	0.8
S&P 500	60	0.2	0.8
NIKKEI	59	0.0	1.3

Thu

7

1955: Clement Attlee resigns as leader of the Labour Party and is made an Earl hours later by the Queen.

FTSE 100	43	0.0	0.6
FTSE 250	52	0.1	0.5
S&P 500	47	0.1	0.7
NIKKEI	59	0.4	1.3

Fri
Feast of the Immaculate Conception
Bodhi Day

8

1864: The Clifton Suspension Bridge over the River Avon officially opens.

FTSE 100	55	0.3	1.5
FTSE 250	50	0.0	1.3
S&P 500	47	0.0	1.0
NIKKEI	41	-0.2	1.6

Sat 9

Sun 10

Interim Ashtead Group, DS Smith, Micro Focus International, Polar Capital Technology Trust, Sports Direct International, Stagecoach Group
Final TUI AG

COMPANY
RESULTS

SANTA RALLY PORTFOLIO

The *Santa Rally Portfolio* comprises the ten best-performing FTSE 350 shares over the Santa Rally period (i.e. roughly the last two weeks of the year) over the last ten years. The characteristics of the ten stocks in the portfolio are:

1. All ten stocks have positive returns over the two-week Santa Rally period for every year since 2006.

2. The ten stocks have the highest average returns of all FTSE 350 stocks over the Santa Rally periods of the last ten years.

The following table lists these ten shares and their average returns over the Santa Rally periods for the last ten years.

Company	TIDM	Avg (%)
Ashtead Group PLC	AHT	7.4
National Express Group PLC	NEX	6.7
FirstGroup PLC	FGP	6.2
Croda International PLC	CRDA	6.0
Informa PLC	INF	5.5
PZ Cussons PLC	PZC	5.5
Vesuvius PLC	VSVS	5.5
PageGroup PLC	PAGE	5.0
G4S PLC	GFS	4.7
Spectris PLC	SXS	4.7

The following chart compares the performance of the Santa Rally Portfolio with the FTSE 350 for the Santa Rally periods of the past ten years.

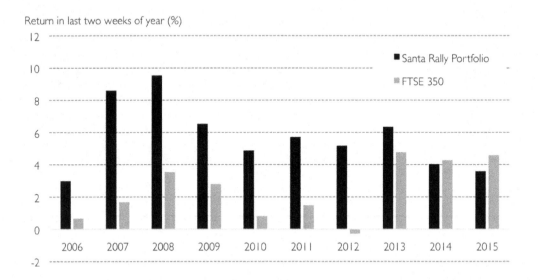

Return in last two weeks of year (%)

Notes:

1. The FTSE 350 has had positive returns in every Santa Rally period since 2005, except 2012. The average return for the index over this period for the last ten years is 2.4%.

2. The Santa Rally Portfolio has had positive returns every year since 2006. The average return for the Portfolio over the last ten years (over the two-week Santa Rally period) is 5.7%, outperforming the FTSE 350 by an average of 3.3 percentage points each year.

Mon

11

1946: The United Nations International Children's Emergency Fund (UNICEF) is established.

FTSE 100	38	-0.3	1.0
FTSE 250	45	0.0	0.8
S&P 500	45	-0.2	0.9
NIKKEI	42	-0.1	1.3

Tue

12

Hanukkah (until 20th)
Two-day FOMC meeting starts

1927: Robert Noyce is born. He goes on to be nicknamed 'the Mayor of Silicon Valley'.

FTSE 100	43	-0.4	1.0
FTSE 250	43	-0.5	0.9
S&P 500	51	-0.1	0.7
NIKKEI	65	0.2	1.5

Wed

13

Geminids Meteor Shower (until 14th)

2012: EU finance ministers agree a deal where the European Central Bank will oversee euro zone banks to try to prevent them failing and triggering another economic crisis.

FTSE 100	64	0.0	0.9
FTSE 250	65	0.0	0.8
S&P 500	52	0.0	0.6
NIKKEI	55	0.1	1.7

Thu

14

MPC interest rate announcement at 12h00
ECB Governing Council meeting (monetary policy)

1959: The Motown record label is founded in Detroit, Michigan, by Berry Gordy.

FTSE 100	50	-0.1	0.9
FTSE 250	52	0.0	0.7
S&P 500	40	-0.2	0.9
NIKKEI	41	-0.2	1.0

Fri

15

Triple Witching

1906: The London Underground's Great Northern, Piccadilly and Brompton Railway opens.

FTSE 100	50	0.0	1.0
FTSE 250	64	0.2	0.6
S&P 500	46	-0.1	0.7
NIKKEI	41	0.1	1.6

Sat 16   100th anniversary of the birth of Arthur C. Clarke

Sun 17

Interim Dixons Carphone, SuperGroup
Final Finsbury Growth & Income Trust

COMPANY
RESULTS

BOUNCEBACK PORTFOLIO

The Bounceback Portfolio had its most successful year ever in 2016.

To recap, the Bounceback Portfolio exploits the fact that stocks that have fallen greatly in a year tend to bounce back in the first three months of the following year.

So, the Bounceback Portfolio is an equally-weighted portfolio that comprises the ten worst performing stocks in the FTSE 350 in a year. The stocks are bought on 31 December and then sold three months later at the end of March.

The chart below plots the Bounceback Portfolio and FTSE 350 returns for the period January-March each year for 2003-2016.

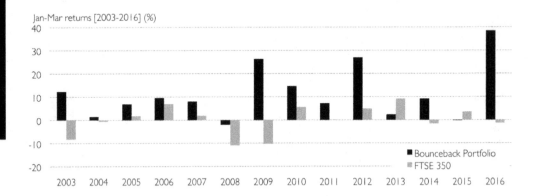

In 2016 the Bounceback Portfolio gained 38.5% against a -1.4% loss for the FTSE 350.

We can also observe:

1. The Bounceback Portfolio has outperformed the FTSE 350 every year since 2003, except in 2013 and 2015.

2. The FTSE 350 has fallen in five years in the Jan-Mar period since 2003, whereas the Bounceback Portfolio has fallen just twice (by relatively small amounts).

3. The Bounceback Portfolio has outperformed the FTSE 350 by an average of 11.3 percentage points each year since 2003.

The following chart plots the cumulative performance of two portfolios that invested in the market only over the January-March period for the years 2003-2016: one portfolio invests in the FTSE 350, the other in that year's Bounceback Portfolio.

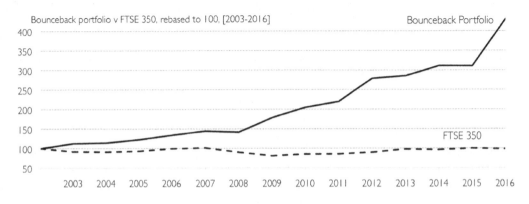

By 2016, the FTSE 350 portfolio value would have fallen 1.7%, while the Bounceback Portfolio would have risen 330.4%.

Mon

18

New Moon
FTSE Index series quarterly changes effective today

1997: HTML 4.0 is published by the World Wide Web Consortium.

FTSE 100	67	0.2	0.9
FTSE 250	68	0.3	0.7
S&P 500	61	0.3	1.2
NIKKEI	50	0.0	1.2

Tue

19

1994: Rolls-Royce announces its future cars will feature a V12 engine which will be produced by BMW.

FTSE 100	61	0.0	0.9
FTSE 250	57	0.1	0.7
S&P 500	43	0.0	0.7
NIKKEI	52	-0.2	1.9

Wed

20

1996: NeXT merges with Apple Computer, starting the path to Mac OS X.

FTSE 100	64	0.2	0.9
FTSE 250	70	0.2	0.6
S&P 500	38	-0.1	0.9
NIKKEI	59	-0.1	1.2

Thu

21

December Solstice
Ursids Meteor Shower (until 22nd)

1898: Scientists Pierre Curie and Marie Curie announce their discovery of the radioactive element, radium.

FTSE 100	55	0.4	0.9
FTSE 250	70	0.4	0.6
S&P 500	68	0.3	0.7
NIKKEI	45	0.0	1.2

Fri

22

1975: British Leyland announces a record loss of £123m for the year.

FTSE 100	73	0.4	0.6
FTSE 250	91	0.4	0.4
S&P 500	62	0.2	0.7
NIKKEI	59	0.1	1.3

Sat 23   Emperor's Birthday (Japan)

Sun 24   Christmas Eve

Final Carnival, GCP Infrastructure Investments

COMPANY
RESULTS

DO THE FIRST FIVE DAYS PREDICT THE FULL YEAR?

The January Effect refers to the tendency of small-cap stocks to outperform large-cap stocks in the month of January. However, the term *January Effect* is used rather loosely and can also refer to stocks generally being strong in the first month of the year, and also to how the direction of the market in January forecasts the market direction of the whole year (this latter effect is also termed the *January Barometer*).

Previous editions of the *Almanac* have looked at these various January effects. In this edition we look at a variant of the January Barometer to see if the **first five days of the year** predict the return for the whole year. We will call this the *January Barometer (5D)*.

The bald figures don't look encouraging: in the 46 years since 1970, the January Barometer (5D) applied to the FTSE All-Share has been right in 26 years (57%). In other words, in just over half the years since 1970 the first five days of the year have accurately forecast the full year.

But let's look at this in more detail to see if we can tease anything out of the figures.

The scatter chart on the right plots the return on the FTSE All-Share for the first five days of a year against the return for the full year, for the period 1970-2015.

There is a positive correlation here (given by the positive sloping trend line), however the measure of correlation (R^2) is very low.

Summary: the chart shows there is a very low level of correlation between returns of the first five days and returns for the full year, but it is far from being significant.

However, strictly, the January Barometer only says the direction (i.e. positive or negative returns) can be forecast, not the size of returns. In which case the bottom chart on the right may be more useful. This plots a binary value for each year:

- 1: if the sign on the full year return was the **same** as the sign for the return for the first five days (i.e. either both positive returns or both negative returns)

- -1: if the sign on the full year return was **different** to the sign for the return for the first five days

In this chart we can see the roughly even split between years when the January Barometer (5D) works and those years when it doesn't. However, the distribution of years when it works is interesting, as there does appear to be a certain clustering of years when the effect works and when it doesn't. For example, in the last 20 years the January Barometer (5D) has been accurate 14 times (a hit rate of 70%). And since 2004 there is a rather odd pattern of the Barometer not working every fourth year.

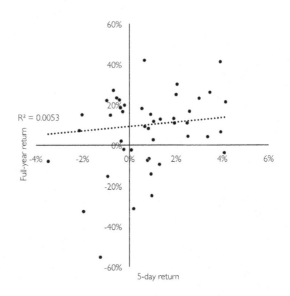

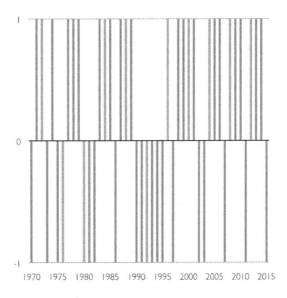

Mon
25

Christmas Day
LSE. NYSE, HKEX closed

1950: The Stone of Scone, traditional coronation stone of British monarchs, is taken from Westminster Abbey by Scottish nationalist students.

NIKKEI	47	0.5	1.3

Tue
26

Boxing Day
LSE, HKEX closed

1933: The Nissan Motor Company is incorporated in Tokyo under the name Dat Jidosha Seizo Co.

S&P 500	84	0.4	0.6
NIKKEI	81	0.6	1.4

Wed
27

Strongest market day

↑

1977: Thousands of people flock to UK cinemas to watch the blockbuster *Star Wars*.

FTSE 100	86	0.5	1.1
FTSE 250	91	0.4	0.3
S&P 500	56	0.1	0.8
NIKKEI	59	0.2	0.8

Thu
28

→

1065: Westminster Abbey is consecrated.

FTSE 100	62	0.2	0.5
FTSE 250	85	0.3	0.3
S&P 500	57	0.0	0.6
NIKKEI	55	-0.1	1.3

Fri
29

9th strongest market day

↑

1782: The first nautical almanac in the US is published by Samuel Stearns.

FTSE 100	77	0.5	1.1
FTSE 250	82	0.3	0.8
S&P 500	55	0.2	0.7
NIKKEI	68	0.2	0.5

Sat 30   New Year's Eve

Sun 31   New Year's Day

Final Victrex

COMPANY
RESULTS

2.
STATISTICS

CONTENTS

MARKET INDICES

DAYS OF THE WEEK

Is the performance of the FTSE 100 influenced by the day of the week?

First, let's review how the index has performed on the different days of the week over a range of periods.

Longer-term analysis

The following chart shows the average returns of the FTSE 100 for the five days of the week over the periods 1984-2016, 2000-2016 and 2012-2016. For example, since 1984 the index has fallen by an average of 0.025% on Mondays.

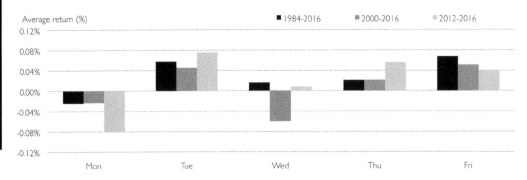

Broadly, a similar profile of behaviour can be seen over the three periods. Namely, the index is weak on Mondays and Wednesdays, and relatively strong on Tuesdays, Thursdays and Fridays. The weakest day is obviously Monday, while the strongest day is Tuesday (this profile has been particularly strong in the last four years).

It is one thing to observe this behaviour, it is another to explain it. The weakness on Mondays might be a result of a reversal of the strength of Fridays, and the strength of Tuesday a reversal of Monday's weakness. Obviously, this sequence of causal price reversals can only be taken so far!

It can be observed that the strength of the market on Fridays has been steadily declining in the three periods shown here.

The following chart is similar to the above, except instead of average returns it shows the proportion of days seeing positive returns. For example, since 1984 the index has risen on 49.7% of Mondays.

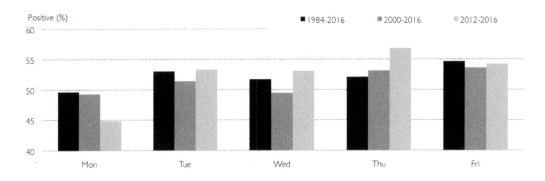

The profile seen here is similar to that seen in the first chart. The weak day again is Monday, although here Thursday is relatively stronger.

So, that's the longer term, let's look now at recent behaviour.

2016

The following chart shows the average returns of the FTSE 100 for the five days of the week over the period Jan-Aug 2016 (the time of writing).

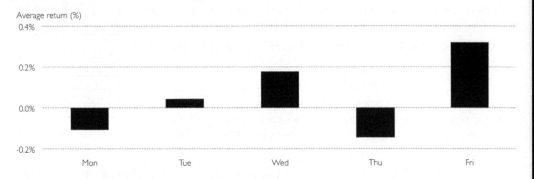

As for the longer term, Mondays are still weak. However, previously strong Thursday is now the weakest day of the week. So far in 2016 it is Friday that has seen the highest average day returns.

The following chart shows the proportion of positive return days for each day of the week in 2016.

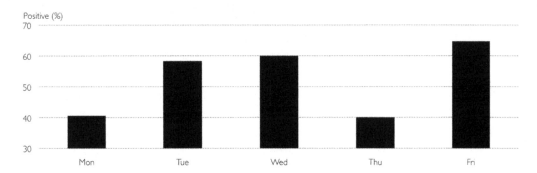

This chart reinforces the observation that Mondays and Thursdays have been weak so far in 2016. Friday can claim to be the strongest day of the week with the highest average returns and positive returns.

The following chart shows the cumulative performance of the index for each respective day of the week. For example, the FTSE 100 has a cumulative return of 11.1% for all Fridays so far in 2016.

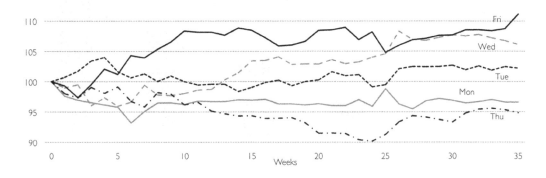

The above chart supports the view that the majority of the positive performance in shares in 2016 has been due to price strength on Wednesdays and Fridays.

VERY LARGE ONE-DAY MARKET FALLS

Analysis of the behaviour of the FTSE 100 for very large one-day falls.

On 20 October 1987, the FTSE 100 fell 12.2% in one day. This is the largest one-day fall in the index since its inception in 1984. The accompanying table shows the ten largest one-day falls in the index since 1984.

Judging by the table it would seem that many of the largest one-day falls have occurred in recent years.

Is the FTSE 100 becoming increasingly volatile?

Since 1984, there have been 224 very large one-day falls, where "very large fall" is defined as a move more than two standard deviations beyond the average daily change in the index. In other words, a very large fall is any decrease over -2.18%. These falls are plotted on the following chart.

Date	Change (%)
20 Oct 87	-12.2
10 Oct 08	-8.8
06 Oct 08	-7.9
15 Oct 08	-7.2
26 Oct 87	-6.2
19 Oct 87	-5.7
06 Nov 08	-5.7
22 Oct 87	-5.7
21 Jan 08	-5.5
15 Jul 02	-5.4

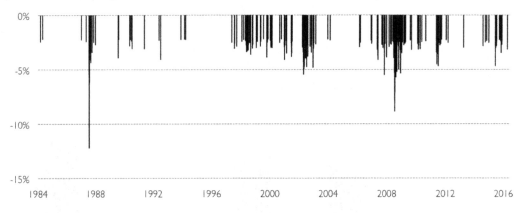

As can be seen in the chart, the periods 1997-2003 and 2007-2010 saw an increased frequency of large one-day falls.

After the fall

The following chart shows how on average the index behaves in the days immediately following a very large fall. The Y-axis is the percentage move from the close of the index on the day of the large fall. For example, by day 5 the index has risen 0.9% above the index close on the day of the large fall.

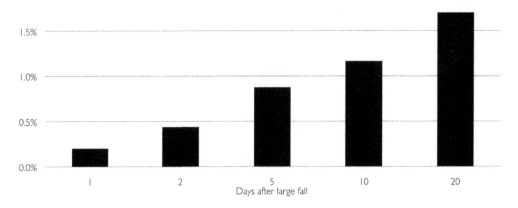

Days after large fall

As can be seen, the index steadily recovers in the days following a very large fall, such that by the 20th day after the fall the index has bounced back 1.7%.

INTRA-DAY VOLATILITY

Since 1985, the average daily Hi-Lo range of the FTSE 100 has been 1.24% (expressing the Hi-Lo difference as a percentage of the close). This means that when the index is at, say, 6000, the average daily difference between the high and low levels of the index is 74 points. The standard deviation of this daily range is 0.9. We could define a very volatile day as one where the day's Hi-Lo range is 2 standard deviations above the average (i.e. above 3.04%).

The chart below plots the Hi-Lo range for the 315 days since 1985 when the range has been over 3.04%.

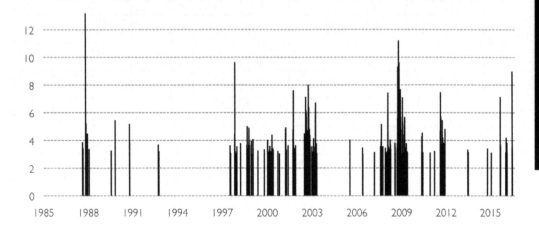

As can be seen, the index has experienced periods of heightened intra-day volatility, notably 1997-2003 and 2007-2009. The record for the greatest Hi-Lo range in a day is still 13.1%, seen on 20 October 1987.

After a greater than 2SD daily return, the average return on the following day is 0.16%, and the average return over the following five-day period is 0.53%.

Hi-Lo-Close

The table below shows the frequency with which the index closes within a certain percentage of the high (or low) of the day. For example, since 1985 the FTSE 100 has closed within 10% of its daily high on 20.8% of all days, and it has closed within 1% of its low on 5.6% of all days.

	10%	5%	1%
Top (%)	20.8	15.1	9.8
Bottom (%)	14.5	9.6	5.6

It's interesting to note that for one in ten days, the index closes within 1% of its high for the day.

Continuing this analysis of where the index closes relative to the Hi-Lo range of the day, the following table shows the performance of the FTSE 100 on the following day. For example, on the days when the index closes within 10% of its low for the day, on average the index return is -0.005% the following day; and when the index closes within 1% of its high for the day, on average the index return is 0.167% the following day.

	10%	5%	1%
Top (%)	0.111	0.132	0.167
Bottom (%)	-0.005	0.001	0.013

COMPARATIVE PERFORMANCE OF FTSE 100 & FTSE 250

The table below shows the monthly outperformance of the FTSE 100 over the mid-cap FTSE 250. For example, in January 1986, the FTSE 100 increased 1.6%, while the FTSE 250 increased 2.6%; the outperformance of the former over the latter was therefore -1.0 percentage points. The cells are highlighted if the number is negative (i.e. the FTSE 250 outperformed the FTSE 100).

	Jan	Feb	Mar	Apr	May	Jun	Jul	Aug	Sep	Oct	Nov	Dec
1986	-1.0	-1.1	0.4	-4.0	-0.1	-1.5	-1.0	2.3	-0.8	-0.3	-2.3	1.5
1987	-1.8	2.6	-2.1	1.3	1.3	-4.8	-2.7	-0.1	-1.3	2.6	1.0	-4.1
1988	-2.0	-1.0	-0.3	-0.5	-1.4	-0.6	-1.3	0.9	0.5	-2.0	0.3	2.0
1989	1.3	-3.6	1.5	2.8	-1.3	2.6	0.1	3.2	-2.1	2.2	2.6	1.8
1990	-1.0	1.4	0.7	-0.3	2.8	-0.8	0.3	4.8	1.9	-1.7	2.9	-1.2
1991	2.7	-4.8	-1.4	1.6	2.2	0.0	2.0	-1.9	-1.9	0.4	0.4	4.0
1992	-1.6	-2.3	-0.2	-3.9	-0.4	1.4	4.8	1.1	1.0	-1.1	-0.1	-6.1
1993	-4.6	-0.6	-2.0	-3.1	-0.1	-0.1	-1.3	-0.3	0.2	1.6	1.1	-0.9
1994	-5.6	-1.6	-2.0	0.5	0.8	2.5	-1.0	0.6	1.5	1.7	0.0	-0.6
1995	1.3	0.2	2.8	-0.3	-0.3	1.5	-2.0	-1.9	0.0	2.0	2.2	-0.9
1996	-0.7	-3.0	-3.4	-2.0	-0.9	2.5	2.6	0.1	2.8	-0.1	1.8	0.1
1997	1.5	-0.5	1.8	4.5	4.2	1.1	5.2	-4.3	3.9	-3.8	-0.5	3.5
1998	4.7	-1.3	-3.4	-1.6	-6.2	6.1	0.5	2.6	1.5	1.5	3.7	3.4
1999	-3.3	0.3	-2.4	-2.8	-1.4	-2.4	-3.3	-0.6	2.0	4.9	-4.7	1.0
2000	-5.5	-4.9	4.6	1.1	0.0	-6.7	-1.9	0.7	-0.3	3.0	-1.4	-0.7
2001	-1.7	-4.7	3.5	0.8	-5.4	1.5	1.4	-3.9	8.1	-2.0	-5.8	-1.3
2002	0.5	-1.0	-2.5	-1.2	-0.3	0.7	4.2	-2.0	-0.2	5.5	0.0	-0.3
2003	-2.5	1.9	0.8	-2.2	-6.6	-3.5	-4.2	-4.9	0.7	-0.1	1.5	1.5
2004	-5.7	-1.8	-2.2	3.1	1.2	-3.0	2.9	0.0	-0.5	0.3	-2.3	-3.1
2005	-2.5	1.2	0.2	3.7	-2.3	-0.6	0.1	-1.6	0.8	0.1	-6.0	-2.0
2006	-1.8	-2.5	-1.3	0.7	0.9	0.6	2.3	-3.0	-3.2	-0.9	-4.2	-1.9
2007	0.4	-0.4	-3.3	0.2	1.1	4.6	-2.1	-0.6	5.0	-1.8	3.6	1.2
2008	-1.7	-1.8	-2.6	5.7	0.2	1.9	-0.6	-1.8	2.9	9.6	1.0	-1.0
2009	-4.7	-4.5	-2.9	-10.0	3.5	-1.7	0.6	-3.7	0.9	1.1	2.5	-0.1
2010	-3.4	2.0	-2.7	-4.2	0.5	-2.4	0.7	0.6	-1.0	-0.7	-0.4	-2.2
2011	0.1	0.9	-1.2	-0.9	-1.7	0.3	1.0	1.6	1.8	1.4	0.9	3.3
2012	-4.6	-3.0	-2.5	0.5	0.3	1.2	-0.7	-1.1	-2.3	-1.0	0.6	-2.3
2013	1.1	-3.8	-0.8	0.1	-0.5	-1.7	-1.3	-0.4	-2.3	0.3	-1.1	-1.5
2014	-1.9	-2.1	-0.4	5.6	-0.3	0.3	1.2	-1.2	0.3	-1.9	0.4	-3.8
2015	1.4	-3.0	-1.4	0.5	0.4	-7.0	1.9	-3.5	-0.5	2.3	-1.9	-1.8
2016	2.9	-0.5	-0.7	1.8	-2.5	9.7	-2.8	-1.8				

The proportion of years that the FTSE 100 has outperformed the FTSE 250 for each month since 1986 is shown in the following chart.

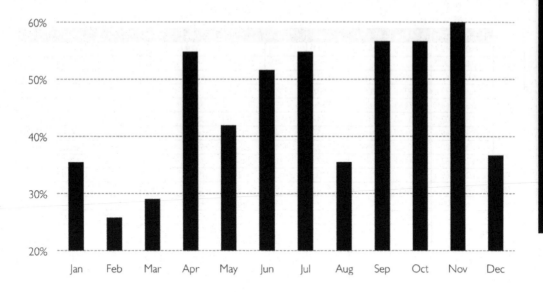

1. The FTSE 250 tends to outperform the FTSE 100 in the first three months of the year and in August and December. For example, as can be seen in the above table, the mid-cap index has outperformed the large-cap index in every March since 2006.

2. The FTSE 100 is strong relative to the FTSE 250 in September and October (and, in recent years, April).

3. In recent years (since 2000), the above characteristics have if anything been even stronger, suggesting a certain degree of persistency.

See also: The FTSE 100/250 Monthly Switching Strategy (page 8).

FTSE 100 MONTH-END VALUES

The following table shows the month-end and year-end values of the FTSE 100.

NB. The FTSE 100 was launched on the first trading day of January 1984, but was given a starting value of 1000 assigned for the last trading day of 1983.

	Jan	Feb	Mar	Apr	May	Jun	Jul	Aug	Sep	Oct	Nov	Dec
1984	1063.0	1040.3	1112.5	1138.3	1021.0	1041.4	1010.1	1103.9	1140.3	1151.0	1181.3	1232.2
1985	1280.8	1259.7	1277.0	1291.0	1313.0	1234.9	1261.7	1341.1	1290.0	1377.2	1439.1	1412.6
1986	1435.0	1543.9	1668.8	1660.5	1602.8	1649.8	1558.1	1661.2	1555.8	1632.1	1636.7	1679.0
1987	1808.3	1979.2	1997.6	2050.5	2203.0	2284.1	2360.9	2249.7	2366.0	1749.8	1579.9	1712.7
1988	1790.8	1768.8	1742.5	1802.2	1784.4	1857.6	1853.6	1753.6	1826.5	1852.4	1792.4	1793.1
1989	2051.8	2002.4	2075.0	2118.0	2114.4	2151.0	2297.0	2387.9	2299.4	2142.6	2276.8	2422.7
1990	2337.3	2255.4	2247.9	2103.4	2345.1	2374.6	2326.2	2162.8	1990.2	2050.3	2149.4	2143.5
1991	2170.3	2380.9	2456.5	2486.2	2499.5	2414.8	2588.8	2645.7	2621.7	2566.0	2420.2	2493.1
1992	2571.2	2562.1	2440.1	2654.1	2707.6	2521.2	2399.6	2312.6	2553.0	2658.3	2778.8	2846.5
1993	2807.2	2868.0	2878.7	2813.1	2840.7	2900.0	2926.5	3100.0	3037.5	3171.0	3166.9	3418.4
1994	3491.8	3328.1	3086.4	3125.3	2970.5	2919.2	3082.6	3251.3	3026.3	3097.4	3081.4	3065.5
1995	2991.6	3009.3	3137.9	3216.7	3319.4	3314.6	3463.3	3477.8	3508.2	3529.1	3664.3	3689.3
1996	3759.3	3727.6	3699.7	3817.9	3747.8	3711.0	3703.2	3867.6	3953.7	3979.1	4058.0	4118.5
1997	4275.8	4308.3	4312.9	4436.0	4621.3	4604.6	4907.5	4817.5	5244.2	4842.3	4831.8	5135.5
1998	5458.5	5767.3	5932.2	5928.3	5870.7	5832.5	5837.0	5249.4	5064.4	5438.4	5743.9	5882.6
1999	5896.0	6175.1	6295.3	6552.2	6226.2	6318.5	6231.9	6246.4	6029.8	6255.7	6597.2	6930.2
2000	6268.5	6232.6	6540.2	6327.4	6359.3	6312.7	6365.3	6672.7	6294.2	6438.4	6142.2	6222.5
2001	6297.5	5917.9	5633.7	5966.9	5796.1	5642.5	5529.1	5345.0	4903.4	5039.7	5203.6	5217.4
2002	5164.8	5101.0	5271.8	5165.6	5085.1	4656.4	4246.2	4227.3	3721.8	4039.7	4169.4	3940.4
2003	3567.4	3655.6	3613.3	3926.0	4048.1	4031.2	4157.0	4161.1	4091.3	4287.6	4342.6	4476.9
2004	4390.7	4492.2	4385.7	4489.7	4430.7	4464.1	4413.1	4459.3	4570.8	4624.2	4703.2	4814.3
2005	4852.3	4968.5	4894.4	4801.7	4964.0	5113.2	5282.3	5296.9	5477.7	5317.3	5423.2	5618.8
2006	5760.3	5791.5	5964.6	6023.1	5723.8	5833.4	5928.3	5906.1	5960.8	6129.2	6048.8	6220.8
2007	6203.1	6171.5	6308.0	6449.2	6621.4	6607.9	6360.1	6303.3	6466.8	6721.6	6432.5	6456.9
2008	5879.8	5884.3	5702.1	6087.3	6053.5	5625.9	5411.9	5636.6	4902.5	4377.3	4288.0	4434.2
2009	4149.6	3830.1	3926.1	4243.7	4417.9	4249.2	4608.4	4908.9	5133.9	5044.5	5190.7	5412.9
2010	5188.5	5354.5	5679.6	5553.3	5188.4	4916.9	5258.0	5225.2	5548.6	5675.2	5528.3	5899.9
2011	5862.9	5994.0	5908.8	6069.9	5990.0	5945.7	5815.2	5394.5	5128.5	5544.2	5505.4	5572.3
2012	5681.6	5871.5	5768.5	5737.8	5320.9	5571.1	5635.3	5711.5	5742.1	5782.7	5866.8	5897.8
2013	6276.9	6360.8	6411.7	6430.1	6583.1	6215.5	6621.1	6483.0	6462.2	6731.4	6650.6	6749.1
2014	6510.4	6809.7	6598.4	6780.0	6844.5	6743.9	6730.1	6819.8	6622.7	6546.5	6722.6	6566.1
2015	6749.4	6946.7	6773.0	6960.6	6984.4	6521.0	6696.3	6247.9	6061.6	6361.1	6356.1	6242.3
2016	6083.8	6097.1	6174.9	6241.9	6230.8	6504.3	6724.4	6781.5				

MONTHLY PERFORMANCE OF THE FTSE 100

The table below shows the percentage performance of the FTSE 100 for every month since 1986. The months where the index fell are highlighted. By scanning the columns it is possible to get a feel for how the market moves in certain months.

	Jan	Feb	Mar	Apr	May	Jun	Jul	Aug	Sep	Oct	Nov	Dec
1980	9.2	4.9	-9.2	3.4	-2.3	11.2	3.7	0.7	3.2	5.9	0.6	-5.3
1981	-1.5	4.3	0.4	6.9	-5.0	1.9	0.4	5.0	-16.6	3.2	10.5	-1.1
1982	4.5	-4.9	3.5	1.1	3.4	-4.3	3.6	2.9	6.1	2.0	0.9	1.7
1983	3.1	0.6	1.8	8.1	0.2	2.8	-2.1	2.6	-2.6	-3.4	5.7	1.9
1984	6.3	-2.1	6.9	2.3	-10.3	2.0	-3.0	9.3	3.3	0.9	2.6	4.3
1985	3.9	-1.6	1.4	1.1	1.7	-5.9	2.2	6.3	-3.8	6.8	4.5	-1.8
1986	1.6	7.6	8.1	-0.5	-3.5	2.9	-5.6	6.6	-6.3	4.9	0.3	2.6
1987	7.7	9.5	0.9	2.6	7.4	3.7	3.4	-4.7	5.2	-26.0	-9.7	8.4
1988	4.6	-1.2	-1.5	3.4	-1.0	4.1	-0.2	-5.4	4.2	1.4	-3.2	0.0
1989	14.4	-2.4	3.6	2.1	-0.2	1.7	6.8	4.0	-3.7	-6.8	6.3	6.4
1990	-3.5	-3.5	-0.3	-6.4	11.5	1.3	-2.0	-7.0	-8.0	3.0	4.8	-0.3
1991	1.3	9.7	3.2	1.2	0.5	-3.4	7.2	2.2	-0.9	-2.1	-5.7	3.0
1992	3.1	-0.4	-4.8	8.8	2.0	-6.9	-4.8	-3.6	10.4	4.1	4.5	2.4
1993	-1.4	2.2	0.4	-2.3	1.0	2.1	0.9	5.9	-2.0	4.4	-0.1	7.9
1994	2.1	-4.7	-7.3	1.3	-5.0	-1.7	5.6	5.5	-6.9	2.3	-0.5	-0.5
1995	-2.4	0.6	4.3	2.5	3.2	-0.1	4.5	0.4	0.9	0.6	3.8	0.7
1996	1.9	-0.8	-0.7	3.2	-1.8	-1.0	-0.2	4.4	2.2	0.6	2.0	1.5
1997	3.8	0.8	0.1	2.9	4.2	-0.4	6.6	-1.8	8.9	-7.7	-0.2	6.3
1998	6.3	5.7	2.9	-0.1	-1.0	-0.7	0.1	-10.1	-3.5	7.4	5.6	2.4
1999	0.2	4.7	1.9	4.1	-5.0	1.5	-1.4	0.2	-3.5	3.7	5.5	5.0
2000	-9.5	-0.6	4.9	-3.3	0.5	-0.7	0.8	4.8	-5.7	2.3	-4.6	1.3
2001	1.2	-6.0	-4.8	5.9	-2.9	-2.7	-2.0	-3.3	-8.3	2.8	3.3	0.3
2002	-1.0	-1.2	3.3	-2.0	-1.6	-8.4	-8.8	-0.4	-12.0	8.5	3.2	-5.5
2003	-9.5	2.5	-1.2	8.7	3.1	-0.4	3.1	0.1	-1.7	4.8	1.3	3.1
2004	-1.9	2.3	-2.4	2.4	-1.3	0.8	-1.1	1.0	2.5	1.2	1.7	2.4
2005	0.8	2.4	-1.5	-1.9	3.4	3.0	3.3	0.3	3.4	-2.9	2.0	3.6
2006	2.5	0.5	3.0	1.0	-5.0	1.9	1.6	-0.4	0.9	2.8	-1.3	2.8
2007	-0.3	-0.5	2.2	2.2	2.7	-0.2	-3.8	-0.9	2.6	3.9	-4.3	0.4
2008	-8.9	0.1	-3.1	6.8	-0.6	-7.1	-3.8	4.2	-13.0	-10.7	-2.0	3.4
2009	-6.4	-7.7	2.5	8.1	4.1	-3.8	8.5	6.5	4.6	-1.7	2.9	4.3
2010	-4.1	3.2	6.1	-2.2	-6.6	-5.2	6.9	-0.6	6.2	2.3	-2.6	6.7
2011	-0.6	2.2	-1.4	2.7	-1.3	-0.7	-2.2	-7.2	-4.9	8.1	-0.7	1.2
2012	2.0	3.3	-1.8	-0.5	-7.3	4.7	1.2	1.4	0.5	0.7	1.5	0.5
2013	6.4	1.3	0.8	0.3	2.4	-5.6	6.5	-2.1	-0.3	4.2	-1.2	1.5
2014	-3.5	4.6	-3.1	2.8	1.0	-1.5	-0.2	1.3	-2.9	-1.2	2.7	-2.3
2015	2.8	2.9	-2.5	2.8	0.3	-6.6	2.7	-6.7	-3.0	4.9	-0.1	-1.8
2016	-2.5	0.2	1.3	1.1	-0.2	4.4	3.4	0.8				

Observations

1. In recent years (i.e. since 2000), the index has been weak in January and June; and strong in April, October and December.

2. In the last 20 years, it can clearly be seen that the strongest month has been December (only down six times in 32 years, although it has now been down in the last two years). However, in the 1970s and 1980s the strongest month was April (which increased every year from 1971 to 1985).

3. Looking across the table, it can be seen that the longest period of consecutive down months was April 2002-September 2002. The longest periods of consecutive up months were Jul 1982-Jun 1983 and June 2012-May 2013 (the only times the FTSE 100 has risen for 12 months without a break).

FTSE 250 MONTH-END VALUES

The following table shows the month-end and year-end values of the FTSE 250.

NB. The FTSE 250 was launched on 12 October 1992, but the base date for the index is 31 December 1985.

	Jan	Feb	Mar	Apr	May	Jun	Jul	Aug	Sep	Oct	Nov	Dec
1986	1449.5	1575.1	1695.8	1755.2	1696.5	1771.0	1690.2	1763.1	1665.5	1751.9	1798.0	1817.9
1987	1990.6	2126.4	2190.2	2219.9	2357.2	2556.2	2710.1	2585.8	2753.7	1964.2	1754.0	1974.0
1988	2103.9	2100.1	2075.3	2156.1	2164.7	2266.2	2291.5	2147.9	2227.1	2303.1	2220.8	2176.1
1989	2461.7	2491.7	2545.5	2526.7	2555.5	2533.1	2701.9	2723.4	2679.3	2438.4	2528.7	2645.8
1990	2578.6	2451.9	2425.4	2276.2	2474.5	2524.8	2465.4	2174.9	1960.4	2052.2	2092.8	2112.9
1991	2082.0	2383.6	2492.9	2483.7	2441.5	2359.7	2482.7	2584.0	2608.6	2543.5	2388.6	2364.6
1992	2476.4	2523.5	2408.2	2712.4	2779.2	2548.7	2302.3	2192.5	2397.4	2521.6	2637.5	2862.9
1993	2954.8	3036.1	3107.8	3132.1	3165.4	3235.7	3306.5	3511.9	3433.2	3528.1	3484.9	3791.3
1994	4084.3	3960.0	3752.9	3781.1	3564.3	3414.1	3640.2	3816.6	3494.8	3516.9	3497.3	3501.8
1995	3370.4	3384.1	3434.7	3530.2	3653.8	3592.6	3826.0	3913.4	3948.8	3894.3	3959.1	4021.3
1996	4125.0	4215.0	4326.7	4551.8	4510.0	4353.2	4230.6	4416.2	4391.1	4422.5	4428.5	4490.4
1997	4595.4	4654.4	4576.2	4498.7	4495.8	4431.3	4492.0	4603.4	4829.9	4643.2	4656.7	4787.6
1998	4861.5	5201.0	5525.4	5610.8	5901.4	5503.8	5482.7	4786.2	4544.2	4811.4	4901.7	4854.7
1999	5024.2	5248.3	5475.2	5849.6	5639.1	5858.2	5969.5	6017.9	5687.1	5622.3	6194.8	6444.9
2000	6181.0	6451.2	6475.1	6194.6	6227.8	6601.0	6779.1	7057.8	6676.9	6629.3	6419.9	6547.5
2001	6735.9	6649.5	6094.7	6409.2	6571.1	6298.9	6082.2	6116.3	5118.6	5364.8	5849.5	5939.1
2002	5849.2	5834.0	6175.5	6123.7	6049.0	5496.6	4783.6	4858.8	4287.1	4417.7	4558.2	4319.3
2003	4016.4	4037.6	3959.8	4389.3	4815.6	4963.4	5325.6	5593.2	5457.8	5724.4	5712.6	5802.3
2004	6023.9	6269.9	6259.4	6210.7	6053.6	6277.9	6023.5	6087.3	6269.1	6321.8	6577.4	6936.8
2005	7166.2	7254.0	7130.5	6728.9	7114.3	7368.7	7605.1	7749.2	7951.1	7711.1	8327.9	8794.3
2006	9172.6	9448.3	9850.3	9878.7	9298.2	9422.7	9355.6	9601.2	9996.8	10372.2	10673.9	11177.8
2007	11100.3	11082.9	11689.3	11929.4	12111.1	11527.6	11337.5	11309.2	11037.4	11666.0	10748.8	10657.8
2008	9881.8	10067.9	10013.2	10122.3	10049.3	9145.8	8856.7	9381.8	7888.2	6282.6	6093.3	6360.9
2009	6250.8	6049.1	6373.9	7529.0	7572.0	7414.6	8000.0	8817.5	9142.3	8885.8	8918.4	9306.9
2010	9237.3	9344.4	10165.3	10366.0	9637.1	9366.1	9948.7	9825.1	10531.8	10843.5	10607.8	11558.8
2011	11471.5	11621.3	11592.0	12013.9	12060.8	11934.0	11552.1	10525.9	9819.4	10479.7	10315.3	10102.9
2012	10769.4	11449.5	11538.9	11417.6	10558.2	10932.1	11136.7	11410.2	11734.1	11935.0	12034.2	12375.0
2013	13030.5	13704.0	13923.0	13949.9	14350.9	13798.2	14872.9	14625.2	14908.2	15480.0	15466.6	15935.4
2014	15674.4	16726.0	16273.7	15817.2	16010.2	15723.6	15495.6	15885.7	15379.7	15501.4	15851.8	16085.4
2015	16305.8	17273.8	17090.6	17474.6	17468.3	17531.5	17677.4	17106.4	16683.0	17117.2	17420.7	17429.8
2016	16487.7	16603.1	16926.1	16801.6	17184.7	16271.1	17282.9	17732.8				

MONTHLY PERFORMANCE OF THE FTSE 250

The table below shows the percentage performance of the FTSE 250 for every month since 1986. The months where the index fell are highlighted. By scanning the columns it is possible to get a feel for how the market moves in certain months.

	Jan	Feb	Mar	Apr	May	Jun	Jul	Aug	Sep	Oct	Nov	Dec
1986	6.8	2.6	8.7	7.7	3.5	-3.3	4.4	-4.6	4.3	-5.5	5.2	2.6
1987	1.1	9.5	6.8	3.0	1.4	6.2	8.4	6.0	-4.6	6.5	-28.7	-10.7
1988	12.5	6.6	-0.2	-1.2	3.9	0.4	4.7	1.1	-6.3	3.7	3.4	-3.6
1989	-2.0	13.1	1.2	2.2	-0.7	1.1	-0.9	6.7	0.8	-1.6	-9.0	3.7
1990	4.6	-2.5	-4.9	-1.1	-6.2	8.7	2.0	-2.4	-11.8	-9.9	4.7	2.0
1991	1.0	-1.5	14.5	4.6	-0.4	-1.7	-3.4	5.2	4.1	0.9	-2.5	-6.1
1992	-1.0	4.7	1.9	-4.6	12.6	2.5	-8.3	-9.7	-4.8	9.3	5.2	4.6
1993	8.5	3.2	2.8	2.4	0.8	1.1	2.2	2.2	6.2	-2.2	2.8	-1.2
1994	8.8	7.7	-3.0	-5.2	0.8	-5.7	-4.2	6.6	4.8	-8.4	0.6	-0.6
1995	0.1	-3.8	0.4	1.5	2.8	3.5	-1.7	6.5	2.3	0.9	-1.4	1.7
1996	1.6	2.6	2.2	2.7	5.2	-0.9	-3.5	-2.8	4.4	-0.6	0.7	0.1
1997	1.4	2.3	1.3	-1.7	-1.7	-0.1	-1.4	1.4	2.5	4.9	-3.9	0.3
1998	2.8	1.5	7.0	6.2	1.5	5.2	-6.7	-0.4	-12.7	-5.1	5.9	1.9
1999	-1.0	3.5	4.5	4.3	6.8	-3.6	3.9	1.9	0.8	-5.5	-1.1	10.2
2000	4.0	-4.1	4.4	0.4	-4.3	0.5	6.0	2.7	4.1	-5.4	-0.7	-3.2
2001	2.0	2.9	-1.3	-8.3	5.2	2.5	-4.1	-3.4	0.6	-16.3	4.8	9.0
2002	1.5	-1.5	-0.3	5.9	-0.8	-1.2	-9.1	-13.0	1.6	-11.8	3.0	3.2
2003	-5.2	-7.0	0.5	-1.9	10.8	9.7	3.1	7.3	5.0	-2.4	4.9	-0.2
2004	1.6	3.8	4.1	-0.2	-0.8	-2.5	3.7	-4.1	1.1	3.0	0.8	4.0
2005	5.5	3.3	1.2	-1.7	-5.6	5.7	3.6	3.2	1.9	2.6	-3.0	8.0
2006	5.6	4.3	3.0	4.3	0.3	-5.9	1.3	-0.7	2.6	4.1	3.8	2.9
2007	4.7	-0.7	-0.2	5.5	2.1	1.5	-4.8	-1.6	-0.2	-2.4	5.7	-7.9
2008	-0.8	-7.3	1.9	-0.5	1.1	-0.7	-9.0	-3.2	5.9	-15.9	-20.4	-3.0
2009	4.4	-1.7	-3.2	5.4	18.1	0.6	-2.1	7.9	10.2	3.7	-2.8	0.4
2010	4.4	-0.7	1.2	8.8	2.0	-7.0	-2.8	6.2	-1.2	7.2	3.0	-2.2
2011	9.0	-0.8	1.3	-0.3	3.6	0.4	-1.1	-3.2	-8.9	-6.7	6.7	-1.6
2012	-2.1	6.6	6.3	0.8	-1.1	-7.5	3.5	1.9	2.5	2.8	1.7	0.8
2013	2.8	5.3	5.2	1.6	0.2	2.9	-3.9	7.8	-1.7	1.9	3.8	-0.1
2014	3.0	-1.6	6.7	-2.7	-2.8	1.2	-1.8	-1.5	2.5	-3.2	0.8	2.3
2015	1.5	1.4	5.9	-1.1	2.2	0.0	0.4	0.8	-3.2	-2.5	2.6	1.8
2016	0.1	-5.4	0.7	1.9	-0.7	2.3	-5.3	6.2	2.6			

Observations

1. Historically the strongest months for the FTSE 250 have been January and March, and the weakest July and October.

2. In recent years (i.e. since 2000), the index has also been strong in September and November.

MONTHLY SEASONALITY WORLDWIDE

Elsewhere in this *Almanac*, the results are given of analysis of the monthly seasonality of the FTSE 100 (page 60). To summarise:

- The three **strongest** months in the year were found to be: April, October and December, and

- The three **weakest** months in the year were: May, June and September.

Such seasonality behaviour is not unique to the UK and most other stock markets around the world display similar behaviour – as found in an academic paper[1] published in June 2013.

The special feature of this latest study on the topic is its scope: it analyses data from 70 of the 78 operational stock markets in the world.

The paper found that across all 70 markets, on average:

- The three **strongest** months were: January, April and December, and

- The three **weakest** months were: August, September and October.

The study also split the results for developed and emerging markets (shown in the following two charts).

The chart on the left shows the mean, median and standard deviation of monthly returns for each month across 70 countries. The chart on the right shows the mean, median and standard deviation of monthly returns for each month across emerging stock markets.

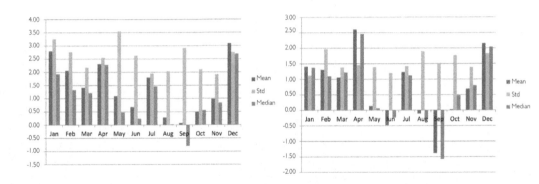

Source: Vichet Sum

The main difference between the two sets of markets is that while April was the strongest month in developed markets, it was January and December that were the strongest months for the emerging markets. In addition, the developed markets were significantly weak in June and September, which was not the case in emerging markets.

1. V. Sum, 'Stock Market Performance: High and Low Months' (5 June 2013)

TURN OF THE MONTH

This study analyses the behaviour of the market on the ten days around each turn of the month (ToM). The days studied are the five last trading days of the month, from ToM(-5) to ToM(-1) (the latter being the last trading day of the month), and the first five trading days of the following month, from ToM(+1) to ToM(+5). The index analysed is the FTSE All-Share.

From 1970

The charts below analyse the 561 ToMs since 1970. The left chart shows the average return on the day, and the right chart is the percentage number of positive days. For example, on ToM(-5) the market has on average risen 49.2% of the time with an average return of -0.05.

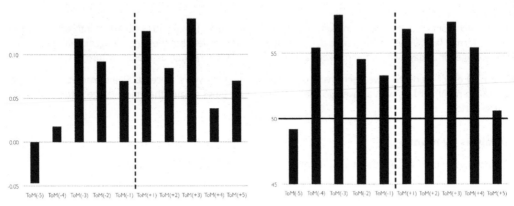

We can see that there is a definite trend for the market to be weak at the beginning of the ten-day period, to then strengthen on the third day before the end of the month, then weaken in the final two days, before starting strong in the new month.

Does this behaviour persist in more recent years?

From 2000

The charts below are the same configuration as above, except they look at a shorter time period: the 201 ToMs from the year 2000 to mid-2016.

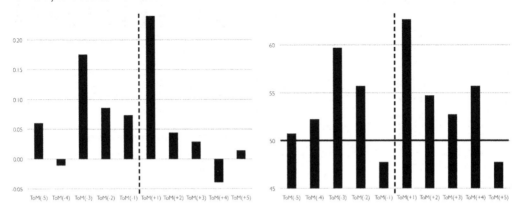

Broadly, the behaviour has been the same for the last few years as that from 1970. The main observation is that the strength of the first trading day of the month, ToM(0), has become ever more pronounced. On average since 2000, the market rises on 63% of all ToM(+1), with an average change of 0.24% (which is eight times the average change on all trading days).

FIRST TRADING DAYS OF THE MONTH

Does the market display any special effect on the first trading day of each month?

FTSE 100 daily data was analysed from 1984 to discover if the UK equity market displayed abnormal returns on the first trading day (FTD) of each month. The results are shown in the table below.

	Number of days	Positive	Positive(%)	Average(%)
All days	8192	4281	52.3	0.03%
First trading day of each month	389	230	59.1	0.20%
First trading day of each month (from 2000)	201	123	61.2	0.23%

Of the 389 months since 1984, the market has risen 230 times (59.1%) on the FTD of each month, with an average daily return of 0.20%. These figures have declined slightly in the last year, but they are still significantly greater than the average for all days, where the market has risen 52.3% of the time with an average return of 0.03%.

The FTD effect seems to have been marginally stronger in recent years. Since 2000, the market has increased 61.2% on months' FTDs with an average rise of 0.23% (eight times greater than the average return for all days in the period).

Analysis by month

The following charts break down the performance of the market on the first trading days by month since 1984.

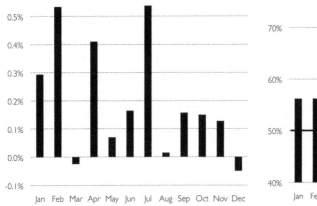 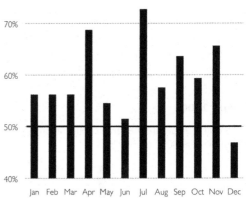

The average returns on the FTDs have been strongest for the months of February, April and July. The average return on the FTD of July has been 0.54% (18 times greater than the average return for all days of the month). Returns have been positive for 73% of all July FTDs.

The weakest month FTD is December – the only month when the market has fallen more often then risen on the first trading day since 1984. This is an unexpected result because December as a whole is one of the stronger months for the market.

LAST TRADING DAYS OF THE MONTH

On the previous page we looked at the first trading day of each month. Here we will look at the last trading days.

The following table shows the results of analysing the performance of the FTSE 100 on the last trading day (LTD) of each month since 1984 and compares this to the average performance on all days in the month.

	Number of days	Positive	Positive(%)	Average(%)
All days	8192	4281	52.3	0.03%
Last trading day of each month	389	203	52.2	0.09%
Last trading day of each month (from 2000)	200	87	43.5	0.04%

Overall, since 1984, the market has a tendency to increase above the average on the LTD of each month. On average, the market has risen 0.09% on months' last trading days against 0.03% for all days in the month; and the market has had a positive return in 52.2% on all LTDs since 1984. However, in recent years (since 2000), the effect has somewhat reversed with the majority of last trading days seeing falls in the market (when the market only rises on 43.5% of month LTDs).

This behaviour is very different from that of the first trading days in the month, which strongly outperform the average for all days, and where the effect has strengthened in recent years.

Analysis by month

The following charts break down the performance of the market on the last trading days by month since 1984.

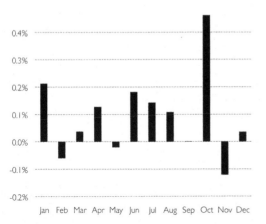
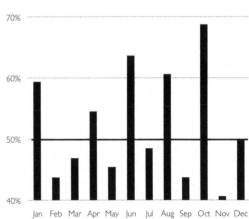

The difference in performance between the months is quite striking. Since 1984, the last trading days in January, June, August and October are all abnormally strong. By contrast, the last trading days of February, September and November are very weak. In recent years, since 2000, the pattern has changed somewhat: the strong months are June and August; the weak months are: February and September.

FTSE 100 QUARTERLY REVIEWS

To keep the FTSE 100 in accordance with its purpose the constituents of the index are periodically reviewed. The reviews take place and are announced on the Wednesday before the first Friday of the month in March, June, September and December.

If any changes are to be made (i.e. companies ejected or introduced), these are announced sometime after the market has closed on the day of the review.

The review dates for 2017 are: 1 March, 31 May, 30 August and 29 November.

Changes to the index following a review are implemented after the close of business on the third Friday of the month.

Since the index's inception in 1984, the company that has danced in and out of the index the most is Tate & Lyle, which has been added six times (and ejected six times).

The accompanying table lists the companies entering and exiting the FTSE 100 in the last few years as a result of the FTSE quarterly reviews.

Date	Company added	TIDM	Company ejected	TIDM
08 Sep 10	Resolution	RSL	Cable and Wireless Worldwide	CWC
08 Sep 10	Tomkins		Home Retail Group	HOME
08 Sep 10	Weir Group	WEIR	Segro	SGRO
08 Dec 10	IMI	IMI	Cobham	COB
09 Mar 11	Wood Group (John)	WG.	Bunzl	BNZL
09 Mar 11	ITV	ITV	Alliance Trust	ATST
09 Mar 11	Hargreaves Lansdown	HL.	African Barrick Gold	ABG
25 May 11	Glencore	GLEN	Invensys	ISYS
08 Jun 11	Tate & Lyle	TATE	TUI Travel	TT.
07 Sep 11	Ashmore Group	ASHM	Wood Group (John)	WG.
07 Sep 11	Bunzl	BNZL	3i Group	III
07 Dec 11	CRH	CRH	Inmarsat	ISAT
07 Dec 11	Evraz	EVR	Investec	INVP
07 Dec 11	Polymetal International	POLY	Lonmin	LMI
07 Mar 12	Croda International	CRDA	Cairn Energy	CNE
07 Mar 12	Aberdeen Asset Management	AND	Essar Energy	ESSR
06 Jun 12	Babcock International Group	BAB	Man Group	EMG
29 Jun 12	Pennon Group	PNN	International Power	
12 Sep 12	Melrose	MRO	ICAP	IAP
12 Sep 12	Wood Group (John)	WG.	Ashmore Group	ASHM
12 Dec 12	TUI Travel	TT.	Pennon Group	PNN
06 Mar 13	Easyjet	EZJ	Intu Properties	INTU
06 Mar 13	London Stock Exchange	LSE	Kazakhmys	KAZ
11 Sep 13	Coca-Cola HBC AG	CCH	Wood Group (John)	WG.
11 Sep 13	Sports Direct International	SPD	Eurasian Natural Resources Corporation*	ENRC
11 Sep 13	Mondi	MNDI	Serco Group	SRP
11 Dec 13	Royal Mail Group	RMG	Croda International	CRDA
11 Dec 13	Ashtead Group	AHT	Vedanta Resources	VED
05 Mar 14	Barratt Developments	BDEV	Amec	AMEC
05 Mar 14	St. James's Place	STJ	Tate & Lyle	TATE
04 Jun 14	3i Group	III	Melrose	MRO
04 Jun 14	Intu Properties	INTU	William Hill	WMH
03 Sep 14	Direct Line Insurance Group	DLG	Barratt Developments	BDEV
03 Sep 14	Dixons Carphone	DC.	Rexam	REX
03 Dec 14	Barratt Developments	BDEV	IMI	IMI
03 Dec 14	Taylor Wimpey	TW.	Petrofac	PFC
04 Mar 15	Hikma Pharmaceuticals	HIK	Tullow Oil	TLW
03 Jun 15	Inmarsat	ISAT	Aggreko	AGK

FTSE INDEX REVIEWS – ACADEMIC RESEARCH

Traders are interested in changes to equity indices due to the potential arbitrage profits; but academics have a wider interest because for them changes to indices act as something like a laboratory for testing theories of stock market efficiency and behavioural finance. Briefly, when a stock joins (or leaves) an index, nothing changes to the company itself and so (in an efficient market) there should be no change to the share price. Below is a brief overview of the major academic papers studying the effects of the FTSE quarterly reviews.

Comovement

Kougoulis and Coakley (2004)[1] found that shares joining the FTSE 100 experienced an increase in comovement (price movement correlation with other shares); shares leaving the index experienced the opposite effect. Mase (2008)[2] supported the previous findings and in addition found that increases in comovement had become larger in recent years, and that the overall increase in comovement was due to new additions to the index rather than previous FTSE 100 constituents rejoining the index.

Price pressures

This is a favourite of academics: if a share price moves without new information is the move temporary (price pressure hypothesis) or permanent (imperfect substitutes hypothesis)? Mazouz and Saadouni (2007)[3] found strong evidence for the price pressure hypothesis: prices increased (decreased) gradually starting before the index change announcement date of inclusion (exclusion) and then reversed completely in less than two weeks after the index change date. The existence of the temporary price changes (price pressure hypothesis) was also found by Opong and Antonios Siganos (2013)[4] and Biktimirov and Li (2014)[5]. Interestingly, Mase (2007)[6] comments that the temporary prices changes to shares joining/leaving the FTSE 100 is in contrast to the case for S&P 500 changes, where permanent price changes have been found.

Information efficiency

Daya, Mazouz and Freeman (2012)[7] (and other papers) found that informational efficiency improved for stocks added to the FTSE 100, but did not diminish after deletion.

Price changes

Gregoriou and Ioannidis (2006)[8] found that price and trading volumes of newly listed firms increased. That confirms what we already knew or suspected. But, interestingly, they (and other papers here) attribute the cause to information efficiency: stocks with more available information increase investor awareness. However, Mase (2007) does say that investor awareness and monitoring due to index membership do not explain the price effects. But not mentioned here is the influence of index funds.

Anticipatory trading

Fernandes and Mergulhao (2011)[9] found that a trading strategy based on addition/deletion probability estimates gave an average daily excess return of 11 basis points over the FTSE 100. Opong and Siganos (2013)[10] found "significant net profitability" from an investment strategy based on firms on the FTSE reserved list. And a strategy based on the FTSE 100 quarterly revisions was profitable if CFDs were used and traders could deal within the bid/ask spread.

1. P. Kougoulis and J. Coakley, 'Comovement and Changes to the FTSE 100 Index', *EFMA 2004 Basel Meetings Paper* (2004).
2. B. Mase, 'Comovement in the FTSE 100 Index', *Applied Financial Economics Letters* 4(1) (2008).
3. K. Mazouz and B. Saadouni, 'The price effects of FTSE 100 index revision: what drives the long-term abnormal return reversal?', *Applied Financial Economics* 17(6) (2007).
4. K. Opong and A. Siganos, .Compositional changes in the FTSE 100 index from the standpoint of an arbitrageur', *Journal of Asset Management* 14 (2013).
5. E. Biktimirov and B. Li, 'Asymmetric stock price and liquidity responses to changes in the FTSE SmallCap index', *Review of Quantitative Finance and Accounting* (2014).
6. B. Mase, 'The Impact of Changes in the FTSE 100 Index', *Financial Review* 42(3) (2007).
7. W. Daya, K. Mazouz and M. Freeman, 'Information efficiency changes following FTSE 100 index revisions', *Journal of International Financial Markets, Institutions and Money* 22(4) (2012).
8. A. Gregoriou and C. Ioannidis, 'Information costs and liquidity effects from changes in the FTSE 100 list', *The European Journal of Finance* 12(4) (2006).
9. M. Fernandes and J. Mergulhao, 'Anticipatory Effects in the FTSE 100 Index Revisions', *Midwest Finance Association*, Annual Meetings Paper (2011).
10. K. Opong and A. Siganos, 'Compositional changes in the FTSE 100 index from the standpoint of an arbitrageur', *Journal of Asset Management* 14 (2013).

COMPARATIVE PERFORMANCE OF UK INDICES

The table below gives the year-end closing values for eight UK stock indices.

Year-end closing values of UK indices

Index	TIDM	2006	2007	2008	2009	2010	2011	2012	2013	2014	2015
FTSE 100	UKX	6,220.80	6,456.90	4,434.17	5,412.88	5,899.94	5,572.28	5,897.81	6,749.09	6,566.09	6,242.30
FTSE 250	MCX	11,177.80	10,657.80	6,360.85	9,306.89	11,558.80	10,102.90	12,375.00	15,935.35	16,085.44	17,429.80
FTSE All-Share	ASX	3,221.42	3,286.67	2,209.29	2,760.80	3,062.85	2,857.88	3,093.41	3,609.63	3,532.74	3,444.26
FTSE Fledgling	NSX	4,389.40	4,022.30	2,321.76	4,035.39	4,789.69	4,081.64	4,751.92	6,453.65	6,849.46	7,725.75
FTSE Small Cap	SMX	3,905.60	3,420.30	1,854.20	2,780.20	3,228.60	2,748.80	3,419.07	4,431.11	4,365.92	4,634.66
FTSE TechMARK Focus	TIX	1,512.38	1,641.10	1,217.00	1,704.80	2,040.00	2,064.10	2,479.80	3,197.32	3,522.00	4,027.41
FTSE4Good UK 50	4UK5	5,267.43	5,428.60	3,787.40	4,577.90	4,852.90	4,529.80	4,864.74	5,636.57	5,496.77	5,205.47
FTSE AIM	AXX	1,054.00	1,049.10	394.32	653.24	933.63	693.18	707.21	850.68	702.00	738.83

The table below gives the annual returns of the eight indices. The light grey cells highlight the best performing index in each respective year; the dark grey cells the worst performing.

Annual performance (%) of UK indices

Index	TIDM	2006	2007	2008	2009	2010	2011	2012	2013	2014	2015
FTSE 100	UKX	10.7	3.8	-31.3	22.1	9.0	-5.6	5.8	14.4	-2.7	-4.9
FTSE 250	MCX	27.1	-4.7	-40.3	46.3	24.2	-12.6	22.5	28.8	0.9	8.4
FTSE All-Share	AXX	13.2	2.0	-32.8	25.0	10.9	-6.7	8.2	16.7	-2.1	-2.5
FTSE Fledgling	ASX	17.1	-8.4	-42.3	73.8	18.7	-14.8	16.4	35.8	6.1	12.8
FTSE Small Cap	NSX	18.2	-12.4	-45.8	49.9	16.1	-14.9	24.4	29.6	-1.5	6.2
FTSE TechMARK Focus	SMX	5.6	8.5	-25.8	40.1	19.7	1.2	20.1	28.9	10.2	14.4
FTSE4Good UK 50	TIX	9.7	3.1	-30.2	20.9	6.0	-6.7	7.4	15.9	-2.5	-5.3
FTSE AIM	4UK5	0.8	-0.5	-62.4	65.7	42.9	-25.8	2.0	20.3	-17.5	5.2

The FTSE Fledgling and FTSE TechMARK 100 indices have been the best performing indices in the year the most number of times, while the FTSE AIM and FTSE 4Good UK 50 indices are at the bottom of the class, having been the worst performing indices in the year the most number of times.

The following chart shows the relative performance of the FTSE 100, FTSE 250, FTSE AIM and FTSE Fledgling (all indices rebased to start at 100).

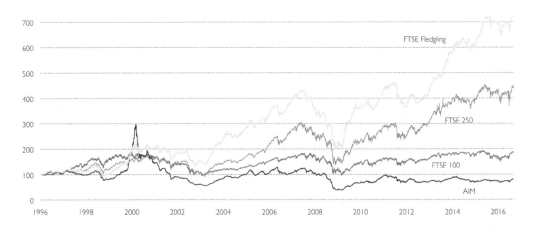

FTSE ALL-SHARE ANNUAL RETURNS

The following chart plots the annual returns of the FTSE All-Share since 1900. [NB. The values for 1973 and 1974 were respectively -55% and 136%, and have been truncated in the chart to make the scale more useful.]

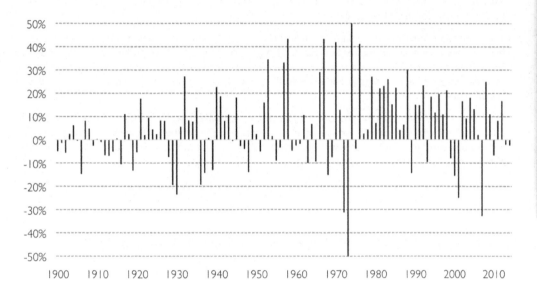

The market fell for two consecutive years in 2014 and 2015. As can be seen from the chart, this is a fairly rare occurrence. The previous time the market fell in two successive years was during the aftermath of the internet bubble, and before that in 1972-73.

The following chart plots the frequency distribution of the annual returns of the FTSE All-Share since 1900. For example, the annual return for the index has been in the range 5%-10% for 15 years since 1900.

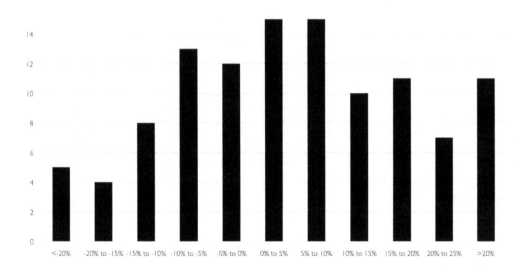

The annual returns can be seen to have roughly a normal distribution (i.e. bell-shaped curve), although very large positive and negative returns have a higher frequency than would be expected under a normal distribution.

MARKET MOMENTUM (UP) ANALYSIS

The table below displays the results of analysis on market momentum – the tendency of the market to increase in one period, having also risen in the previous period(s). Notes on the analysis:

1. The index analysed was the FTSE All-Share from 1969. The number of observations to September 2016 (for each frequency) is indicated in column 0. For example, 12,017 days to September 2016 (from Jan 1969) was the sample data for the "Daily" analysis.

2. The first rows ("Total") of the columns display the number of consecutive periods that the index rose for that frequency. For example, the market rose 6351 days (out of the total 12,017); 3560 times it rose on two consecutive days; and 340 times it rose six days in a row. The second rows ("% Total") express the first row as a percentage of the total sample. For example, the market rose six days in a row 2.8% of the whole period (12,017 days).

3. The rows "% 1 up" expresses the proportion of times that the market rose for n consecutive periods following the market rising for one period (expressed as a percentage of the number of times the market rose once). For example: after the market had risen for one day, the market rose for a second day in 56.1% of all cases; after the market had risen for one day, the market went on to rise six days consecutively in 5.4% of all cases.

4. The subsequent rows display the tendency of the market to rise following n consecutive increases. For example: after the market has risen four days consecutively, the market rose for a fifth day in 55.9% of all cases; after the market had risen three years in a row, the market rose again the following year in 72.4% of all cases.

Frequency		0	1	2	3	4	5	6
Daily	Total	12017	6351	3560	1965	1101	616	340
	% Total		52.9	29.6	16.4	9.2	5.1	2.8
	% 1 up			56.1	30.9	17.3	9.7	5.4
	% 2 up				55.2	30.9	17.3	9.6
	% 3 up					56.0	31.3	17.3
	% 4 up						55.9	30.9
	% 5 up							55.2
Weekly	Total	2695	1484	818	462	261	151	81
	% Total		55.1	30.4	17.1	9.7	5.6	3.0
	% 1 up			55.1	31.1	17.6	10.2	5.5
	% 2 up				56.5	31.9	18.5	9.9
	% 3 up					56.5	32.7	17.5
	% 4 up						57.9	31.0
	% 5 up							53.6
Monthly	Total	847	517	322	201	131	90	61
	% Total		61.0	38.0	23.7	15.5	10.6	7.2
	% 1 up			62.3	38.9	25.3	17.4	11.8
	% 2 up				62.4	40.7	28.0	18.9
	% 3 up					65.2	44.8	30.3
	% 4 up						68.7	46.6
	% 5 up							67.8
Yearly	Total	116	70	46	29	21	15	10
	% Total		60.3	39.7	25.0	18.1	12.9	8.6
	% 1 up			65.7	41.4	30.0	21.4	14.3
	% 2 up				63.0	45.7	32.6	21.7
	% 3 up					72.4	51.7	34.5
	% 4 up						71.4	47.6
	% 5 up							66.7

Observations

The market would appear to display a degree of fractal behaviour – where its properties are similar whatever time frame one looks at. Trends do seem to become more established the longer they last. For example, the probability of the market rising in a week increases the longer the period of previous consecutive up weeks – although this trend falls off after five consecutive up periods.

The market displays greater momentum for longer frequencies. For example, the market only rose six days consecutively 2.8% of the time, whereas it rose six years consecutively 8.6% of the time. In addition, the market rose for a sixth year (after five years of consecutive increases) 66.7% of the time, against just 55.2% for daily increases.

MARKET MOMENTUM (DOWN) ANALYSIS

The table on the previous page looked at market momentum for the market going up. The table below shows the results of analysis of market momentum when the market falls.

The structure of the table is similar to that on the previous page (where an explanation of the figures is given).

Frequency		0	1	2	3	4	5	6
Daily	Total	12017	5649	2859	1410	669	313	145
	% Total		47.0	23.8	11.7	5.6	2.6	1.2
	% 1 down			50.6	25.0	11.8	5.5	2.6
	% 2 down				49.3	23.4	10.9	5.1
	% 3 down					47.4	22.2	10.3
	% 4 down						46.8	21.7
	% 5 down							46.3
Weekly	Total	2695	1206	537	258	130	61	33
	% Total		44.7	19.9	9.6	4.8	2.3	1.2
	% 1 down			44.5	21.4	10.8	5.1	2.7
	% 2 down				48.0	24.2	11.4	6.1
	% 3 down					50.4	23.6	12.8
	% 4 down						46.9	25.4
	% 5 down							54.1
Monthly	Total	847	328	135	54	20	10	3
	% Total		38.7	15.9	6.4	2.4	1.2	0.4
	% 1 down			41.2	16.5	6.1	3.0	0.9
	% 2 down				40.0	14.8	7.4	2.2
	% 3 down					37.0	18.5	5.6
	% 4 down						50.0	15.0
	% 5 down							30.0
Yearly	Total	116	46	21	8	2	0	0
	% Total		39.7	18.1	6.9	1.7	0.0	0.0
	% 1 down			45.7	17.4	4.3	0.0	0.0
	% 2 down				38.1	9.5	0.0	0.0
	% 3 down					25.0	0.0	0.0
	% 4 down						0.0	0.0
	% 5 down							0.0

Observations

1. Since 1969, the market has fallen on six consecutive days on 145 occasions (the last time was December 2015). The most consecutive days the market has fallen is 13, which it has done once (in June 1974).

2. Since 1946 the market has only fallen four consecutive months on 20 occasions (2.4%). Random chance would suggest 6.3%.

3. Since 1900, the market has never fallen for five consecutive years. The market has fallen for three consecutive years on eight occasions, but having done so the market continued to fall for a fourth year only twice.

4. As with up markets (previous page), down markets appear to display a degree of fractal behaviour, where properties are similar whatever time frame one looks at.

5. Down markets display far less momentum tendency than that seen for up markets. For example, if the market rises for three consecutive months, there's a 65.2% probability that the market will continue to rise for a fourth month as well. However, if the market falls for three consecutive months, there's only a 37.0% probability that the market will fall for a fourth month as well.

COMPANY PROFILE OF THE FTSE 100

Rank 2016	Company	TIDM	Turnover (£m)	Profit (£m)	Profit margin (%)	Capital (£m)	Weighting (%)	Cumulative weighting (%)
1	Royal Dutch Shell	RDSB	172,540	1,333	2.2	149,227	8.0	8.0
2	HSBC Holdings	HSBA	45,462	12,286		113,558	6.1	14.0
3	British American Tobacco	BATS	13,104	5,855	37.7	88,238	4.7	18.7
4	GlaxoSmithKline	GSK	23,923	10,526	18.7	79,119	4.2	22.9
5	BP	BP.	145,140	-6,232	-3.0	79,111	4.2	27.1
6	SABMiller	SAB	13,173	2,706	19.0	72,051	3.8	31.0
7	AstraZeneca	AZN	16,089	1,999	17.3	63,153	3.4	34.3
8	Vodafone Group	VOD	40,973	-449	5.0	58,342	3.1	37.4
9	Diageo	DGE	10,485	2,858	26.6	53,325	2.8	40.3
10	Reckitt Benckiser Group	RB.	8,874	2,208	26.9	50,242	2.7	43.0
11	Unilever	ULVR	38,760	5,253	14.0	45,518	2.4	45.4
12	Shire	SHP	4,331	935	33.5	44,354	2.4	47.7
13	Lloyds Banking Group	LLOY	0	1,644		40,490	2.2	49.9
14	National Grid	NG.	15,115	3,032	27.0	39,435	2.1	52.0
15	Imperial Brands	IMB	25,289	1,756	9.8	37,821	2.0	54.0
16	BT Group	BT.A	19,042	3,029	19.9	37,816	2.0	56.0
17	Prudential	PRU	0	3,148		35,145	1.9	57.9
18	Rio Tinto	RIO	22,680	-473	19.4	31,574	1.7	59.6
19	Barclays	BARC	23,873	2,073		28,664	1.5	61.1
20	Glencore	GLEN	111,020	-5,220	0.1	26,342	1.4	62.5
21	Compass Group	CPG	17,590	1,159	7.1	24,150	1.3	63.8
22	Royal Bank of Scotland Group (The)	RBS	13,650	-2,703		22,898	1.2	65.0
23	WPP Group	WPP	12,235	1,493	14.1	22,780	1.2	66.2
24	Associated British Foods	ABF	12,800	717	7.8	21,581	1.1	67.4
25	BHP Billiton	BLT	20,867	-4,900	-20.2	21,163	1.1	68.5
26	CRH	CRH	17,196	752	5.6	20,874	1.1	69.6
27	Standard Chartered	STAN	6,959	-992		20,495	1.1	70.7
28	Aviva	AV.	23,728	1,390		17,726	0.9	71.7
29	BAE Systems	BA.	16,787	1,090	8.7	17,412	0.9	72.6
30	RELX	REL	5,971	1,312	23.9	15,648	0.8	73.4
31	SSE	SSE	28,781	593	4.7	15,346	0.8	74.2
32	Experian	EXPN	3,022	682	23.3	14,798	0.8	75.0
33	Sky	SKY	11,965	752	10.2	14,319	0.8	75.8
34	Tesco	TSCO	54,433	162	2.4	13,868	0.7	76.5
35	Rolls-Royce Group	RR.	13,725	160	10.5	13,414	0.7	77.3
36	Legal & General Group	LGEN	12,701	1,355		12,565	0.7	77.9
37	Centrica	CNA	27,971	-1,136	4.4	12,449	0.7	78.6
38	Fresnillo	FRES	975	143	14.3	12,129	0.6	79.2
39	Anglo American	AAL	13,320	-3,552	9.3	11,379	0.6	79.8
40	Wolseley	WOS	13,332	508	6.0	11,050	0.6	80.4
41	Smith & Nephew	SN.	3,018	364	16.6	10,953	0.6	81.0
42	London Stock Exchange Group	LSE	1,419	336	29.3	9,556	0.5	81.5
43	Old Mutual	OML	10,375	1,319		9,381	0.5	82.0
44	International Consolidated Airlines Group SA	IAG	16,631	1,310	10.0	8,885	0.5	82.5
45	Kingfisher	KGF	10,441	512	6.9	8,214	0.4	82.9
46	Land Securities Group	LAND	943	1,336	105.9	8,010	0.4	83.4
47	ITV	ITV	2,972	641	22.8	7,982	0.4	83.8
48	Sage Group (The)	SGE	1,436	276	25.0	7,878	0.4	84.2
49	Mondi	MNDI	5,033	588	13.7	7,716	0.4	84.6
50	Bunzl	BNZL	6,490	323	5.6	7,711	0.4	85.0
51	Whitbread	WTB	2,922	488	18.1	7,396	0.4	85.4
52	Paddy Power Betfair	PPB	807	125	16.2	7,387	0.4	85.8
53	Next	NXT	4,177	836	20.7	7,302	0.4	86.2
54	Schroders	SDR	2,043	589	26.1	7,299	0.4	86.6
55	Mediclinic International	MDC	2,107	245	13.6	6,941	0.4	87.0
56	Randgold Resources Ltd	RRS	676	176	18.8	6,924	0.4	87.3
57	Standard Life	SL.	8,760	415		6,787	0.4	87.7
58	United Utilities Group	UU.	1,730	354	44.2	6,683	0.4	88.0
59	Carnival	CCL	10,259	1,174	16.5	6,667	0.4	88.4
60	Capita	CPI	4,837	112	6.4	6,584	0.4	88.8
61	Pearson	PSON	4,468	-433	-17.1	6,409	0.3	89.1

Rank 2016	Company	TIDM	Turnover (£m)	Profit (£m)	Profit margin (%)	Capital (£m)	Weighting (%)	Cumulative weighting (%)
62	InterContinental Hotels Group	IHG	1,174	919	36.7	6,396	0.3	89.4
63	British Land Co	BLND	590	1,331	171.0	6,368	0.3	89.8
64	Johnson Matthey	JMAT	10,714	386	3.8	6,269	0.3	90.1
65	Coca-Cola HBC AG	CCH	4,617	260	8.0	6,247	0.3	90.4
66	Ashtead Group	AHT	2,546	617	26.0	6,183	0.3	90.8
67	3i Group	III	0	0		6,172	0.3	91.1
68	DCC	DCC	10,601	216	2.5	6,129	0.3	91.4
69	Hargreaves Lansdown	HL.	388	219	56.2	6,038	0.3	91.7
70	TUI AG	TUI	14,989	401	4.6	6,026	0.3	92.1
71	Worldpay Group	WPG	982	19	16.8	5,962	0.3	92.4
72	Admiral Group	ADM	0	369		5,689	0.3	92.7
73	Severn Trent	SVT	1,787	322	29.0	5,663	0.3	93.0
74	Intertek Group	ITRK	2,166	-308	14.4	5,626	0.3	93.3
75	Burberry Group	BRBY	2,515	416	17.0	5,587	0.3	93.6
76	Babcock International Group	BAB	4,158	330	8.3	5,557	0.3	93.9
77	Persimmon	PSN	2,902	630	21.6	5,463	0.3	94.2
78	GKN	GKN	7,231	245	4.1	5,450	0.3	94.5
79	RSA Insurance Group	RSA	7,415	106		5,406	0.3	94.8
80	Smiths Group	SMIN	2,897	325	15.8	5,350	0.3	95.0
81	Sainsbury (J)	SBRY	23,506	548	2.2	5,248	0.3	95.3
82	Royal Mail Group	RMG	9,251	267	3.6	5,165	0.3	95.6
83	Hikma Pharmaceuticals	HIK	972	215	26.8	5,118	0.3	95.9
84	Direct Line Insurance Group	DLG	0	508		5,108	0.3	96.1
85	Marks & Spencer Group	MKS	10,555	489	7.3	5,092	0.3	96.4
86	St James's Place	STJ	3,090	151		4,975	0.3	96.7
87	Micro Focus International	MCRO	830	130	25.7	4,953	0.3	96.9
88	Taylor Wimpey	TW.	3,140	603	20.1	4,897	0.3	97.2
89	Morrison (Wm) Supermarkets	MRW	16,122	217	1.3	4,860	0.3	97.5
90	Antofagasta	ANTO	2,291	175	10.3	4,825	0.3	97.7
91	Merlin Entertainments	MERL	1,278	237	22.8	4,801	0.3	98.0
92	Barratt Developments	BDEV	4,235	682	15.8	4,785	0.3	98.2
93	Informa	INF	1,212	220	21.6	4,721	0.3	98.5
94	Hammerson	HMSO	236	732	180.3	4,462	0.2	98.7
95	easyJet	EZJ	4,686	686	14.7	4,310	0.2	98.9
96	Provident Financial	PFG	1,113	274	18.7	4,296	0.2	99.2
97	Dixons Carphone	DC.	9,738	263	4.4	4,233	0.2	99.4
98	Travis Perkins	TPK	5,942	224	5.1	3,923	0.2	99.6
99	Intu Properties	INTU	572	513	106.7	3,839	0.2	99.8
100	Berkeley Group Holdings (The)	BKG	2,048	531	24.6	3,529	0.2	100.0

Notes to the table

1. The *Weighting* column expresses a company's market capitalisation as a percentage of the total capitalisation of all companies in the FTSE 100. The table is ranked (in descending order) by this column.

2. Figures accurate as of August 2016.

Observations

1. The five largest companies in the FTSE 100 account for 27.1% of the total market capitalisation. This figure has fallen quite considerably in the last few years – in 2004 the top five companies accounted for 36% of the FTSE 100 and by 2013 it had decreased to 29% – albeit it has grown from last year's figure of 23.7%.

2. The 14 largest companies in the index account for just over half of the total capitalisation (2004: 10).

3. The 21 smallest companies in the index account for only 5% of total capitalisation. In other words, the individual movements of these 25 companies have very little impact on the level of the index.

4. The aggregate capitalisation of all 100 companies in the index is £1,877bn (2015: £1,764bn; 2012: £1,640bn; 2006: £1,397bn). When the index started in 1984 the aggregate capitalisation was £100 billion.

INDEX PROFILES – SHARE PRICES

The table below presents a range of share-price related characteristics for six UK stock market indices.

	FTSE 100	FTSE 250	Small Cap	Fledgling	AIM	techMARK Focus
Number of companies in index	100	250	274	104	1,012	34
Market capitalisation, mean (£m)	18,770	1,594	305	49	83	3,416
Market capitalisation, standard deviation	24,703	935	227	41	214	8,178
Market capitalisation, median (£m)	7,553	1,257	264	44	22	921
Market capitalisation, largest company (£m)	0	4,420	3,132	301	3,770	44,354
Market capitalisation, smallest company (£m)	3,529	271	52			52
Share price, average (£)	17.01	8.85	6.66	1.76	1.24	9.87
Number of companies paying a dividend	97	214	227	66	280	27
Number of companies paying a dividend (%)	97	86	83	63	28	79
Dividend yield, average (%)	3.2	3.0	4.4	5.1	24.5	2.6
Dividend yield, standard deviation	1.6	1.6	14.9	8.5	349.6	1.4
PE ratio, average	26.9	30.0	47.6	54.1	33.3	41.1
PE ratio, standard deviation	29.3	47.7	86.2	92.2	62.8	87.4
PEG, average	1.4	1.7	1.5	0.8	1.4	1.7
Correlation (FTSE 100), average	0.5	0.4	0.3	0.2	0.1	0.3
Correlation (FTSE 100), standard deviation	0.1	0.2	0.2	0.1	0.1	0.1
Beta (FTSE 100), average	0.8	0.6	0.4	0.2	0.2	0.5
Beta (FTSE 100), standard deviation	0.3	0.3	0.2	0.2	0.4	0.2

Notes and observations

1. As for the table *Index profiles – company financials* on the opposite page, care should be taken with some of the figures above – especially those of indices with few companies (such as the FTSE Fledgling and techMARK).

2. Just 28% of AIM companies pay a dividend. The figures for all the indices have changed very little since 2007. (NB. The average dividend yield is an average for the companies that pay a dividend – not all the companies in the index.)

3. The average PE for FTSE 100 companies is 26.9 (last year: 21.9), with the PE values fairly tightly clustered around this average level. The PEs for companies in the other indices have a very wide range around the average (i.e. a high standard deviation).

4. Correlation is calculated relative to the FTSE 100. (Note: the averages calculated here are equally weighted, not market capitalisation weighted.)

5. Beta is calculated relative to the FTSE 100.

Data compiled September 2016.

INDEX PROFILES – COMPANY FINANCIALS

The table below presents a range of company financials characteristics for six UK stock market indices. For example, the average turnover for the 288 companies in the FTSE Small Cap is £199m.

	FTSE 100	FTSE 250	Small Cap	Fledgling	AIM	techMARK Focus
Number of companies in index	100	250	274	104	1,012	34
Turnover, average (£m)	13,578	996	199	51	53	1,238
Turnover growth last five years, average (%)	152	102	135	-2	336	45
Turnover growth last five years, median (%)	17	29	22	-6	41	25
Turnover to capitalisation ratio, average	1.2	0.9	1.6	1.6	2.0	0.4
Number of companies making a profit	88	188	115	40	394	25
Number of companies making a profit (%)	88	75	42	38	39	74
Profit, average (£m)	728.0	66.7	-4.7	-2.0	-1.0	113.4
Profit, median (£m)	488.3	72.8	0.0	0.0	-0.4	29.4
Profit growth last five years, average (%)	186	198	147	175	277	30
Profit growth last five years, median (%)	27	45	37	-4	62	8
Profit / turnover, average (%)	59	58	55	49		62
Current ratio, average	1.1	2.1	1.6	1.6	5.3	1.8
Net cash, average (£m)	5,420	208	37	8	11	159
Net cash, median (£m)	707	74	12	4	3	58
Net cash, sum total (£m)	542,000	51,673	9,847	828	10,661	5,236
Net borrowings, average (£m)	45,212	865	66	10	7	205
Net borrowings, sum total (£m)	4,521,176	215,474	17,411	1,023	7,313	6,761
Net gearing, average	447	117	46	96	-19	-47
Interest cover, average	15	28	25	21	32	34
Dividend cover, average	2	3	2	2	2	3
ROCE, average (%)	18	-1	16	-5	-92	1
ROCE, standard deviation	52	198	51	70	2,211	74

Notes and observations

1. Care should be taken with some of the figures above – especially those of indices with few companies (such as the FTSE Fledgling and techMARK Focus) – as the averages can be significantly affected by one or two outlier numbers. In addition, techMARK is very non-homogenous, combining very large and very small companies in the same index. In such cases, a median figure can be more informative than an average.

2. Only 38% of Fledgling companies and 39% of AIM companies reported a profit for the latest year.

3. On average, FTSE 100 companies have £5,420m net cash (median value: £712m), while FTSE 250 companies have average net cash of £208m.

Data compiled September 2016.

DIVERSIFICATION WITH ETFS

The following chart shows the 40 ETFs with the highest trading volumes on the London Stock Exchange (LSE) and their correlations with the FTSE 100. The ETFs are ranked by the correlation value; the ETFs at the top of the chart have the closest correlation with the FTSE 100.

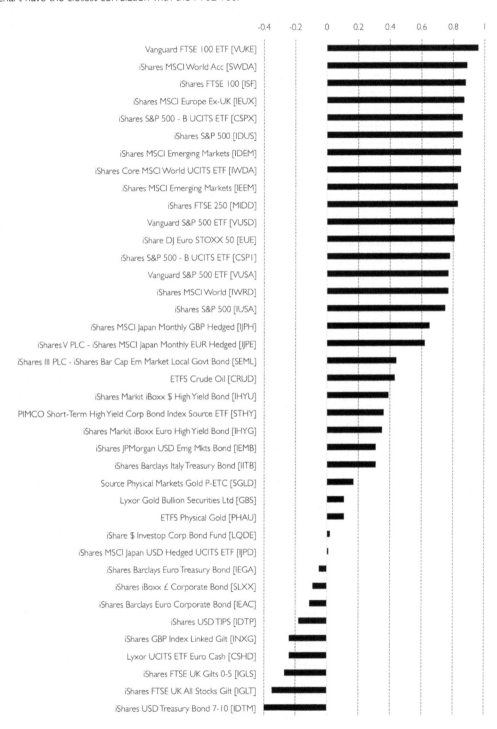

An attractive feature of ETFs is that they can offer cheap and easy diversification. But how effective really is that diversification? A few notes follow on the diversification properties of the most traded ETFs on the LSE, with reference to the chart on the facing page.

As might be expected, the FTSE 100 tracker ETFs are at the top of the ranking – led by the **Vanguard ETF [VUKE]**.

Rather surprisingly, second in the ranking is **iShares MSCI World Acc [SWDA]**, which invests in a broad range of developed companies and has a UK weighting of only 7.5%. This ETF has a higher correlation with the FTSE 100 than the **iShares FTSE 100 [ISF]**!

Also near the top of the ranking are **iShares MSCI Europe Ex-UK [IEUX]** and **iShares S&P 500 [IDUS]**.

Most surprising perhaps is the very high ranking of **iShares MSCI Emerging Markets [IDEM and IEEM]**.

In summary, don't expect much diversification (away from the FTSE 100) by investing in any of these ETFs.

The gold ETFs (**Source Physical Markets Gold P-ETC [SGLD]**, **Lyxor Gold Bullion Securities Ltd [GBS]** and **ETFS Physical Gold [PHAU]**) are ranked near the bottom. But note that while their correlations are low, they are not negative.

For maximum diversification away from the FTSE 100, an investor needs to look at the bottom of the list; at those ETFs with an actual negative correlation with the FTSE 100. Namely, the gilt and T-Bond ETFs (**iShares FTSE UK All Stocks Gilt [IGLT]** and **iShares USD Treasury Bond 7-10 [IDTM]**).

AN AVERAGE YEAR

What does an average year for the FTSE 100 look like?

The summary pages for each month in the diary section of the *Almanac* carry charts that show the average cumulative behaviour of the market day-by-day. These charts are produced by calculating the daily mean return for each day in the trading year over a specific period (in this case from 1984).

For example, if we take the index returns on the first trading day of January for the 29 years since 1985, we can calculate the average return to be 0.29%. With this we can say that on average the FTSE 100 increased 0.29% on the first trading day of January over the period 1985-2016. We can repeat this process for the second trading day of January, and the third, etc., until we have a set of average returns for all the trading days of January.

With this set of returns we can plot an average index for the market in January (we set the index to start at 100). For example, the average return for the market on the first trading day is 0.29%, and so the average index would close at 100.29 on the first trading day of January.

By concatenating the average index data for each month, we can create an average index chart for the whole year. This is shown in the following chart.

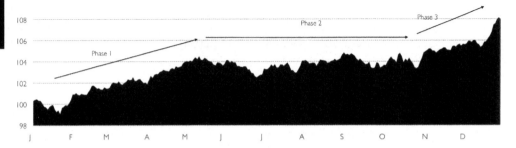

In the above chart we can see that, on average, the year appears to have three phases:

1. **Phase 1**: after a weak three weeks, the market is strong until May.

2. **Phase 2**: from May to October the market is fairly flat.

3. **Phase 3**: the market rises strongly in the final two months of the year.

This annual market behaviour profile concurs with what we already knew about the market, but it is illustrated simply and efficiently in this one chart.

Beyond simple mean returns, it is also useful to look at volatility. The following chart shows the (five-day moving average of the) standard deviation of the daily returns throughout the year for the FTSE 100 from 1984 to 2016. In plain English: the chart plots the range of daily fluctuations of the FTSE 100 for each trading day throughout the year.

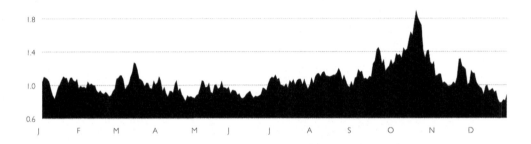

It can be seen that the volatility of daily returns is fairly even for the first eight months of the year; it then starts to increase in September and peaks in October before trailing off for the remainder of the year. So, according to this study of daily returns throughout the year, October has been the most volatile month since 1984.

AN AVERAGE MONTH

What does an average month for the FTSE 100 look like?

The summary pages for each month in the diary section of the *Almanac* carry charts that show the average cumulative behaviour of the market day-by-day. These charts are produced by calculating the daily mean return for each day in the trading year over a specific period (in this case from 1984). These charts then show the average behaviour of the market for the 12 calendar months for each day of the month. But we can also combine those 12 month charts into one, to show the average behaviour of the market on each day in any month.

The following chart plots the average daily returns for each day in the month for the FTSE 100 over the period 1984-2016. For example, since 1984 the market has traded 246 times on the first calendar day of all the months, and the average return of the FTSE 100 on those 246 days has been 0.23% (the first data point plotted in the chart).[1]

Note: the chart here plots the average returns on the *calendar days* of the months, whereas elsewhere in the *Almanac* we look at the trading days.

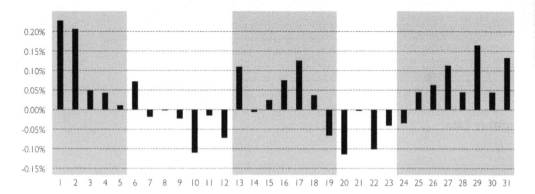

From this data we can calculate the average cumulative performance of the FTSE 100 in a month based on each day's average gain/loss (see following chart).

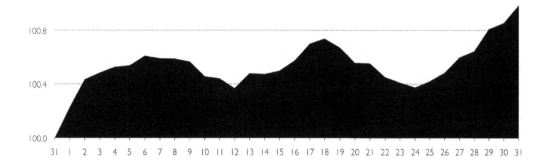

So, in an average month the FTSE 100 rises to the 5th of the month, falls back until the 12th, then increases again briefly to the 19th, before it falls back and then bottoms on the 23rd, and then rises quite strongly from there to the end of the month.

In conclusion, we have the rather remarkable fact that 76% of all the index gains in a month come from the first six days and last six days of the month. For more about this see the articles Turn of the Month (page 125) and Turn of the Month Strategy (page 28).

1. Credit to Crossing Wall Street (www.crossingwallstreet.com) for the idea for this bar chart.

PRICE HISTORY PROFILE OF THE FTSE ALL-SHARE

The FTSE All-Share is the aggregation of the FTSE 100, FTSE 250 and FTSE Small Cap. Effectively, all those LSE-listed companies with a market capitalisation above the lower limit for inclusion in the FTSE Small Cap (in 2016 this was around £80m), are included in the FTSE All-Share. The FTSE All-Share is the standard benchmark for measuring the performance of the broad UK market.

The following tables list some statistical data on the yearly, monthly and daily performance of the index.

Yearly data

Data starts	1899 (117 years)
Largest one-year rise	136.3% (1975)
Largest one-year fall	-55.3% (1974)
Average annual return (standard deviation)	5.71% (20.29)
Number of times the index has risen 5 years in a row (last time)	15 (2003-2007)
Number of times the index has risen 8 years in a row (last time)	6 (1983-1989)
Number of times the index has risen 10 years in a row (last time)	4 (1980-1989)
Most number of consecutive years risen	13 (1977-1989)
Number of times the index has fallen 3 years in a row (last time)	8 (2000-2002)
Number of times the index has fallen 4 years in a row (last time)	2 (1912-1915)
Number of times the index has fallen 5 years in a row	0

Monthly data

Data starts	1946 (847 months)
Largest one-month rise	52.7% (Jan 1975)
Largest one-month fall	-26.6% (Oct 1987)
Average monthly change (standard deviation)	0.66% (5.05)
Number of times the index has risen 6 months in a row (last time)	61 (Feb 16-Aug 16)
Number of times the index has risen 8 months in a row (last time)	21 (Oct 12-May 13)
Number of times the index has risen 10 months in a row (last time)	9 (Sep 12-May 13)
Most number of consecutive months risen (last time)	12 (Jun 12-May 13)
Number of times the index has fallen 4 months in a row (last time)	20 (Jun 11-Sep 11)
Number of times the index has fallen 6 months in a row (last time)	3 (Apr 02-Sep 02)
Number of times the index has fallen 7 months in a row	0

Daily data

Data starts	2 Jan 1969 (12,017)
Largest one-day rise	9.4% (24 Jan 75)
Largest one-day fall	-11.2% (20 Oct 87)
Average daily change (standard deviation)	0.03% (1.06)
Number of times the index has risen 5 days in a row	616
Number of times the index has risen 8 days in a row (last time)	106 (4 Aug 16 – 15 Aug 16)
Number of times the index has risen 10 days in a row (last time)	34 (9 May 12 – 2 May 12)
Most number of consecutive days risen	18 (19/12/86 – 16/01/87)
Number of times the index has fallen 5 days in a row	313
Number of times the index has fallen 8 days in a row (last time)	26 (3 Dec 15 14 Dec 15)
Number of times the index has fallen 10 days in a row (last time)	7 (14 Jan 03 – 27 Jan 03)
Most number of consecutive days fallen	13 (6 Jun 74 – 24 Jun 74)

SECTORS

SECTOR QUARTERLY PERFORMANCE

The following four tables show the performance of FTSE 350 sectors in the four quarters of the year for the past ten years.

Notes:

1. The tables are ranked by the *Avg* column – the average performance for each sector over the ten years.

2. For each year the top five performing sectors are highlighted in light grey, the bottom five in dark grey.

The general clustering of light grey highlights at the top of the table, and dark grey at the bottom, suggests that certain sectors consistently perform well (or badly) in certain quarters. This effect is the strongest in the first quarter and weakest in the third.

The table on the right gives a subjective listing of the three strongest and three weakest sectors in each quarter (sectors with just one or two constituents are not included here).

Quarter	Strong	Weak
1	Oil Equip; Srvs & Dist	Pharm & Biotech
	Industrial Engineering	Banks
	Techn Hardware & Equip	Mobile Telecoms
2	Personal Goods	Construction & Materials
	Pharm & Biotech	Food & Drug Retailers
	Electronic & Elect Equip	Aerospace & Defense
3	Tech Hardware & Equip	Oil & Gas Producers
	Nonlife Insurance	Industrial Transportation
	Life Insurance	Mining
4	Chemicals	Banks
	Food Producers	Real Estate Inv Trusts
	Mobile Telecom	Oil Equip, Services & Dist

First quarter

Sector	Avg	2007	2008	2009	2010	2011	2012	2013	2014	2015	2016
Industrial Metals	16.2	14.4	21.0	80.7	39.5	0.1	5.1	-18.5	-24.7	21.5	22.87
Forestry & Paper	12.6		-1.6	-27.4	38.5	16.7	29.6	33.5	0.3	23.6	0.15
Oil Equip; Srvs & Dist	9.0	4.0	-0.3	19.6	11.1	2.5	20.1	3.1	11.1	11.6	6.95
Industrial Engineering	8.7	9.6	3.2	10.2	21.0	1.6	7.8	17.3	2.5	3.3	10.32
Technology Hard & Equip	7.8	5.2	-28.1	27.1	19.7	22.9	8.2	19.4	-4.0	9.5	-1.81
Chemicals	6.3	10.0	7.4	-3.0	14.0	-4.1	25.5	6.7	2.2	2.7	1.85
Household Goods	6.0	5.8	-4.4	3.6	5.6	-5.0	14.2	23.9	4.1	10.8	1.62
Automobiles & Parts	5.4	37.2	7.9	-29.6	17.9	-9.6	12.6	15.6	4.6	4.2	-6.36
Software & Comp Srvs	5.3	2.2	-11.7	10.8	15.8	0.9	14.5	11.5	2.2	4	2.61
Health Care Equip & Srvs	4.9	22.6	6.9	-2.3	2.1	3.1	1.2	9.9	7.1	0.8	-2.2
Construction & Materials	4.8	5.2	-2.7	-2.3	10.8	5.8	1.5	11	7.4	12.7	-1.15
Personal Goods	4.2	2.7	-18.6	6.7	11.7	1.8	21.2	8.3	-6.2	7	7.86
Mining	4.2	9.5	-0.9	13.4	11.5	-4.2	2.7	-10.1	1.4	-4.2	22.51
Industrial Transportation	4.2	-3.2	-12.6	3.2	19.7	3.0	15.8	7.5	1.7	-0.3	6.76
Electronic & Elect Equip	4.1	8.6	-2.0	-20.8	12.3	3.8	25.6	12.3	-6.1	5.3	2.23
Support Services	3.9	5.7	-4.8	-6.9	8.7	1.5	14.7	15.8	1.8	5.2	-2.31
Real Estate Inv & Srvs	3.8			-0.6	2.8	5.9	11.9	7.8	11.5	-12.4
General Industrials	3.8	5.9	-4.7	-20.6	12.6	5.9	21.1	9.6	-8.8	11.6	5.42
Media	3.7	7.5	-13.5	-4.2	11.3	3.8	9.4	13.7	-5.9	13.8	1.38
Aerospace & Defense	3.1	8.2	-9.4	-12.2	10.1	0.1	9.9	22.5	-9.3	7.6	3.78
General Retailers	2.6	3.4	-19.1	20.6	-3.8	-9.0	19.9	7.3	11.2	3.3	-7.89
Financial Services	2.5	4.6	-15.6	-2.9	-1.2	-4.0	17.5	18.2	2.2	11.4	-4.93
Tobacco	2.4	9.7	-7.9	-12.1	9.3	0.5	3.4	8.5	3.2	1.1	8.21
Equity Inv Instruments	2.1	3.1	-5.8	-2.4	6.7	-0.1	7.7	9.6	0.3	4.3	-2.77
Travel & Leisure	1.8	4.2	-16.5	-6.5	17.8	-8.3	8.5	14.4	0.5	9	-5.16
Nonlife Insurance	1.8	1.5	-10.4	-8.2	7.5	2.3	7.7	6.3	1.2	7.7	2.01
Food & Drug Retailers	0.7	16.3	-19.3	-7.2	2.3	-7.6	-12.5	12.5	-11.0	16.1	17.67
Beverages	0.6	1.2	-9.2	-15.5	3.9	-1.2	8.6	18.4	-5.7	2.5	2.67
Food Producers	-0.7	6.7	-9.7	-15.6	2.6	-3.3	-2.0	17.5	3.4	-6.9	0.19
Gas; Water & Multiutilities	-1.0	5.3	-13.6	-18.6	1.0	1.5	5.1	8.6	3.0	-5.4	3.35
Life Insurance	-1.0	-2.8	-10.7	-28.5	-4.6	9.5	15.3	11.3	-1.9	12.6	-10.37
Oil & Gas Producers	-1.3	-3.4	-14.4	-7.2	2.6	5.7	-2.7	4.3	-2.6	-3.1	8.07
Electricity	-1.5	1.3	-7.0	-10.5	-3.3	2.1	2.5	5.7	5.0	-9.1	-1.51
Real Estate Inv Trusts	-1.5	-5.0	1.8	-31.5	-2.1	4.8	9.6	0.5	5.3	8.7	-7.02
Fixed Line Telecoms	-1.6	1.8	-19.9	-32.5	-4.6	-0.5	17.1	19.7	0.2	8.8	-5.82
Pharm & Biotech	-1.7	2.3	-15.3	-14.3	-0.7	-1.7	-5.5	14	2.5	9.1	-7.01
Mobile Telecom	-1.7	-4.1	-19.6	-11.2	5.9	5.9	-3.4	20.8	-10.3	-0.1	-0.99
Banks	-4.1	-3.1	-10.1	-27.4	6.7	-2.3	17.0	7.5	-8.8	-1.7	18.5

Second quarter

Sector	Avg	2007	2008	2009	2010	2011	2012	2013	2014	2015	2016
Personal Goods	7.3	5.0	-1.1	35.2	7.0	17.1	-11.5	0.8	0.9	-3.4	22.59
Pharm & Biotech	6.7	-3.9	6.0	2.3	-2.8	10.4	2.2	2.5	9.8	-11.8	52.44
Automobiles & Parts	5.1	4.4	-26.7	81.7	-15.7	15.4	-12.4	13.9	-7.0	-6.7	4.42
Electronic & Elect Equip	4.9	13.2	9.1	23.6	12.1	13.7	-4.6	-14.3	-8.4	0.5	4.06
Fixed Line Telecoms	3.7	10.0	-6.5	16.9	2.8	5.4	-2.9	8.7	0.1	4	-1.09
Software & Comp Srvs	3.6	-3.5	7.1	20.8	-8.2	5.1	-0.5	4.4	-4.0	12.9	1.51
Beverages	3.2	5.1	-5.2	13.9	-3.1	5.2	5.7	-8.9	4.4	-2.9	17.69
Electricity	3.1	-0.8	6.8	2.8	-0.7	12.3	4.4	1.5	2.5	1.9	0.74
Oil Equip; Srvs & Dist	2.1	8.4	21.0	21.8	-3.8	-1.3	-17.8	-10.7	-0.2	-2.4	5.62
Industrial Engineering	1.7	6.2	14.7	4.8	-1.2	8.7	-11.4	-5.4	-2.7	-6	9.72
Equity Inv Instruments	1.3	2.5	-2.7	10.7	-6.3	1.7	-4.7	-2.3	1.0	-1.3	13.99
Mobile Telecom	1.1	23.4	-0.7	-4.0	-8.3	-6.4	4.2	0.5	-10.8	3.9	8.87
Oil & Gas Producers	0.9	15.1	16.4	1.4	-25.9	-3.2	-5.0	-2.2	9.1	-4.3	7.43
Chemicals	0.8	15.2	-6.5	7.6	-4.6	9.4	-3.4	-3.0	-8.1	-5.1	6.39
Tobacco	0.5	5.0	-7.8	2.8	-6.1	8.7	1.1	-3.6	5.4	-0.4	-0.35
Real Estate Inv & Srvs	0.5				-14.5	8.6	1.2	11.8	-9.3	5.3	0.06
Technology Hard & Equip	0.4	14.5	-4.8	31.5	4.4	0.4	-15.2	-13.1	-12.0	-4	2.08
General Retailers	0.2	-8.8	-15.9	14.5	-10.3	9.8	-5.8	9.2	-7.6	3.1	14.05
Support Services	0.2	2.3	-9.4	11.0	-5.0	3.1	-4.8	-2.9	-5.1	3.6	9.3
Travel & Leisure	-0.4	-3.9	-7.6	6.3	-11.7	3.1	1.3	3.3	-1.0	-4.9	11.51
General Industrials	-0.4	-1.7	-1.8	13.1	-6.6	0.9	-6.2	1.0	0.4	1.9	-4.72
Food Producers	-0.6	3.9	-13.1	7.2	-6.2	5.0	2.7	-4.7	4.5	0.1	-5.14
Life Insurance	-0.8	-0.7	-18.5	31.8	-13.1	0.9	-6.5	0.6	4.2	-8.5	1.44
Financial Services	-0.9	1.3	-3.6	21.7	-8.1	-1.5	-8.7	-0.1	0.8	-1.6	-9.07
Banks	-1.0	-1.0	-21.2	34.9	-11.9	-4.7	-7.6	-2.2	-3.2	2.2	5.17
Gas; Water & Multiutilities	-1.1	-3.8	-2.1	2.4	-5.4	2.7	5.4	-2.2	1.4	-2.6	-6.61
Nonlife Insurance	-1.1	-6.5	-7.8	-3.3	0.4	5.8	3.8	1.7	4.1	-0.7	-8.93
Mining	-1.8	18.5	16.9	17.2	-21.6	-2.0	-13.2	-18.3	-0.8	-7.8	-6.83
Health Care Equip & Srvs	-2.1	-0.5	-22.0	6.8	-2.6	-4.3	0.9	-2.6	12.3	-6.4	-2.35
Forestry & Paper	-2.4		-29.1	39.9	-17.2	3.5	-7.5	-8.5	1.2	5.6	-9.36
Industrial Transportation	-2.6	-4.0	-19.0	14.6	-7.0	3.8	-6.8	5.5	-9.3	8.6	-12.27
Media	-2.7	3.2	-14.5	1.0	-5.8	3.1	-3.2	0.2	0.5	-4	-7.36
Household Goods	-2.8	-6.3	-24.9	5.3	-15.3	7.1	-3.8	1.7	0.4	5.4	2.58
Real Estate Inv Trusts	-2.9	-15.3	-21.7	15.9	-13.9	9.0	3.1	3.8	3.0	-4	-9.07
Aerospace & Defense	-3.1	-1.5	-9.6	8.2	-9.5	1.7	0.4	0.6	2.1	-10.1	-13.06
Construction & Materials	-4.4	14.4	-16.5	0.0	-17.8	9.8	-1.7	-5.1	-11.3	2.8	0.94
Food & Drug Retailers	-4.7	-1.2	-3.4	2.9	-10.7	4.5	-6.3	-8.9	-6.5	-5.1	-12.56
Industrial Metals	-6.1		-2.9	79.2	-25.0	-8.1	-29.4	-48.9	4.5	-34.4	9.83

Third quarter

Sector	Avg	2006	2007	2008	2009	2010	2011	2012	2013	2014	2015
Technology Hard & Equip	6.7	-7.4	-6.0	6.5	23.2	29.8	-6.9	12.4	18.9	3.3	-6.5
Nonlife Insurance	6.0	13.9	3.8	18.3	16.5	8.5	-16.1	5.7	-1.1	-1.8	11.9
Life Insurance	5.4	5.4	-2.2	-3.5	35.8	26.2	-21.4	10.7	8.9	1.7	-7.9
Personal Goods	4.7	18.9	-3.4	-7.9	20.3	35.8	-16.4	-21.2	21.5	2.8	-3.7
Forestry & Paper	4.5		-45.0	-13.0	49.2	33.9	-23.7	15.6	27.5	-4.8	0.9
Household Goods	4.4	10.4	-6.9	6.7	14.3	11.1	-6.4	8.2	-2.2	3.4	5.8
Gas; Water & Multiutilities	4.3	13.9	1.6	3.8	6.7	9.1	-0.3	1.9	0.7	1.6	4.2
Automobiles & Parts	4.0	5.2	-11.1	-12.2	35.9	45.7	-24.1	18.9	13.5	-12.1	-19.9
Health Care Equip & Srvs	3.9	15.3	-5.8	5.6	24.6	-7.3	-12.0	6.6	4.3	0.1	7.2
Software & Comp Srvs	3.8	2.3	3.6	-5.4	23.8	14.0	-7.1	9.3	3.0	-2.2	-2.9
Tobacco	3.7	5.8	0.9	1.5	16.4	8.0	1.3	-3.2	-1.9	0.4	8.1
Real Estate Inv Trusts	3.5	6.0	-9.4	4.4	27.8	13.2	-21.9	3.7	4.3	1.2	5.5
Mobile Telecom	3.5	6.3	5.3	-17.4	18.9	12.0	0.2	-1.4	14.7	4.2	-8.3
Food Producers	3.3	9.4	-11.3	-0.1	30.2	2.4	0.0	4.2	-5.7	-.9	12.4
Beverages	3.2	4.4	4.1	-1.0	15.2	5.4	-5.3	6.2	2.9	-2.3	2.7
Industrial Engineering	3.1	-0.4	-1.7	-20.5	47.6	25.1	-20.4	11.5	13.7	-5.6	-18
Media	2.6	1.6	-5.2	-8.2	24.7	9.2	-16.1	7.5	11.3	2.4	-0.9
Banks	2.2	4.8	-8.5	-1.4	39.2	10.7	-24.1	7.8	2.7	4.5	-13.3
Chemicals	1.7	6.7	2.1	-21.4	23.0	25.4	-20.3	9.8	6.6	-6.1	-8.6
Pharm & Biotech	1.7	-2.4	-3.4	10.4	11.9	6.2	-2.7	0.2	-0.6	-0.7	-2.4
Aerospace & Defense	1.6	5.9	8.2	-5.8	15.6	6.7	-12.4	3.5	6.2	-3.1	-8.6
General Industrials	1.5	-1.4	-3.8	-6.1	24.8	20.0	-21.2	5.7	8.2	-4.8	-6.1
Oil Equip; Srvs & Dist	1.5	4.6	7.1	-26.9	24.5	26.1	-22.3	14.5	8.7	-7.7	-13.6
General Retailers	1.5	6.5	-10.7	-12.1	16.2	10.8	-10.8	5.1	14.6	-2.2	-2.7
Food & Drug Retailers	1.2	9.3	1.9	4.0	12.3	12.7	-7.2	7.6	9.1	-27.7	-9.9
Travel & Leisure	1.1	7.8	-9.2	-11.2	22.1	8.5	-16.8	5.6	3.9	-0.6	1
Electricity	1.0	8.1	1.4	-1.0	7.7	8.3	-6.7	-1.2	-0.4	-1	-4.9
Fixed Line Telecoms	0.9	11.4	-7.0	-14.1	21.5	2.9	-14.6	8.5	10.0	-1.8	-7.5
Equity Inv Instruments	0.7	4.0	2.5	-14.4	16.5	8.5	-13.6	3.8	3.6	2.1	-5.9
Support Services	0.5	5.9	-10.9	-10.5	19.4	8.8	-13.7	9.0	6.8	-1.8	-8.3
Construction & Materials	0.3	16.8	-0.6	-24.2	10.9	13.1	-15.7	-1.3	12.7	-6.4	-2.1
Electronic & Elect Equip	-0.1	4.0	-8.8	-18.1	24.4	22.0	-26.9	7.1	11.5	-8.6	-7.9
Financial Services	-0.2	6.5	-4.0	-21.9	21.6	12.4	-21.8	7.2	8.8	-5.3	-5.1
Real Estate Inv & Srvs	-0.2					7.9	-18.8	6.7	6.0	-3	0
Industrial Transportation	-3.1	3.0	-9.9	-19.1	26.9	7.1	-19.3	-1.3	8.3	-12.1	-14.1
Oil & Gas Producers	-3.5	-6.0	-2.5	-21.9	13.0	19.2	-12.2	0.1	-1.8	-7.2	-15.8
Mining	-3.9	-5.1	12.8	-44.1	26.5	19.1	-30.9	3.2	14.4	-3.6	-31.7
Industrial Metals	-13.1	-15.0	-65.5	-60.8	10.9	30.6	-44.7	-7.5	32.7	29.2	-40.8

Fourth quarter

Sector	Avg	2006	2007	2008	2009	2010	2011	2012	2013	2014	2015
Food Producers	7.6	5.6	14.9	2.2	6.1	7.9	6.2	7.8	7.6	14.1	3.8
Chemicals	7.3	9.1	9.2	-21.3	12.0	16.3	10.3	1.8	10.2	18.2	6.9
Mobile Telecom	6.7	15.3	6.7	12.8	3.3	5.4	9.3	-11.8	9.6	9.2	6.7
Beverages	6.3	8.5	3.4	3.8	16.3	9.0	11.0	3.3	0.7	0.7	6.5
Real Estate Inv & Srvs	5.4					6.8	8.8	7.8	6.6	4.6	-2.2
Health Care Equip & Srvs	5.3	6.3	3.2	-27.6	13.1	16.7	6.7	0.8	12.0	15.6	6.4
Travel & Leisure	5.2	16.6	-7.6	-13.6	0.9	10.0	6.9	7.9	12.4	11.1	7.3
Electronic & Elect Equip	5.1	16.3	-15.7	-21.6	1.1	18.0	8.2	10.5	13.1	13	7.7
Tobacco	4.8	7.7	15.4	-0.9	4.5	3.7	12.0	-0.4	-0.3	2.2	4
Fixed Line Telecoms	4.7	12.6	-9.2	-13.7	2.5	18.7	5.9	0.9	13.0	5.3	11.2
Personal Goods	4.5	19.2	-1.8	-23.0	18.7	8.6	-1.3	22.3	-4.9	2.3	5.3
Oil & Gas Producers	4.5	-0.3	10.1	8.1	6.5	11.0	16.6	-4.6	7.9	-12.2	1.6
Media	3.7	1.7	-4.7	-2.9	6.4	6.2	9.3	4.7	6.3	4.7	4.9
Construction & Materials	3.6	4.5	-12.6	4.3	-8.4	16.3	8.0	1.9	4.0	7.5	10.6
Household Goods	3.5	11.9	-7.9	-6.8	5.0	1.6	-0.5	11	9.6	6.4	4.2
Support Services	3.4	10.3	-6.3	-5.7	4.3	6.5	8.0	1.1	5.4	4.2	5.7
Financial Services	3.1	10.6	0.3	-29.9	-2.7	19.0	-3.2	7.4	10.8	11.9	6.6
Technology Hard & Equip	3.0	-8.1	-12.6	-22.2	12.5	5.0	5.9	22.0	9.6	8.4	9.1
Aerospace & Defense	2.8	5.4	4.4	-6.2	5.4	1.3	13.3	2.3	5.2	-1.7	-1.4
Gas; Water & Multiutilities	2.6	9.9	4.3	-6.4	11.8	3.5	-1.1	0.3	1.0	2	0.9
Life Insurance	2.6	6.6	-4.8	-19.2	-1.1	-2.5	9.7	11.3	11.6	4.9	9.2
Software & Comp Srvs	2.3	9.7	-9.5	-17.5	-1.1	2.0	3.6	3.3	4.8	11.1	16.1
Mining	2.1	10.6	2.7	-31.5	24.1	22.8	8.5	8.8	-0.5	-10.2	-14.7
Nonlife Insurance	2.0	12.0	-4.8	3.5	-5.0	0.4	-3.4	4.8	4.2	2.2	6.1
Equity Inv Instruments	1.8	6.6	-1.7	-18.6	4.3	9.3	1.5	3.3	3.4	3.5	6.3
Electricity	1.6	13.7	4.6	-14.8	-0.1	9.6	1.4	2.6	-3.1	-0.1	2
Pharm & Biotech	1.5	-9.3	-4.7	8.9	6.2	-3.6	8.4	-3.9	7.4	-2.6	8
Industrial Metals	1.5	36.7	10.0	-65.0	13.5	26.3	-9.6	2.8	-6.9	6.3	0.5
General Industrials	1.3	1.4	-13.2	-20.4	10.0	9.0	4.1	7.4	11.7	-3.2	5.7
Food & Drug Retailers	1.1	10.2	2.7	-4.3	4.9	-1.1	7.5	-0.3	-4.8	6.9	-11
General Retailers	0.7	2.6	-12.1	-12.9	9.2	2.0	-1.0	11.5	-1.3	11.9	-2.6
Industrial Engineering	0.6	6.3	-18.8	-26.8	7.3	19.2	17.5	7.8	0.9	-9.6	1.7
Automobiles & Parts	0.3	-3.2	-20.3	-50.4	2.9	31.2	4.0	6.5	9.2	7.8	15.1
Industrial Transportation	0.0	10.2	-5.3	-32.2	1.5	5.3	1.7	6.4	6.3	7.7	-1.3
Real Estate Inv Trusts	-0.6	11.0	-12.8	-33.6	4.7	7.6	-2.1	7.2	5.8	9.5	-3.2
Forestry & Paper	-2.0		-8.6	-21.0	8.4	-0.2	-3.9	6.3	0.3	3.9	-3.5
Oil Equip; Srvs & Dist	-2.2	23.8	14.5	-38.3	3.6	15.9	14.0	-6.1	-6.4	-27.3	-16
Banks	-4.5	3.2	-10.3	-38.2	-9.2	-4.0	-0.3	15.4	-0.2	-1.9	0.2

SECTOR ANNUAL PERFORMANCE

The table below shows the year-on-year percentage performance of the FTSE 350 sectors for the past ten years. The three best [worst] performing sectors in each year are highlighted in light grey [dark grey]. The table is ranked by the final column – the average annual return for the sector for the period 2006-2015.

Sector performance 2005-2014 (percentage change YoY)

EPIC	Sector	2006	2007	2008	2009	2010	2011	2012	2013	2014	2015	Avg
NMX9570	Technology Hardware & Equipment	-10.4	-1.2	-43.3	131.6	70.4	21.6	25.7	35.1	-5.4	7.1	23.1
NMX3760	Personal Goods	40.7	2.2	-42.9	105.8	76.1	-1.6	3.4	26.2	-0.5	4.9	21.4
NMX1350	Chemicals	33.6	41.3	-37.8	43.8	58.5	-7.8	35.5	21.5	4.2	-4.8	18.8
NMX2750	Industrial Engineering	19.8	-7.2	-31.1	83.1	78.2	3.2	14.7	27.5	-14.9	-19.1	15.4
NMX3350	Automobiles & Parts	-3.5	1.4	-65.6	78.7	89.9	-17.6	25.0	63.2	-7.8	-10.4	15.3
NMX1730	Forestry & Paper		-49.7	-52.1	64.4	53.3	-11.4	47.1	56.2	0.4	27.1	15.0
NMX9530	Software & Computer Services	-2.9	-7.5	-26.2	63.9	23.7	2.1	28.8	25.6	6.6	32.4	14.6
NMX1750	Industrial Metals	79.8	-56.6	-83.9	307.3	72.4	-54.0	-29.4	-48.6	8.0	-52.6	14.2
NMX2730	Electronic & Electrical Equipment	23.4	-5.5	-31.4	23.0	81.2	-6.6	41.8	21.3	-11.1	4.9	14.1
NMX8630	Real Estate Investment & Services					-2.0	-1.3	23.4	41.4	-0.8	14.8	12.6
NMX3530	Beverages	16.5	14.4	-11.6	28.9	15.6	9.3	25.8	11.7	-3.1	8.9	11.6
NMX3780	Tobacco	14.8	34.0	-14.6	9.9	15.0	23.9	0.8	2.3	11.7	13.3	11.1
NMX4530	Health Care Equipment & Services	-2.9	18.6	-36.3	47.0	7.5	-7.2	9.7	25.0	39.3	7.6	10.8
NMX3720	Household Goods		-15.0	-28.6	30.9	1.0	-5.2	31.9	35.1	14.9	28.8	10.4
NMX8770	Financial Services	37.9	2.0	-55.4	39.7	21.5	-28.5	23.5	42.3	9.1	10.8	10.3
NMX6530	Fixed Line Telecommunications	32.9	-5.4	-44.5	-1.7	19.8	-5.2	24.4	61.8	3.6	16.4	10.2
NMX8530	Nonlife Insurance	28.6	-6.2	1.2	-1.7	17.6	-12.3	23.8	11.4	5.7	27.1	9.5
NMX3570	Food Producers	9.8	12.9	-19.9	25.1	6.3	7.8	13.2	13.7	12.1	8.8	9.0
NMX0570	Oil Equipment; Services & Distribution		38.1	-45.7	87.8	56.3	-10.4	6.2	-6.3	-25.7	-20.9	8.8
NMX5750	Travel & Leisure	27.6	-15.9	-40.8	22.5	24.2	-15.9	25.2	38.1	9.9	12.4	8.7
NMX5550	Media	4.0	0.2	-34.1	28.3	21.5	-1.9	19.2	34.9	1.4	13.5	8.7
NMX5370	General Retailers	16.6	-25.9	-47.8	75.2	-2.5	-11.7	32.4	32.6	12.4	0.9	8.2
NMX2790	Support Services	20.4	-9.7	-27.2	28.7	19.7	-2.4	20.2	26.6	-1.1	5.7	8.1
NMX6570	Mobile Telecommunications		32.9	-25.7	4.6	14.7	8.6	-12.5	52.7	-8.9	1.7	7.6
NMX2720	General Industrials		-13.1	-30.0	23.2	37.6	-12.3	28.9	33.9	-15.7	12.9	7.3
NMX8570	Life Insurance	18.5	-10.1	-43.3	26.5	2.0	-4.6	32.8	36.0	9.1	3.7	7.1
NMX7530	Electricity	41.2	6.5	-16.2	-1.0	14.0	8.5	8.4	3.6	6.4	-10.2	6.1
NMX2770	Industrial Transportation	49.9	-20.8	-61.2	52.3	25.7	-12.2	13.4	30.7	-12.6	-8.1	5.7
NMX7570	Gas; Water & Multiutilities	31.0	7.3	-17.8	-0.6	7.9	2.8	13.2	8.0	8.2	-3.2	5.7
NMX8980	Equity Investment Instruments	12.4	6.5	-36.1	31.3	18.5	-10.9	10.1	14.6	7.0	3.0	5.6
NMX2710	Aerospace & Defense	6.0	20.4	-27.6	15.8	7.7	1.1	16.9	37.6	-11.8	-12.9	5.3
NMX2350	Construction & Materials	29.0	4.5	-35.7	-0.7	19.6	-13.1	0.3	23.4	-4.1	25.4	4.9
NMX1770	Mining	22.9	50.4	-55.7	108.5	27.8	-29.7	0.2	-16.3	-13.0	-48.6	4.7
NMX4570	Pharmaceuticals & Biotechnology	-5.1	-9.5	8.0	4.2	-1.2	14.5	-7.0	24.8	8.7	1.4	3.9
NMX8670	Real Estate Investment Trusts	33.8	-36.5	-44.7	6.2	2.7	-12.6	25.7	15.1	20.2	6.6	1.7
NMX0530	Oil & Gas Producers	-2.0	19.3	-16.0	13.3	0.5	4.8	-11.8	8.1	-13.4	-20.6	-1.8
NMX5330	Food & Drug Retailers	23.6	20.2	-22.5	12.5	1.8	-3.6	-12.0	6.5	-35.6	-11.7	-2.1
NMX8350	Banks	10.0	-21.3	-56.8	23.8	-0.1	-29.6	34.5	7.8	-9.5	-12.7	-5.4

Notes

Since 2006, the best performing sector has been Technology Hardware & Equipment (with an average annual return of 23.1%). The worst performing sector has been Banks (average annual return: -5.4%).

SECTOR PROFILES OF THE FTSE 100 AND FTSE 250

The chart below shows the FTSE 350 sector weightings in the FTSE 100 and FTSE 250.

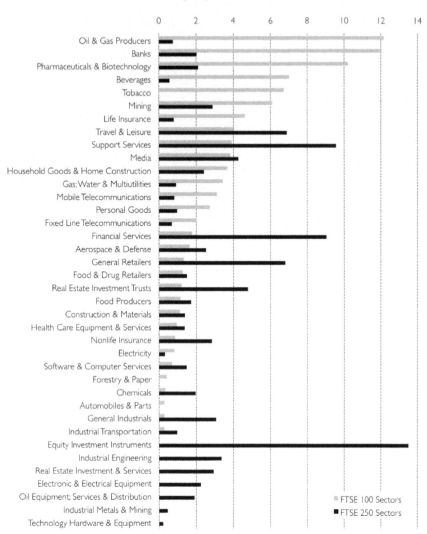

Note: Figures as of September 2016.

OBSERVATIONS

1. The top four FTSE 350 sectors (oil and gas producers, banks, pharmaceuticals, and beverages) together account for 41% of the total market capitalisation of the FTSE 100. (In 2006, the top four sectors accounted for 55% of the index capitalisation.)

2. In the last year, oil and gas producers has displaced banks as the largest sector in the FTSE 100.

3. In 1935, the FT 30 was dominated by engineering and machinery companies. Today, the sector isn't represented at all in the FTSE 100.

4. The FTSE 100 is still dominated by the old industries of oil, banks, mining, beverages, and tobacco, while the FTSE 250 has proportionately a greater representation of service (support, financial, and computer) companies.

COMPANIES

COMPANY RANKINGS

On the following pages are tables with companies ranked according to various criteria. The tables are grouped into the following categories:

1. FTSE 350

2. AIM

3. Investment Trusts

Table index

A summary of the tables is given below.

1. 10 largest companies by **market capitalisation** [FTSE 350]

2. 10 companies with largest average **daily trade value** [FTSE 350]

3. 5-year **share performance** [FTSE 350]

4. 10-year **share performance** [FTSE 350]

5. 10 companies with highest **turnover** [FTSE 350]

6. 10 companies with greatest **turnover growth** in 5 the last years [FTSE 350]

7. 10 companies with highest **ROCE** [FTSE 350]

8. 10 companies with highest **profits** [FTSE 350]

9. 10 companies with greatest **profit growth** in the last 5 years [FTSE 350]

10. 10 companies with highest **operating margins** [FTSE 350]

11. 10 companies with highest **EPS growth** in the last 5 years [FTSE 350]

12. 10 companies with highest **dividend growth** in the last 5 years [FTSE 350]

13. 10 companies paying the most **tax** in last year [FTSE 350]

14. 10 companies with largest **market capitalisation** [AIM]

15. 10 companies with largest average daily trade value [AIM]

16. 5-year **share performance** [AIM]

17. 10 companies with largest **turnover** [AIM]

18. 10 companies with largest **profits** [AIM]

19. 10 companies with highest **ROCE** [AIM]

20. 10 largest investment trusts by **capitalisation [ITs]**

21. 10 **best performing** investment trusts in the last 5 years **[ITs]**

22. 10 investment trusts with highest average **daily trading value [ITs]**

Note: All figures accurate as of September 2016.

FTSE 350

Size, volume and performance

Table 1: 10 largest companies by market capitalisation [FTSE 350]

Rank	Company	TIDM	Capital (£m)
1	Royal Dutch Shell	RDSB	149,227
2	HSBC Holdings	HSBA	113,558
3	British American Tobacco	BATS	88,238
4	GlaxoSmithKline	GSK	79,119
5	BP	BP.	79,111
6	SABMiller	SAB	72,051
7	AstraZeneca	AZN	63,153
8	Vodafone Group	VOD	58,342
9	Diageo	DGE	53,325
10	Reckitt Benckiser Group	RB.	50,242

Table 2: 10 companies with largest average daily trade value [FTSE 350]

Rank	Company	TIDM	Average daily trade value (£m)
1	HSBC Holdings	HSBA	151
2	Royal Dutch Shell	RDSB	138
3	BP	BP.	137
4	GlaxoSmithKline	GSK	124
5	SABMiller	SAB	119
6	Vodafone Group	VOD	117
7	AstraZeneca	AZN	115
8	British American Tobacco	BATS	111
9	Lloyds Banking Group	LLOY	110
10	Rio Tinto	RIO	110

Table 3: 5-year share performance [FTSE 350]

Rank	Company	TIDM	5-yr change (%)
1	Paysafe Group	PAYS	1,877
2	Ashtead Group	AHT	745
3	Greencore Group	GNC	597
4	JD Sports Fashion	JD.	567
5	Micro Focus International	MCRO	538
6	Barratt Developments	BDEV	489
7	Hill & Smith Holdings	HILS	392
8	Taylor Wimpey	TW.	360
9	Smurfit Kappa Group	SKG	348
10	IP Group	IPO	320

Table 4: 10-year share performance [FTSE 350]

Rank	Company	TIDM	10-yr change (%)
1	Micro Focus International	MCRO	1,928
2	JD Sports Fashion	JD.	1,694
3	Booker Group	BOK	1,153
4	Rightmove	RMV	1,090
5	Paddy Power Betfair	PPB	803
6	Ashtead Group	AHT	767
7	NCC Group	NCC	754
8	Telecom plus	TEP	739
9	Domino's Pizza UK & IRL	DOM	627
10	Randgold Resources Ltd	RRS	568

Turnover

Table 5: 10 companies with highest turnover [FTSE 350]

Rank	Company	TIDM	Turnover (£m)
1	Royal Dutch Shell	RDSB	172,500
2	BP	BP.	145,100
3	Glencore	GLEN	111,000
4	Tesco	TSCO	54,430
5	HSBC Holdings	HSBA	45,460
6	Vodafone Group	VOD	40,970
7	Unilever	ULVR	38,760
8	SSE	SSE	28,780
9	Centrica	CNA	27,970
10	Imperial Brands	IMB	25,290

Table 6: 10 companies with greatest turnover growth in the last 5 years [FTSE 350]

Rank	Company	TIDM	Turnover 5-yr growth (%)
1	Dixons Carphone	DC.	9,999+
2	IP Group	IPO	4,368
3	John Laing Inf, Fund Ltd	JLIF	3,984
4	Paysafe Group	PAYS	939
5	Centamin	CEY	518
6	BTG	BTG	302
7	Playtech	PTEC	276
8	AO World	AO.	265
9	Bovis Homes Group	BVS	217
10	Redrow	RDW	205

Table 7: 10 companies with highest ROCE [FTSE 350]

Rank	Company	TIDM	ROCE (%)
1	Hargreaves Lansdown	HL.	505
2	Softcat	SCT	146
3	Wizz Air Holding	WIZZ	138
4	PayPoint	PAY	130
5	Paddy Power Betfair	PPB	128
6	Domino's Pizza UK & IRL	DOM	111
7	WH Smith	SMWH	85
8	Jardine Lloyd Thompson Group	JLT	77
9	Howden Joinery Group	HWDN	70
10	QinetiQ Group	QQ.	69

Profits

Table 8: 10 companies with highest profits [FTSE 350]

Rank	Company	TIDM	Profit (£m)
1	HSBC Holdings	HSBA	12,286
2	GlaxoSmithKline	GSK	10,526
3	British American Tobacco	BATS	5,855
4	Unilever	ULVR	5,253
5	Prudential	PRU	3,148
6	National Grid	NG.	3,032
7	BT Group	BT.A	3,029
8	Diageo	DGE	2,858
9	SABMiller	SAB	2,706
10	Reckitt Benckiser Group	RB.	2,208

Table 9: 10 companies with greatest profit growth in the last 5 years [FTSE 350]

Rank	Company	TIDM	5-yr profit growth (%)
1	Ashtead Group	AHT	9,999
2	IP Group	IPO	4,072
3	Phoenix Group Holdings	PHNX	2,983
4	Regus	RGU	1,768
5	IG Group Holdings	IGG	1,563
6	Big Yellow Group	BYG	1,527
7	UNITE Group	UTG	1,505
8	John Laing Infrastructure Fund Ltd	JLIF	1,026
9	Rentokil Initial	RTO	997
10	Redrow	RDW	888

Table 10: 10 companies with highest operating margins [FTSE 350]

Rank	Company	TIDM	Operating margin (%)
1	Great Portland Estates	GPOR	626
2	Shaftesbury	SHB	503
3	Capital & Counties Properties	CAPC	473
4	Workspace Group	WKP	398
5	Derwent London	DLN	395
6	Tritax Big Box REIT	BBOX	316
7	Segro	SGRO	249
8	Hammerson	HMSO	180
9	Kennedy Wilson Eur. Real Estate	KWE	173
10	CLS Holdings	CLI	171

Table 11: 10 companies with highest EPS growth in the last 5 years [FTSE 350]

Rank	Company	TIDM	EPS 5-yr growth (%)
1	Ashtead Group	AHT	2,126
2	IP Group	IPO	1,915
3	Electra Private Equity	ELTA	1,815
4	Barratt Developments	BDEV	1,319
5	UNITE Group	UTG	1,141
6	Merlin Entertainments	MERL	1,035
7	Paysafe Group	PAYS	823
8	Redrow	RDW	823
9	Moneysupermarket.com Group	MONY	806
10	Bovis Homes Group	BVS	754

Dividends

Table 12: 10 companies with highest dividend growth in the last 5 years [FTSE 350]

Rank	Company	TIDM	5-yr div growth (%)
1	Persimmon	PSN	1367
2	John Laing Infrastructure Fund Ltd	JLIF	1265
3	Bovis Homes Group	BVS	1233
4	Booker Group	BOK	705
5	Bellway	BWY	670
6	RIT Capital Partners	RCP	663
7	Ashtead Group	AHT	650
8	Fidelity China Special Situation	FCSS	620
9	BP	BP.	516
10	3i Group	III	419

Tax

Table 13: 10 companies paying the most tax in last year [FTSE 350]

Rank	Company	TIDM	Tax paid (£m)
1	Vodafone Group	VOD	3,370
2	HSBC Holdings	HSBA	2,460
3	GlaxoSmithKline	GSK	2,150
4	Barclays	BARC	1,450
5	Unilever	ULVR	1,430
6	British American Tobacco	BATS	1,330
7	SABMiller	SAB	765
8	Lloyds Banking Group	LLOY	688
9	Rio Tinto	RIO	647
10	Prudential	PRU	569

AIM

Table 14: 10 companies with largest market capitalisation [AIM]

Rank	Name	TIDM	Capital (£m)
1	ASOS	ASC	3,770
2	New Europe Property Invs	NEPI	2,571
3	GW Pharmaceuticals	GWP	1,940
4	Abcam	ABC	1,648
5	BCA Marketplace	BCA	1,490
6	Fevertree Drinks	FEVR	1,137
7	Hutchison China Meditech Ltd	HCM	1,113
8	boohoo.com	BOO	1,033
9	Breedon Group	BREE	966
10	James Halstead	JHD	938

Table 15: 10 companies with largest average daily trade value [AIM]

Rank	Name	TIDM	Average daily trade value (£m)
1	ASOS	ASC	22.8
2	Abcam	ABC	3.9
3	Sirius Minerals	SXX	3.7
4	Fevertree Drinks	FEVR	3.4
5	Dart Group	DTG	3.2
6	boohoo.com	BOO	2.8
7	Plus500 Ltd	PLUS	2.7
8	Clinigen Group	CLIN	2.7
9	Secure Income REIT	SIR	2.6
10	GW Pharmaceuticals	GWP	2.1

Table 16: 5-year share performance [AIM]

Rank	Name	TIDM	5-yr share price (%)
1	Somero Enterprises Inc	SOM	1,695
2	Trakm8 Holdings	TRAK	1,134
3	Best of the Best	BOTB	1,108
4	CVS Group	CVSG	941
5	Accesso Technology Group	ACSO	837
6	Sigma Capital Group	SGM	826
7	Crawshaw Group	CRAW	774
8	Tracsis	TRCS	732
9	GB Group	GBG	667
10	Public Service Properties Invs Ltd	PSPI	646

Table 17: 10 companies with largest turnover [AIM]

Rank	Name	TIDM	Turnover (£m)
1	Datatec Ltd	DTC	4,268
2	Vertu Motors	VTU	2,423
3	Total Produce	TOT	2,122
4	Impellam Group	IPEL	1,777
5	Origin Enterprises	OGN	1,458
6	Dart Group	DTG	1,405
7	Ambrian	AMBR	1,242
8	Marshall Motor Holdings	MMH	1,233
9	BCA Marketplace	BCA	1,153
10	ASOS	ASC	1,151

Table 18: 10 companies with largest profits [AIM]

Rank	Name	TIDM	Profit (£m)
1	New Europe Property Investments	NEPI	180
2	Asian Growth Properties Ltd	AGP	115
3	Dart Group	DTG	104
4	Origin Enterprises	OGN	86
5	Plus500 Ltd	PLUS	83
6	Summit Germany Ltd	SMTG	71
7	Globalworth Real Estate Invs Ltd	GWI	63
8	Abbey	ABBY	62
9	Datatec Ltd	DTC	58
10	Sirius Real Estate Ltd	SRE	57

Table 19: 10 companies with highest ROCE [AIM]

Rank	Name	TIDM	ROCE
1	GoldStone Resources Ltd	GRL	17,000
2	Asiamet Resources Ltd	ARS	7,770
3	32Red	TTR	4,330
4	Gloo Networks	GLOO	4,090
5	Tiziana Life Sciences	TILS	3,700
6	Pathfinder Minerals	PFP	2,940
7	Applied Graphene Materials	AGM	2,890
8	Shield Therapeutics	STX	2,860
9	EVR Holdings	EVRH	2,720
10	Maxcyte Inc	MXCT	2,400

Investment Trusts

Table 20: 10 largest investment trusts by capitalisation

Rank	Investment Trust	TIDM	Capital (£m)
1	Land Securities Group	LAND	8,010
2	British Land Co	BLND	6,368
3	3i Group	III	6,172
4	Hammerson	HMSO	4,462
5	Scottish Mortgage Inv Trust	SMT	4,018
6	Intu Properties	INTU	3,839
7	Segro	SGRO	3,629
8	Alliance Trust	ATST	2,933
9	Derwent London	DLN	2,810
10	Foreign & Colonial Inv Trust	FRCL	2,726

Table 21: 10 best performing investment trusts in the last 5 years

Rank	Investment Trust	TIDM	5-yr price change (%)
1	Downing Two VCT D	DP3E	9910
2	Hazel Renewable Energy VCT 1	HR1A	4950
3	Hazel Renewable Energy VCT 2	HR2A	4950
4	Downing Two VCT E	DP2E	4910
5	Premier Veterinary Group	PVG	3250
6	Downing Structured Opps VCT 1	DO1C	2410
7	Public Service Properties Invs Ltd	PSPI	646
8	EPE Special Opportunities	ESO	325
9	Chelverton Growth Trust	CGW	314
10	Biotech Growth Trust (The)	BIOG	308

Table 22: 10 investment trusts with highest average daily trading value

Rank	Investment Trust	TIDM	Average daily trade value (£m)
1	British Land Co	BLND	29.31
2	Land Securities Group	LAND	27.88
3	Hammerson	HMSO	13.40
4	3i Group	III	9.75
5	Derwent London	DLN	8.23
6	Intu Properties	INTU	7.78
7	Great Portland Estates	GPOR	7.75
8	Segro	SGRO	7.06
9	Shaftesbury	SHB	4.76
10	Scottish Mortgage Investment Trust	SMT	4.20

TEN BAGGERS

The term *ten bagger* was coined by Peter Lynch, the legendary manager of the Fidelity Magellan fund, in his book *One Up on Wall Street*. The term ten bagger comes from baseball and Lynch used it to describe stocks that rise ten times in value.

The table below shows the UK stocks that rose ten times or more in the ten years to September 2016.

UK ten baggers over ten years to August 2016

Company	TIDM	Price increase 10Y (%)	Capital (£m)	Sector	Index
Accesso Technology Group	ACSO	6,336	336	Software & Computer Srvs	AIM 100
ASOS	ASC	4,852	3,770	General Retailers	AIM 100
Advanced Medical Solutions Group	AMS	1,989	494	Health Care Equipment & Srvs	AIM 100
Micro Focus International	MCRO	1,928	4,953	Software & Computer Srvs	FTSE 100
JD Sports Fashion	JD.	1,694	2,793	General Retailers	FTSE 250
First Derivatives	FDP	1,450	483	Software & Computer Srvs	AIM 100
Judges Scientific	JDG	1,376	86	Electronic & Electrical Eqp	AIM All-Share
Abcam	ABC	1,367	1,648	Pharmaceuticals & Biotech	AIM 100
Booker Group	BOK	1,153	3,223	Food & Drug Retailers	FTSE 250
Rightmove	RMV	1,090	3,897	Media	FTSE 250
Scapa Group	SCPA	1,062	395	Chemicals	AIM 100
Sirius Minerals	SXX	1,046	862	Mining	AIM 100

Observations

1. The table above does not include those companies that rose ten times in the interim, only to see their share prices fall back again. For example, companies such as Ashtead, Aveva, Babcock Intl, Domino's Pizza, Dragon Oil, Goodwin, and Randgold Resources, have all been ten baggers at some point.

2. Jim Slater's comment that "elephants don't gallop" would seem to hold true. Many of the above ten baggers were very small companies ten years ago.

3. It can be seen that the ten baggers come from quite a wide range of sectors. In other words, it's not necessary to look for ten baggers in just a few glamour sectors.

As Peter Lynch says:

"The very best way to make money in a market is in a small growth company that has been profitable for a couple of years and simply goes on growing."

ANNOUNCEMENT DATES OF COMPANY RESULTS

Companies listed on the London Stock Exchange are required to release certain information to the public. Some of these statements are one-offs and unpredictable, such as news of takeovers or board changes, while others follow a more regular timetable. For investors, two important announcements each year are:

1. **Interim results** (known as *interims*): usually reported about eight months into a company's financial year, they relate to the unaudited headline figures for the first half of the company's year.

2. **Preliminary results** (known as *prems*): unaudited figures published prior to the full annual report at the end of the company's financial year. (Note that although these are termed "preliminary", these are very much the real final results.)

These announcements are watched very carefully and have the potential to significantly move the share price of a company.

FTSE 100

The following chart plots the frequency distribution of the dates of these announcements for FTSE 100 companies.

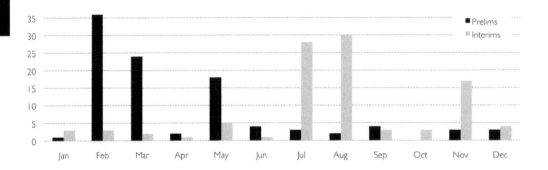

As can be seen, the majority of interim results are announced in July and August, while preliminary results are clustered in February and March (60 companies announce their prems in this two-month period).

FTSE 250

The following chart is similar to that above, except this time the companies are in the FTSE 250.

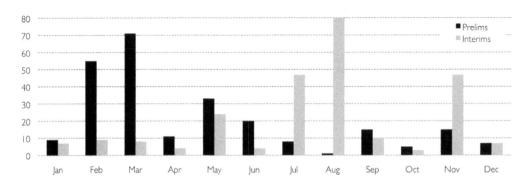

For the FTSE 250 companies, the announcements are a little more evenly distributed throughout the year, but the main months are the same as those for the FTSE 100: July/August are the busiest months (with November) for interims, and February/March are the busiest for the prems.

LONG TERM

CORRELATION BETWEEN UK AND US MARKETS

Here we look at how close the movements of the US and UK markets are on a monthly basis and how this has changed over time.

The following charts plot the correlation of monthly returns of the FTSE All-Share and S&P 500 for each decade since the 1960s.

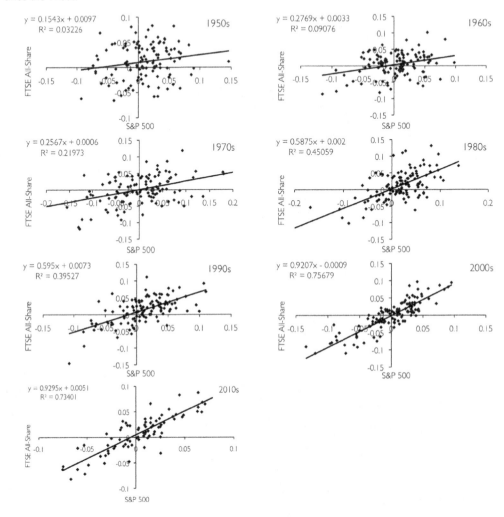

There is obviously a trend of increasing correlation throughout the decades. In the 1960s and 1970s, there was negligible correlation (measured by the R^2 value in the charts) between the UK and US markets on a monthly basis. The US equity market might rise one month and the UK would respond by rising or falling. In the 1970s some evidence of correlation can be seen for the first time – although it was still very weak.

But in the 1980s, the monthly correlation of the two markets jumped and became statistically significant. There could be many reasons for this increase in correlation, but one contributing factor was undoubtedly the increasing presence of computers in trading rooms. And, of course, the October crash in 1987 would have alerted many for the first time to the scale of interconnectedness of worldwide markets.

Correlation rose somewhat again in the 1990s, and then increased hugely in the 2000s. This can be clearly seen in the last two charts, where the points are closely aligned along the line of best fit.

The correlation of monthly returns for the two markets since 2010 has been a high 0.73, albeit this correlation is slightly lower than that seen in the 2000s.

CORRELATION BETWEEN UK AND WORLD MARKETS

This is an update of the analysis of the correlation of the UK equity market with six other markets worldwide.

The charts on this page show the correlation of monthly returns between the FT All-Share and six international indices for the period 2000-2016.

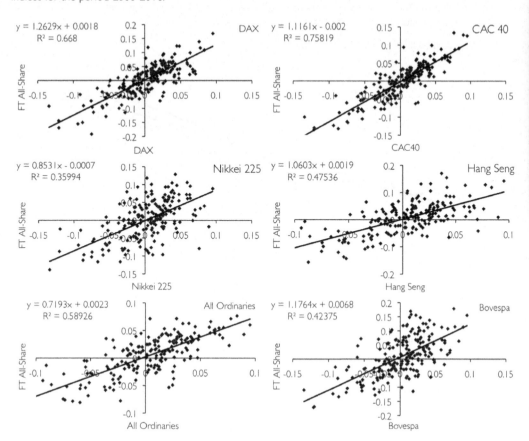

Analysis

The first observation is that all of the markets are positively correlated with the UK market.

The next question is how closely correlated are they?

The table on the right summarises the R^2 values for the correlation between the FT All-Share and the six international indices. The values are also given for previous years. The higher the R^2 figure, the closer the correlation (R-Squared is a measure of correlation – in effect, how close the points are to the line of best fit).

Index	2016 R^2	2015 R^2	2014 R^2	2013 R^2
CAC 40	0.76	0.77	0.78	0.79
DAX	0.67	0.67	0.69	0.70
All Ordinaries	0.59	0.60	0.61	0.62
Hang Seng	0.48	0.47	0.48	0.49
Bovespa	0.42	0.43	0.45	0.47
Nikkei 225	0.36	0.36	0.37	0.39

By visual inspection it can be seen that in the charts of CAC 40 and DAX the points are more closely distributed around the line of best fit. This is confirmed in the table where it can be seen these two markets have the highest R^2 values (the CAC 40 value of 0.76 is higher than that of 0.73 for the S&P 500). Among the sample, the index with the lowest correlation with the UK market is the Nikkei.

The practical impact of this is that if a UK investor is looking to internationally diversify a portfolio they would do better by investing in markets at the bottom of the table (low R^2) than at the top. And the good news for investors looking for diversification is that the correlation between the UK market and all the international markets in this study has slightly fallen in the past two years.

THE LONG-TERM FORMULA

An update on the Almanac's famous UK stock market Long-Term Formula.

The chart below plots the FTSE All-Share from 1946 to the present day.

1. The Y-scale is logarithmic, which presents percentage (rather than absolute) changes better over long periods, and so is more suitable for long-term charts.

2. The straight line is a line of best fit calculated by regression analysis.

$$y = 0.8465e^{0.0002x}$$
$$R^2 = 0.95774$$

Observations

1. The R^2 for the line of best fit is 0.96, which is impressively high for such a simple model (i.e. the line of best fit fairly accurately approximates the real data points).

2. The FTSE All-Share fluctuated closely around the trend line (line of best fit) from 1946 to 1973; it then traded consistently below the trend line until 1983, when it crossed over to trade above the trend line until 2001. From 2001 the index was close to the trend, but then in 2008 fell significantly below it and has yet to revert to the long-term trend line.

Forecasts

The equation of the line of best fit in the chart above (with a little more precision) is:

$$y = 0.846531e^{0.000207x}$$

This equation allows us to make forecasts for the FTSE All-Share. It is, in effect, the Holy Grail, the key to the stock market – as simple as that!

For example, at the time of writing the FTSE All-Share is 3675, while the above equation forecasts a value today (according to the long-term trend line) of 5809. This suggests the index is currently underpriced relative to the long-term trend line. But as can be seen in the above chart, the index can spend long periods trading above or below the long-term trend line.

Now, if we think that the trend of the market in the last 70 years will broadly continue, we can use the equation to forecast the level of the FTSE All-Share in the future. And this is what has been done in the table to the right. Equivalent forecasts for the FTSE 100 have also been given.

Date	FTAS forecast	FTSE 100 forecast	Chng(%)
Dec 2017	6,403	11,726	74
Dec 2020	8,036	14,716	119
Dec 2030	17,128	31,366	366
Dec 2040	36,513	66,867	894

- The equation says that the trend line value for FTSE 100 at the end 2017 will be 11,726 (74% above its current level in September 2016, the time of writing).

- By end 2020, the forecast is for a FTSE 100 level of 14716 (+119%), and by end 2040 the equation forecasts a FTSE 100 value of 66,867 (+894%).

THE MARKET'S DECENNIAL CYCLE

The following table shows the annual performance of the FTSE All-Share since 1801. The table is arranged to compare the performance of the market for the same year in each decade. For example, in the third year of the 1801-1810 decade (1803), the market fell 21.9%, while in the third year of the 1811-1820 decade (1813), the market fell 0.2%. Years are highlighted in which the market fell.

Decades	1st	2nd	3rd	4th	5th	6th	7th	8th	9th	10th
1801-1810	11.0	1.4	-21.9	10.3	8.5	0.7	3.5	4.7	10.4	-9.2
1811-1820	-14.6	-7.5	-0.2	2.4	-6.2	-12.2	32.6	5.5	-8.3	3.2
1821-1830	4.5	9.4	9.2	90.7	-22.7	-20.1	4.6	-14.5	3.3	-14.8
1831-1840	-15.7	2.2	16.5	-9.3	5.0	5.2	-8.5	-3.6	-12.7	3.1
1841-1850	-9.7	7.1	12.3	16.5	-2.1	-1.8	-13.9	-13.5	-7.3	14.4
1851-1860	-0.2	9.6	-6.8	-3.2	-3.4	5.4	-5.9	6.5	-2.0	11.1
1861-1870	3.1	16.6	12.8	5.0	1.4	-22.4	-2.2	6.8	7.4	8.6
1871-1880	18.9	4.0	3.6	-5.2	-7.9	-2.4	-9.6	-11.0	12.1	4.9
1881-1890	-0.6	-6.3	-5.0	-2.1	0.2	0.6	-3.6	5.8	13.1	-6.2
1891-1900	0.7	-0.1	1.6	6.0	11.2	22.0	5.2	0.3	-2.0	-0.9
1901-1910	-4.9	-1.3	-5.6	2.5	6.2	-0.4	-14.7	8.1	4.8	-2.5
1911-1920	0.3	-0.9	-6.7	-6.9	-5.1	0.5	-10.5	11.0	2.4	-13.3
1921-1930	-5.4	17.6	2.0	9.5	4.4	2.4	8.3	8.1	-7.4	-19.4
1931-1940	-23.5	5.6	27.2	8.3	7.8	13.9	-19.3	-14.3	0.8	-13.0
1941-1950	22.6	18.6	8.1	10.7	-0.6	18.1	-2.7	-4.0	-13.9	6.4
1951-1960	2.4	-5.1	16.0	34.5	1.6	-9.0	-3.3	33.2	43.4	-4.7
1961-1970	-2.5	-1.8	10.6	-10.0	6.7	-9.3	29.0	43.4	-15.2	-7.5
1971-1980	41.9	12.8	-31.4	-55.3	136.3	-3.9	41.2	2.7	4.3	27.1
1981-1990	7.2	22.1	23.1	26.0	15.2	22.3	4.2	6.5	30.0	-14.3
1991-2000	15.1	14.8	23.3	-9.6	18.5	11.7	19.7	10.9	21.2	-8.0
2001-2010	-15.4	-25.0	16.6	9.2	18.1	13.2	2.0	-32.8	25.0	10.9
2011-2020	-6.7	8.2	16.7	-2.1	-2.4					
Analysis										
Since 1801										
Positive	50%	64%	68%	59%	64%	57%	48%	67%	62%	43%
Average(%)	1.3	4.6	5.5	5.8	8.7	1.6	2.7	2.9	5.2	-1.2
Since 1921										
Positive	50%	70%	90%	60%	80%	67%	67%	67%	67%	33%
Average(%)	3.6	6.8	11.2	2.1	20.6	6.6	8.8	6.0	9.8	-2.5
Since 1951										
Positive	57%	57%	86%	43%	86%	50%	83%	83%	83%	33%
Average(%)	6.0	3.7	10.7	-1.0	27.7	4.2	15.5	10.6	18.1	0.6

Observations

1. Since 1801, the strongest years have been the second, third and fifth years in the decades. The market has risen with an average annual return over 4% in each of these years. But the single year champion has got to be the 5th year in each decade, which has risen an average of 8.7%.

2. The standout weakest year in the decade since 1801 has been the tenth – this is the only year to have risen less than ten times in the 21 decades, and also the only year to have a negative average return (-1.2%).

3. Generally, performance in the more recent decades has not changed too much from the long-term picture. In the six decades since 1951, the strong years are still the third and fifth years, although they are now also joined by the seventh and ninth years. And the tenth year continues to be weakest, with positive returns only twice in the past six decades.

4. Concerning 2017, the seventh year of decades are currently on a roll, without a down year since 1957.

BUY AND HOLD

An update on whether buy and hold still works.

The last decade or so has not been the best for buy-and-hold investors. At the time of writing (September 2016), the FTSE 100 is at 6730, which is 12 points below where it closed on 3 December 1999 – almost 17 years ago.

The question must be asked: is buy and hold dead?

Such thinking inspired Richard Bernstein to write a paper[1] in July 2012 called, appropriately, 'Is buy and hold dead?' In the paper, which advocates longer-term investing, Bernstein says:

> There are sound economic reasons why extending one's time horizon can benefit investment returns. Changes within the economy tend to be very gradual, and significant adjustments rarely happen within a short period of time. Certainly, there is plenty of daily news, but how much of that news is actually important and worth acting on? The data suggest very little of that information is meaningful and valuable. Most of it is simply noise.

He also writes:

> investment returns can be significantly hurt by strategies based on short-term, noise-driven strategies. The data clearly and consistently showed that extending one's investment time horizon was a simple method for improving investment returns.

In the paper he presents a chart showing the probability of sustaining a loss over different time horizons for an investment in the S&P 500.

The chart on this page does the same for the FTSE All-Share. The analysis was carried out on daily data for the FTSE All-Share from 1970 to 2016.

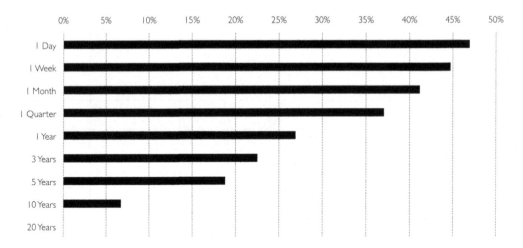

The analysis found that if an investment was made in the index on any day since 1970, the chance of the index being lower one week later (i.e. five trading days later) was 45%. Similarly, since 1970, investing on any day would see a 41% chance the market would be lower a month later.

As can be seen in the chart, the longer the time horizon of an investment, the lower the chance of loss. Conversely, the shorter the time horizon, the closer the probability of loss tends towards 50/50 (i.e. the closer it becomes to a simple coin toss). By the time one gets to a holding period of ten years, the chance of loss is down to 7%; and it is zero with a holding period of 20 years (based on the historic behaviour since 1970).

Finally, the paper makes the useful point that while longer time horizons tend to progressively improve investment returns in many financial assets (e.g. shares), this is not necessarily the case for real assets such as gold and other commodities.

1. www.rbadvisors.com

ULTIMATE DEATH CROSS

An update on the Almanac's study of the Ultimate Death Cross.

A previous edition of the *Almanac* showed a chart with the FTSE All-Share poised to make an *ultimate death cross* (when the 50-month moving average moves down through the 200-month moving average). Readers were left hanging with the comment, "If the 50-month average *does* fall below the 200-month average, will that signal a lost decade(s) for the UK market as in Japan?"

So, what happened?

The chart below updates the action.

As can be (just) seen, the 50M MAV narrowly avoided crossing the 200M MAV. We were saved. And, in fact, the narrow avoidance of an ultimate death cross in the past has been a strong buy signal for an ensuing massive bull market.

The last time the FTSE All-Share made an ultimate death cross was 1945. So, this signal is fairly rare. But this has not always been the case. The following chart plots the FTSE All-Share with 50-month and 200-month moving averages for the period 1845-1945.

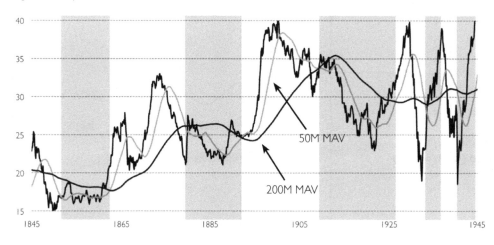

As can be seen, for the 100 years prior to 1945 ultimate death crosses were not uncommon. In fact, the 50-month MAV was below the 200-month MAV (shaded in the chart) for 51 of the 100 years.

POLITICS AND FINANCIAL MARKETS

FTSE All-Share index

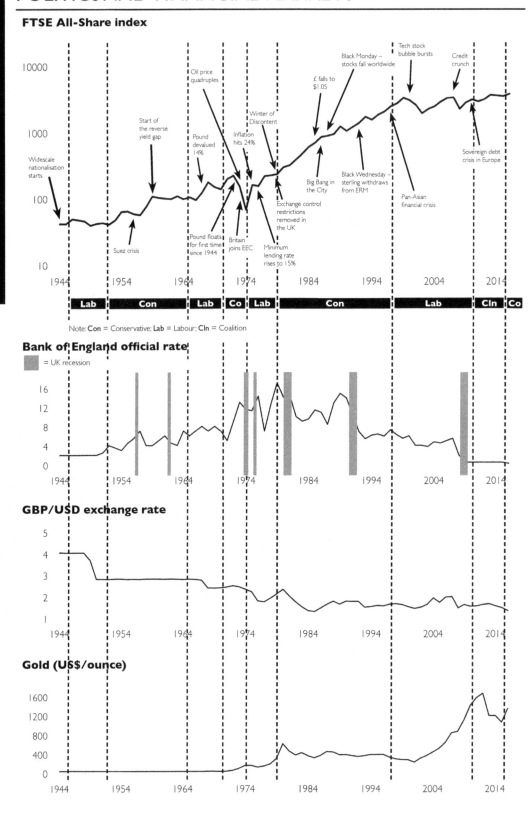

Widescale nationalisation starts

Suez crisis

Start of the reverse yield gap

Oil price quadruples

Pound devalued 14%

Pound floats for first time since 1944

Britain joins EEC

Inflation hits 24%

Winter of Discontent

Minimum lending rate rises to 15%

Exchange control restrictions removed in the UK

£ falls to $1.05

Big Bang in the City

Black Monday – stocks fall worldwide

Black Wednesday – sterling withdraws from ERM

Tech stock bubble bursts

Pan-Asian financial crisis

Credit crunch

Sovereign debt crisis in Europe

| Lab | Con | Lab | Co | Lab | Con | Lab | Cln | Co |

Note: **Con** = Conservative; **Lab** = Labour; **Cln** = Coalition

Bank of England official rate

▨ = UK recession

GBP/USD exchange rate

Gold (US$/ounce)

INTEREST RATES

UK INTEREST RATE CYCLE

A brief analysis of the interest rate cycle in the UK.

When growth in an economy is thought to be too low, interest rates may be reduced to increase consumption and investment. However, at a certain stage low interest rates may lead to inflation, with over-investment in property and other assets. At this point, to limit inflation, interest rates may be raised.

This cycle of interest rates increasing and decreasing is roughly related to the economic cycle: low growth leads to lower interest rates, and high growth leads to higher interest rates.

When central banks are lowering interest rates this is often referred to as the *easing phase* of the interest rate cycle; when rates are being raised this is the *tightening phase* of the cycle.

For the purposes of the study here, rates are said to be in an easing phase if the previous rate change was down. They stay in this phase until a positive rate change occurs, at which point rates move into a tightening phase.

We'll now look in some more detail at these alternating phases of easing and tightening.

Firstly, for a brief recap, the chart below plots the level of the bank rate since 1901.

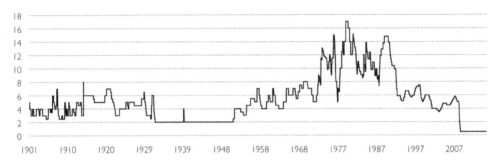

Now, the following chart reproduces the above chart but overlays vertical bars to highlight the **tightening phase** of the interest rate cycle (i.e. periods when the bank rate is being increased). The periods without grey bars are therefore **easing phases**.

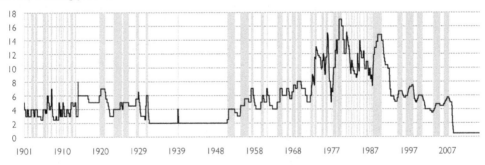

The table to the right gives a summary of the length of time the base rate stayed in the respective phases.

Over the whole period, rates stayed in an easing phase (68%) for twice as long as they did in a tightening phase (32%).

Period	Market Days	Easing	Tightening
1901-1969	17,995	70%	30%
1970-1999	7,590	59%	41%
2000-2016	3,994	74%	26%
1901-2016	29,579	68%	32%

The following chart is similar to the above, but zooms into the shorter time period: 1970-2016.

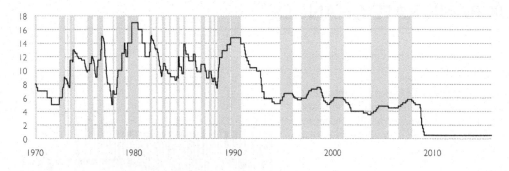

It can be seen that before 1988, monetary policy changed direction frequently (i.e. the average interest rate cycle was short). After 1988, monetary policy settled down and the interest rate cycle became much longer.

For example, in the five years from 1983-1988, there were seven full rate cycles (i.e. an easing phase followed by a tightening phase) – the same number as occurred in the 28 years since 1988.

For reference, the following chart overlays the FTSE All-Share on the BoE base rate.

It can be seen that the period of great credit expansion that occurred from 1980-2000 was accompanied by an overall decline in interest rates from 17% to 5%.

The following chart (crudely) shows what happened to equities over this period during the discrete periods of interest rates being eased and tightened, using three model portfolios:

1. **Portfolio EASE**: a portfolio invested in the equity market only during the easing phase of interest rates.

2. **Portfolio TIGHT**: a portfolio invested in the equity market only during the tightening phase of interest rates.

3. **Portfolio FTAS**: a buy-and-hold portfolio invested continuously in the FTSE All-Share.

All portfolio values start at 100.

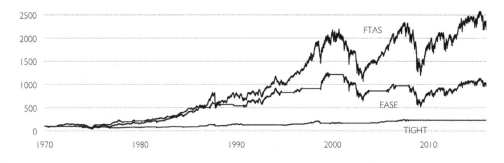

By 2016, the Easing Portfolio had a value of 986, while the Tightening Portfolio a value of 228. Obviously some of this difference in performance is attributable to the fact that the Easing Portfolio was invested in the market for twice as long as the Tightening Portfolio.

UK BANK RATE CHANGES

A brief analysis of the changes made to the bank rate since 1694.

Since 1694, the Bank of England has made 828 changes to the bank rate. Changes to the bank rate today are recommended by the Monetary Policy Committee (MPC), which meets once a month.

The top chart plots all the changes to the bank rate from 1694. The size of each respective change is shown on the Y-axis. (NB. the Y-axis is truncated at plus and minus 3 for legibility; in 1914 the rate did see changes of +4 and -4.)

Until the beginning of the 20th century, the great majority of rate changes were +/- 0.5 and +/- 1. And also the balance of the size of positive and negative rate changes was roughly equal.

Towards the end of the 20th century the Bank started experimenting with larger and smaller increments of change. And the balance of rate changes also changed: periods of small negative changes would be interrupted by larger positive rate adjustments.

In 1982, the Bank began a cautious period of frequent rate reductions of just 0.125 (the smallest rate reduction up to this time). The last time the bank rate was reduced by such a small amount was in 1989.

The frequency distribution of size of rate changes is shown in the middle chart.

As can be seen, the most common rate change has been a reduction of half a percentage point. (Since 1694, 33% of all rate changes have been for -0.5.) After that the most frequent rate change was plus one percentage point.

The above chart supports the (well-known) observation that rates are reduced cautiously with small increments and increased with more aggressive, larger increments.

The bottom chart breaks this frequency distribution down by century.

The above chart supports the previous observation that whereas in the 19th century the Bank restricted its changes to a narrow band of increments, in the 20th century the size of the rate changes were more varied.

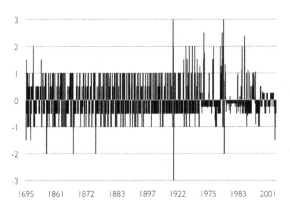

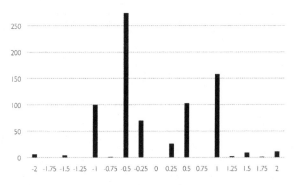

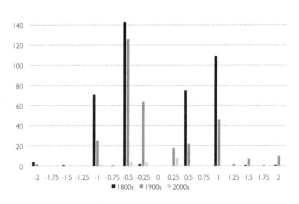

SINCLAIR NUMBERS

SINCLAIR NOS – DAY, WEEK & MONTH MARKET BEHAVIOUR

By analysing past share price data it is possible to calculate the historic average returns on all days, weeks and months of the year. For example, since 1984 the LSE has traded 24 times on 8 January with an average return (of the FTSE 100) of -0.05%. Similarly, over the same period the FTSE 100 has had an average return of -0.54% in the second week of the year.

Sinclair Numbers

The Almanac has conducted such analysis of the historic behaviour for four stock indices:

1. FTSE 100 [from 1984]

2. FTSE 250 [from 1985]

3. S&P 500 [from 1950]

4. Nikkei 225 [from 1984]

The analysis produces three numbers (the Sinclair Numbers) for each day, week and month of the year:

1. **Positive (%):** The proportion of historic returns on the day/week/month that were positive. For example, since 1984 the FTSE 100 has risen 16 times and fallen 6 times on 28 July; it therefore has a Positive (%) value of 73%. If you look at week 30 in the Diary section you will see this figure of 73% in the Sinclair table on the right for the FTSE 100 on 28 July.

2. **Average Change (%):** The average (mean) change of the index on the day/week/month. For example, since 1984 the FTSE 100 has risen an average of 0.2% in the fourth week of the year. If you look at week 4 in the Diary section you will see the second figure on the top line is 0.2.

3. **Std Dev:** This is the standard deviation of the returns for the day/week/month. In the above example, the average return for the fourth week was seen to be 0.2% and the standard deviation for that week is 1.9, which means that 68% of all returns in the fourth week have been in the range -1.7% (0.2 - 1.9) to 2.1% (0.2 + 1.9). The standard deviation measures how closely all the returns in the period cluster around the average return. A high number for the standard deviation suggests that clustering is not close and therefore confidence in forecasting future returns being close to the average is decreased. Conversely, a low standard deviation suggests good clustering and increases the confidence in forecasting future returns being close to the historic average.

These Sinclair Numbers are referred to often in the *Almanac*. An explanation of their occurrence in the Diary section can be found in the Introduction (page xii).

For the weekly Sinclair Numbers, the ISO week numbering system is used.

The rest of this section provides a comprehensive listing of the Sinclair Numbers calculated for the FTSE 100 for all the days, weeks and months of the year. The best and worst performing days/weeks/months in the year are also highlighted.

MARKET BEHAVIOUR – BY DAY

The two tables below list the historic ten strongest and weakest days for the FTSE 100 since 1984. The tables are ranked by the Positive (%) value – the percentage of years that the market has a positive return on the day.

10 strongest days in the year

Date	Positive (%)	Avg Change (%)	Std Dev
27 Dec	86	0.5	1.1
24 Dec	83	0.2	0.5
23 Dec	83	0.6	0.7
26 Jan	82	0.7	1.0
16 Dec	78	0.7	0.8
17 Feb	78	0.5	1.0
29 Jul	78	0.5	1.3
2 May	78	0.5	0.8
29 Dec	77	0.5	1.1
5 Oct	77	0.4	1.7

10 weakest days in the year

Date	Positive (%)	Avg Change (%)	Std Dev
30 May	21	-0.4	1.2
4 Aug	27	-0.3	0.9
8 Apr	27	-0.2	0.7
4 Dec	29	-0.2	0.7
9 Sep	30	-0.2	0.8
8 Jul	30	-0.2	1.0
11 Sep	30	-0.1	0.8
10 Aug	32	-0.5	1.3
19 Nov	33	-0.4	1.5
7 Jan	33	-0.2	1.0

Note: The above best and worst days for the market are marked in the Diary section by their performance data being in bold in the Sinclair numbers table to the right of the day's entry.

Historically, the very best day of the whole year has been 27 December; the market has risen on this day in 86% of all years. And on this day the market has risen by an average of 0.5%. The second strongest day of the year is 24 December.

Considering a combination of the average change on days and their standard deviation, the strongest day of the year could be considered 23 December.

On the downside, the worst day of the year is 30 May – the market has only risen on this day in 21% of previous years and has fallen by an average of 0.4% on this day.

Analysis of all days

Average Positive (%) [Std Dev]	52.5 [10.7]
Average Return (%) [Std Dev]	0.03 [0.23]

Since 1984 the market has risen on 53% of all days with an average daily return of 0.03%.

The standard deviation is 11 for the average Positive (%) value, which means that:

- days that have a Positive (%) value over 64 (the average plus one standard deviation) can be considered strong days, and

- days that have a Positive (%) value under 42 (the average minus one standard deviation) can be considered weak days.

The tables beginning on the next page list the FTSE 100 Sinclair Numbers for all days in the year. The rows for the ten strongest [weakest] days are highlighted light grey [dark grey].

Date	Positive (%)	Avg Change (%)	Std Dev
02 Jan	53	0.3	1.1
03 Jan	72	0.3	1.1
04 Jan	55	0.1	1.4
05 Jan	45	-0.1	1.0
06 Jan	55	0.2	0.9
07 Jan	33	-0.2	1.0
08 Jan	42	-0.1	0.8
09 Jan	41	-0.2	1.0
10 Jan	41	-0.1	0.8
11 Jan	36	-0.2	0.7
12 Jan	45	-0.3	0.7
13 Jan	43	-0.1	0.8
14 Jan	54	-0.3	1.4
15 Jan	63	0.2	1.3
16 Jan	57	0.2	0.9
17 Jan	59	0.2	0.8
18 Jan	59	0.2	1.1
19 Jan	45	-0.1	0.9
20 Jan	35	-0.5	1.0
21 Jan	46	-0.3	1.4
22 Jan	50	0.2	1.2
23 Jan	41	-0.3	0.8
24 Jan	59	0.4	1.2
25 Jan	36	-0.2	0.7
26 Jan	82	0.7	1.0
27 Jan	48	0.1	1.2
28 Jan	58	0.1	1.0
29 Jan	42	-0.1	1.0
30 Jan	52	0.2	1.0
31 Jan	59	0.2	0.7
01 Feb	64	0.6	1.0
02 Feb	73	0.2	1.0
03 Feb	48	0.3	1.2
04 Feb	42	-0.2	1.0
05 Feb	50	-0.1	1.1
06 Feb	61	0.0	0.9
07 Feb	55	0.0	1.1
08 Feb	55	0.1	1.1
09 Feb	50	0.0	0.7
10 Feb	39	-0.2	0.8
11 Feb	58	0.3	1.1
12 Feb	48	0.1	1.3
13 Feb	65	0.2	0.5
14 Feb	45	0.0	0.7
15 Feb	64	0.1	0.8
16 Feb	45	0.2	1.0
17 Feb	78	0.5	1.0
18 Feb	41	0.0	0.7
19 Feb	46	0.0	1.0
20 Feb	50	-0.2	1.0
21 Feb	45	-0.1	0.8
22 Feb	45	0.0	0.7
23 Feb	41	-0.2	0.9
24 Feb	43	-0.1	0.9
25 Feb	67	0.4	1.1
26 Feb	58	0.2	0.9
27 Feb	48	-0.1	0.8
28 Feb	45	-0.2	1.1

Date	Positive (%)	Avg Change (%)	Std Dev
29 Feb	50	0.0	1.1
01 Mar	68	0.3	1.0
02 Mar	45	-0.1	1.3
03 Mar	48	0.0	1.0
04 Mar	63	0.5	1.1
05 Mar	55	0.1	1.2
06 Mar	52	0.2	0.9
07 Mar	43	-0.2	0.7
08 Mar	64	0.1	0.7
09 Mar	45	0.0	0.7
10 Mar	61	0.1	1.4
11 Mar	50	-0.1	1.0
12 Mar	43	-0.3	1.3
13 Mar	39	0.0	1.5
14 Mar	61	0.3	1.2
15 Mar	45	0.1	0.9
16 Mar	50	0.1	1.2
17 Mar	61	0.0	1.3
18 Mar	50	0.2	1.1
19 Mar	61	0.1	0.7
20 Mar	48	0.1	1.0
21 Mar	45	0.0	0.9
22 Mar	45	-0.4	1.1
23 Mar	50	0.1	0.9
24 Mar	43	-0.3	1.3
25 Mar	45	0.2	1.1
26 Mar	57	0.2	0.9
27 Mar	45	0.0	1.0
28 Mar	42	-0.3	0.7
29 Mar	53	0.2	0.7
30 Mar	50	-0.3	1.2
31 Mar	38	-0.1	1.3
01 Apr	74	0.5	1.1
02 Apr	71	0.6	1.1
03 Apr	39	-0.3	1.0
04 Apr	57	0.1	0.8
05 Apr	63	0.1	0.8
06 Apr	65	0.2	0.7
07 Apr	43	0.2	1.1
08 Apr	27	-0.2	0.7
09 Apr	70	0.4	0.7
10 Apr	59	0.4	1.6
11 Apr	38	-0.2	0.9
12 Apr	57	0.1	0.7
13 Apr	61	0.2	0.7
14 Apr	38	-0.3	0.8
15 Apr	58	0.2	0.9
16 Apr	55	0.1	1.1
17 Apr	55	0.0	1.1
18 Apr	50	0.0	0.9
19 Apr	59	0.2	0.7
20 Apr	65	0.0	1.1
21 Apr	40	-0.1	0.5
22 Apr	43	0.0	0.8
23 Apr	42	-0.1	0.9
24 Apr	57	0.1	1.0
25 Apr	57	0.0	0.5
26 Apr	70	0.3	0.6

Date	Positive (%)	Avg Change (%)	Std Dev
27 Apr	55	-0.2	1.1
28 Apr	52	0.1	1.0
29 Apr	48	0.2	0.9
30 Apr	58	0.2	0.6
01 May	60	0.1	0.7
02 May	78	0.5	0.8
03 May	58	-0.2	1.0
04 May	50	-0.2	1.2
05 May	50	0.0	1.0
06 May	67	0.2	0.9
07 May	37	-0.4	0.8
08 May	57	0.2	1.1
09 May	38	-0.1	0.6
10 May	48	0.3	1.4
11 May	52	0.1	1.0
12 May	52	-0.1	0.9
13 May	63	0.2	0.8
14 May	42	-0.4	1.3
15 May	50	0.1	0.8
16 May	46	0.1	0.5
17 May	52	-0.1	1.2
18 May	57	0.2	0.9
19 May	52	-0.2	1.3
20 May	54	-0.1	1.0
21 May	63	0.0	0.7
22 May	54	0.0	1.0
23 May	38	-0.4	1.1
24 May	43	-0.1	0.8
25 May	56	-0.1	1.1
26 May	56	0.2	0.8
27 May	50	0.0	1.0
28 May	60	0.2	0.7
29 May	63	0.2	0.9
30 May	21	-0.4	1.2
31 May	53	0.0	0.6
01 Jun	57	0.3	1.0
02 Jun	50	0.1	0.9
03 Jun	61	0.1	0.7
04 Jun	50	0.0	1.0
05 Jun	48	0.0	0.9
06 Jun	58	0.0	1.0
07 Jun	52	0.0	0.8
08 Jun	41	-0.1	0.8
09 Jun	43	0.1	0.8
10 Jun	46	-0.1	0.8
11 Jun	50	-0.1	0.9
12 Jun	42	-0.2	0.8
13 Jun	50	-0.2	0.8
14 Jun	43	-0.1	1.1
15 Jun	48	-0.1	0.9
16 Jun	57	0.1	0.5
17 Jun	67	0.3	0.9
18 Jun	46	-0.2	0.7
19 Jun	50	0.0	0.9
20 Jun	42	-0.3	1.2
21 Jun	57	0.0	0.7
22 Jun	48	-0.2	0.9
23 Jun	39	-0.2	0.8

Date	Positive (%)	Avg Change (%)	Std Dev
24 Jun	38	-0.5	1.0
25 Jun	54	0.1	0.8
26 Jun	42	-0.4	1.0
27 Jun	58	0.1	0.9
28 Jun	65	0.3	1.0
29 Jun	57	0.2	1.4
30 Jun	57	0.0	1.0
01 Jul	71	0.4	1.4
02 Jul	58	0.0	1.0
03 Jul	63	0.2	1.1
04 Jul	54	0.3	1.0
05 Jul	43	0.1	1.0
06 Jul	48	0.0	1.0
07 Jul	55	0.3	1.0
08 Jul	30	-0.2	1.0
09 Jul	58	0.1	0.8
10 Jul	38	-0.3	0.9
11 Jul	57	-0.2	1.4
12 Jul	36	-0.2	0.7
13 Jul	73	0.3	0.9
14 Jul	64	0.3	0.9
15 Jul	45	-0.1	1.5
16 Jul	50	0.1	0.7
17 Jul	58	0.2	1.2
18 Jul	43	-0.1	1.0
19 Jul	50	-0.1	1.2
20 Jul	45	-0.1	0.8
21 Jul	41	-0.2	0.8
22 Jul	43	-0.4	1.4
23 Jul	54	-0.1	1.0
24 Jul	46	-0.4	1.0
25 Jul	39	0.1	1.1
26 Jul	55	0.1	1.0
27 Jul	55	0.1	0.9
28 Jul	73	0.2	0.6
29 Jul	78	0.5	1.3
30 Jul	58	0.3	0.8
31 Jul	46	0.2	0.9
01 Aug	57	-0.2	1.3
02 Aug	73	0.5	1.0
03 Aug	41	-0.1	1.1
04 Aug	27	-0.3	0.9
05 Aug	52	-0.1	1.2
06 Aug	38	-0.2	1.3
07 Aug	58	0.1	0.9
08 Aug	61	0.1	1.2
09 Aug	59	0.1	1.0
10 Aug	32	-0.5	1.3
11 Aug	45	0.0	1.3
12 Aug	61	0.3	1.0
13 Aug	58	0.2	1.0
14 Aug	67	0.2	0.9
15 Aug	57	0.0	1.1
16 Aug	59	-0.1	1.1
17 Aug	59	0.1	1.2
18 Aug	55	0.0	1.4
19 Aug	43	-0.3	1.2
20 Aug	46	0.0	0.7

Date	Positive (%)	Avg Change (%)	Std Dev	Date	Positive (%)	Avg Change (%)	Std Dev
21 Aug	63	0.0	1.3	18 Oct	55	-0.1	0.8
22 Aug	52	0.2	0.9	19 Oct	45	-0.2	1.6
23 Aug	55	0.0	0.8	20 Oct	45	-0.3	3.0
24 Aug	71	0.0	1.3	21 Oct	65	0.4	1.8
25 Aug	71	0.2	1.2	22 Oct	42	-0.5	1.6
26 Aug	47	-0.2	0.8	23 Oct	58	-0.1	1.3
27 Aug	58	0.3	1.3	24 Oct	48	-0.2	1.4
28 Aug	45	-0.2	1.3	25 Oct	41	-0.3	0.7
29 Aug	53	0.0	0.8	26 Oct	41	-0.3	1.5
30 Aug	67	0.3	1.0	27 Oct	50	0.0	1.2
31 Aug	59	0.2	0.9	28 Oct	70	0.2	1.2
01 Sep	64	0.1	1.3	29 Oct	54	0.5	2.0
02 Sep	59	0.1	0.9	30 Oct	67	0.3	1.3
03 Sep	58	0.1	1.4	31 Oct	74	0.4	1.0
04 Sep	58	-0.1	1.0	01 Nov	59	-0.1	0.9
05 Sep	48	-0.3	1.0	02 Nov	59	0.2	0.8
06 Sep	68	0.1	1.1	03 Nov	55	0.1	1.2
07 Sep	55	0.1	1.4	04 Nov	43	0.4	1.5
08 Sep	41	0.0	1.1	05 Nov	58	-0.1	1.1
09 Sep	30	-0.2	0.8	06 Nov	58	-0.1	1.3
10 Sep	42	-0.3	1.1	07 Nov	48	-0.2	0.9
11 Sep	30	-0.1	0.8	08 Nov	59	0.1	0.6
12 Sep	48	-0.2	1.1	09 Nov	41	-0.3	1.1
13 Sep	50	0.1	0.8	10 Nov	50	0.0	0.5
14 Sep	55	0.0	1.4	11 Nov	61	0.2	1.4
15 Sep	50	-0.1	1.3	12 Nov	50	0.1	1.2
16 Sep	61	0.0	1.1	13 Nov	46	-0.2	1.0
17 Sep	42	0.0	1.5	14 Nov	57	0.2	0.7
18 Sep	46	-0.2	1.3	15 Nov	59	0.1	0.7
19 Sep	57	0.3	2.1	16 Nov	64	0.1	0.9
20 Sep	45	-0.1	1.3	17 Nov	45	-0.1	1.1
21 Sep	36	-0.4	0.9	18 Nov	65	0.1	0.7
22 Sep	45	-0.4	1.4	19 Nov	33	-0.4	1.5
23 Sep	35	-0.2	1.1	20 Nov	50	0.0	1.1
24 Sep	42	-0.1	1.2	21 Nov	57	0.0	1.2
25 Sep	46	0.0	1.1	22 Nov	45	-0.1	0.9
26 Sep	57	0.2	1.4	23 Nov	55	0.3	1.2
27 Sep	73	0.6	1.1	24 Nov	50	0.5	2.2
28 Sep	50	0.0	1.2	25 Nov	65	0.1	0.9
29 Sep	41	-0.3	1.3	26 Nov	46	-0.2	1.0
30 Sep	43	-0.1	1.3	27 Nov	58	0.2	0.7
01 Oct	71	0.4	1.4	28 Nov	48	0.1	1.1
02 Oct	38	-0.1	1.2	29 Nov	68	0.1	0.7
03 Oct	61	0.3	1.0	30 Nov	41	-0.2	1.4
04 Oct	64	0.1	1.0	01 Dec	57	0.1	1.8
05 Oct	77	0.4	1.7	02 Dec	52	0.1	0.9
06 Oct	59	0.3	2.2	03 Dec	46	-0.1	0.9
07 Oct	48	0.0	0.6	04 Dec	29	-0.2	0.7
08 Oct	42	-0.3	1.4	05 Dec	57	0.3	1.1
09 Oct	42	-0.2	1.1	06 Dec	55	0.0	0.7
10 Oct	43	-0.3	2.1	07 Dec	43	0.0	0.6
11 Oct	67	0.4	1.2	08 Dec	55	0.3	1.5
12 Oct	45	0.2	1.2	09 Dec	48	0.0	1.0
13 Oct	59	0.6	1.9	10 Dec	33	-0.2	0.7
14 Oct	48	0.1	1.1	11 Dec	38	-0.3	1.0
15 Oct	50	-0.3	2.0	12 Dec	43	-0.4	1.0
16 Oct	46	-0.6	1.8	13 Dec	64	0.0	0.9
17 Oct	70	0.5	1.5	14 Dec	50	-0.1	0.9

Date	Positive (%)	Avg Change (%)	Std Dev
15 Dec	50	0.0	1.0
16 Dec	78	0.7	0.8
17 Dec	46	-0.1	0.9
18 Dec	67	0.2	0.9
19 Dec	61	0.0	0.9
20 Dec	64	0.2	0.9
21 Dec	55	0.4	0.9
22 Dec	73	0.4	0.6
23 Dec	83	0.6	0.7
24 Dec	83	0.2	0.5
27 Dec	86	0.5	1.1
28 Dec	62	0.2	0.5
29 Dec	77	0.5	1.1
30 Dec	52	0.1	0.9
31 Dec	55	0.0	1.0

MARKET BEHAVIOUR – BY WEEK

The two tables below list the historic ten strongest and weakest weeks for the FTSE 100 since 1984. The tables are ranked by the Positive (%) value – the percentage of years that the market has a positive return on the week.

10 strongest weeks in the year

Week	Positive (%)	Avg Change (%)	Std Dev
52	78	1.1	1.5
51	78	1.0	1.7
31	78	0.6	2.5
34	72	0.2	2.1
7	68	0.5	1.4
27	67	0.8	2.0
14	66	0.6	1.9
1	63	0.9	2.7
40	63	0.7	2.4
45	63	0.1	1.9

10 weakest weeks in the year

Week	Positive (%)	Avg Change (%)	Std Dev
2	28	-0.5	1.7
25	36	-0.7	1.8
30	38	-0.5	2.2
22	39	0.2	1.8
28	41	-0.5	2.4
37	44	-0.4	2.2
50	44	-0.4	2.4
38	44	-0.2	2.8
21	45	-0.2	2.0
36	47	-0.5	2.3

Note: The above best and worst weeks for the market are marked in the Diary section by their performance data at the top of the week's page being in bold.

The strongest week of the whole year – when the market has historically increased the most – is the 52nd; in this week the market has risen in 78% of years, with an average return of 1.1%. It is worth noting that there have only been six occurrences of a week 53 since 1984 and so its data sample is smaller than for the other weeks. For this reason, week 53 has been excluded from the rankings.

The week with the worst record is the 2nd week. This is perhaps not surprising: the market is correcting after the historically strong final and first weeks of the year. The market has only risen in this week 28% of years and has an average return of -0.5%.

Analysis of all weeks

Average Positive (%) [Std Dev]	54.8 [10.4]
Average Change (%) [Std Dev]	0.12 [0.45]

Since 1984 the market has risen 55% of weeks with an average weekly return of 0.12%.

The standard deviation is 10 for the average Positive (%) value, which means that:

- weeks that have a Positive (%) value over 65 (the average plus one standard deviation) can be considered strong weeks, and

- weeks that have a Positive (%) value under 45 (the average minus one standard deviation) can be considered weak weeks.

The table on the following page lists the Sinclair Numbers for all weeks in the year. The rows for the ten strongest [weakest] weeks are highlighted light grey [dark grey].

Week	Positive (%)	Avg Change (%)	Std Dev
1	63	0.9	2.7
2	28	-0.5	1.7
3	53	-0.1	2.5
4	56	0.2	1.9
5	59	0.6	2.2
6	59	0.3	2.0
7	68	0.5	1.4
8	56	0.2	2.3
9	56	0.6	1.9
10	50	-0.1	2.3
11	53	0.0	2.2
12	47	0.3	2.6
13	47	0.0	1.8
14	66	0.6	1.9
15	48	0.2	2.2
16	61	0.5	1.4
17	55	0.0	1.6
18	61	0.3	2.2
19	61	0.3	1.9
20	58	-0.2	2.3
21	45	-0.2	2.0
22	39	0.2	1.8
23	58	0.0	1.8
24	52	-0.4	2.0
25	36	-0.7	1.8
26	48	0.1	2.2
27	67	0.8	2.0
28	41	-0.5	2.4
29	59	0.3	2.2
30	38	-0.5	2.2
31	78	0.6	2.5
32	50	-0.1	2.2
33	56	0.0	2.1
34	72	0.2	2.1
35	56	0.4	2.2
36	47	-0.5	2.3
37	44	-0.4	2.2
38	44	-0.2	2.8
39	47	0.1	2.5
40	63	0.7	2.4
41	59	-0.3	4.3
42	59	0.2	2.6
43	50	-0.6	3.9
44	56	0.7	3.2
45	63	0.1	1.9
46	56	0.2	1.7
47	50	0.0	3.1
48	56	0.9	3.0
49	47	-0.3	2.3
50	44	-0.4	2.4
51	78	1.0	1.7
52	78	1.1	1.5
53	67	-0.5	1.7

MARKET BEHAVIOUR – BY MONTH

The table below ranks the 12 months by their historic FTSE 100 performance since 1984. The table is ranked by the Positive (%) value – the percentage of years that the market has a positive return on the month.

Date	Positive (%)	Avg Change (%)	Std Dev
Dec	81	2.2	3.0
Oct	75	0.9	6.5
Apr	72	1.8	3.3
Feb	63	1.1	3.9
Nov	56	0.7	3.6
Mar	56	0.5	3.3
Jan	56	0.3	5.0
Aug	56	0.3	4.7
Jul	55	1.0	4.1
May	48	-0.2	4.2
Sep	44	-1.1	5.5
Jun	39	-0.9	3.6

The best month of the whole year – when the market has historically increased most often – is December. The proportion of years when the market has increased in December is 81% and on average the market increases 2.2% in this month (with the lowest standard deviation of any month).

Surprisingly, perhaps, the second strongest month is October – but note the very high standard deviation, indicating the volatility of the market in this month.

The month with the worst record is June. The market has only risen in June in 39% of all Junes and the average return is -0.9%.

The following two charts plot the Positive (%) and Average Return (%) values from the above table.

FTSE 100 monthly positive returns (%)

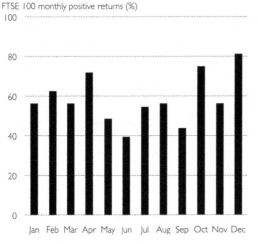

FTSE 100 average month (%)

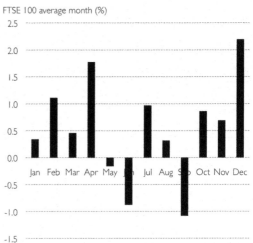

3.
REFERENCE

CONTENTS

STOCK INDICES

FT Ordinary Share Index (FT 30)

The FT 30 was first calculated in 1935 by the *Financial Times*. The index started at a base level of 100, and was calculated from a subjective collection of 30 major companies – which in the early years were concentrated in the industrial and retailing sectors.

For a long time the index was the best known performance measure of the UK stock market. But the index become less representative of the whole market. Also the index was price-weighted (like the DJIA), and not market-capitalisation-weighted. Although the index was calculated every hour, the increasing sophistication of the market needed an index calculated every minute and so the FT 30 has been usurped by the FTSE 100.

FTSE 100

Today, the FTSE 100 (sometimes called the "footsie") is the best known index tracking the performance of the UK market. The index comprises 100 of the top capitalised stocks listed on the LSE, and represents approximately 80% of the total market (by capitalisation). It is market capitalisation weighted and the composition of the index is reviewed every three months. The FTSE 100 is commonly used as the basis for investment funds and derivatives. The index was first calculated on 3 January 1984 with a base value of 1000.

The FTSE 100, and all the FTSE indices, are calculated by FTSE International – which started life as a joint venture between the *Financial Times* and the London Stock Exchange, but is now wholly owned by the LSE.

FTSE 250

Similar in construction to the FTSE 100, except this index comprises the next 250 highest capitalised stocks listed on the LSE after the top 100. It's sometimes referred to as the index of 'mid-cap' stocks, and comprises approximately 18% of the total market capitalisation.

FTSE 350

The FTSE 350 is an index comprising all the stocks in the FTSE 100 and FTSE 250.

FTSE Small Cap

Comprised of companies with a market capitalisation below the FTSE 250 but above a fixed limit. This lower limit is periodically reviewed. Consequently the FTSE Small Cap does not have a fixed number of constituents. By mid-2016, there were 275 companies in the index, which represented about 2% of the total market by capitalisation.

FTSE All-Share

The FTSE All-Share is the aggregation of the FTSE 100, FTSE 250 and FTSE Small Cap indices. Effectively it is comprised of all those LSE listed companies with a market capitalisation above the lower limit for inclusion in the FTSE Small Cap. The FTSE All-Share is the standard benchmark for measuring the performance of the broad UK market and represents 98% to 99% of the total UK market capitalisation.

FTSE Fledgling

This index comprises the companies that do not meet the minimum size requirement of the FTSE Small Cap and are therefore outside of the FTSE All-Share. There are fewer than 200 companies in the FTSE Fledgling.

FTSE All-Small

This consists of all the companies in the FTSE Small Cap and FTSE Fledgling indices.

FTSE TMT

Reflects the performance of companies in the Technology, Media and Telecommunications sectors.

FTSE techMARK All-Share

An index of all companies included in the LSE's techMARK sector.

FTSE techMARK 100

The top 100 companies of the FTSE techMARK All-Share, under £4bn by full market capitalisation.

FTSE AIM UK 50

Comprises the 50 largest UK companies quoted on the Alternative Investment Market (AIM).

FTSE AIM 100

Comprises the 100 largest companies quoted on the Alternative Investment Market (AIM).

FTSE AIM All-Share

All AIM-quoted companies.

STOCK INDICES – INTERNATIONAL

Dow Jones Industrial Average (DJIA)

The DJIA is the oldest continuing stock index of the US market and probably the most famous in the world. Created in 1896, it originally comprised 12 stocks, but over the years has expanded to reach the point where today it includes 30 stocks. The index is weighted by price, which is unusual for a stock index. It is calculated by summing the prices of the 30 stocks and dividing by the divisor. Originally the divisor was 30, but this has been adjusted periodically to reflect capital changes such as stock splits, and is currently about 0.13. This means that companies with high stock prices have the greatest influence on the index – not those with large market values. The longest established company in the index is General Electric, which joined in 1907.

Standard & Poor's 500 (S&P 500)

This is the main benchmark index for the performance of the US market. The index is weighted by market value and constituents are chosen based upon their market size, liquidity and sector. The index was created in 1957, although values for it have been back-calculated several decades.

NASDAQ 100

This index tracks the performance of the 100 largest stocks listed on the NASDAQ exchange. The index is calculated using a modified capitalisation weighting method ("modified" so that large companies like Apple don't overwhelm it). NASDAQ companies tend to be smaller and younger than those listed on the NYSE and although there is no attempt to select technology stocks, it is regarded as the tech stock index. The index can be traded as there's an ETF associated with it (the most actively traded ETF in the US). The ETF has the symbol QQQ and is sometimes referred to as the "Qs" or "Qubes".

Nikkei 225

The Nikkei 225 is owned by the Nihon Keizai Shimbun ("Nikkei") newspaper. It was first calculated in 1949 (when it was known as the Nikkei-Dow index) and is the most widely watched stock index in Japan. It is a price-weighted index of 225 top-rated Japanese companies listed in the First Section of the Tokyo Stock Exchange. The calculation method is therefore similar to that of the Dow Jones Industrial Average (upon which it was modelled).

TOPIX

The TOPIX is calculated by the Tokyo Stock Exchange. Unlike the Nikkei 255, TOPIX is a market capitalisation-weighted index. TOPIX is calculated from all members of the First Section of the Tokyo SE, which is about 1500 companies. For these reasons, TOPIX is preferred over the Nikkei 225 as a benchmark for Japanese equity portfolios.

Hang Seng

The Hang Seng was first calculated in 1964. Today it has 48 constituents representing some 60% of the total Hong Kong market by capitalisation.

CAC 40

The CAC 40 is the main benchmark for Euronext Paris (what used to be the Paris Bourse). The index contains 40 stocks selected among the top 100 by market capitalisation and the most active stocks listed on Euronext Paris. The base value was 1000 at 31 December 1987.

DAX 30

The DAX 30 is published by the Frankfurt Stock Exchange and is the main real-time German share index. It contains 30 stocks from the leading German stock markets. The DAX is a total return index (which is uncommon), whereby it measures not only the price appreciation of its constituents but also the return provided by the dividends paid.

EPIC, TIDM, SEDOL, CUSIP AND ISIN CODES

This page describes the common codes associated with securities.

EPIC

Some time ago the London Stock Exchange devised a system of code names for listed companies. These provide a short and unambiguous way to reference stocks. For example, the code for Marks & Spencer is MKS. This is easier to use than wondering whether one should call the company Marks & Spencer, Marks and Spencer or Marks & Spencer plc. These codes were called EPIC codes, after the name of the Stock Exchange's central computer prior to 1996.

TIDM

After the introduction of the Sequence trading platform, EPIC codes were renamed Tradable Instrument Display Mnemonics (TIDMs), or Mnemonics for short. So, strictly, we should now be calling them TIDMs or Mnemonics – but almost everyone still refers to them as EPIC codes.

SEDOL

SEDOL stands for Stock Exchange Daily Official List. These are seven digit security identifiers assigned by the London Stock Exchange. They are only assigned to UK-listed securities.

CUSIP

CUSIP (Committee on Uniform Securities Identification Procedures) codes are nine-character alphanumeric identifiers used for Canadian and US securities.

ISIN

ISIN stands for International Securities Identification Number. These are 12-digit alphanumeric identifiers assigned by the International Standards Organisation (ISO) in order to provide standardisation of international securities. The first two letters represent the country code; the next nine characters usually use some other code, such as CUSIP in the United States or SEDOL in the UK, with leading spaces padded with 0. The final digit is a check digit.

DAILY TIMETABLE OF THE UK TRADING DAY

This table displays the basic structure of the UK trading day, with some comments from a trader.

07.00	**Regulatory News Services open** The period before the market opens at 08.00 is the most important hour of the day. By the time the opening auction begins at 07.50 traders will have a clear idea at what price any particular major stock should be opening at. Scheduled announcements are normally in the Regulatory News. Having a good idea of what companies are reporting for the forthcoming week is essential. Quite a few banks, brokers and websites provide comprehensive forward diaries. As well as checking the movement of the major stock indices overnight, check the early show for the futures contracts on the main indices, as well as any US company results that were released after hours. Unlike the UK, in the US it is common for companies to release results after the markets close.
07.50–08.00	**Pre-market auction** There are fewer opportunities in the opening auction than the closing auction, partly because there are lower volumes in the opening auction. It is safer to trade against an 'at-market' order than against several orders from several other participants that appear to be at the wrong price – almost certainly they have seen something that you haven't. Despite representing only a small proportion of the total day's volume, the opening uncrossing trade will often be (or very close to) the high or low trade of the day for that stock.
08.00	**UK market and FTSE 100 Index Futures open** By 08.00 as the UK market opens you should be fully prepared for the day's trading.
08.00–16.30	**Continuous trading** Trading is continuous until 16.30. During the day there is a calendar of key economic figures to look out for, as well as both ad-hoc and scheduled announcements. Some company-scheduled trading figures come out at midday, particularly companies that are dual-quoted. US index futures should be monitored throughout the day as well as other influential continental indices such as Germany's DAX. Traders will often concentrate on watching the high volatility shares as these provide the most trading opportunities, although many will add 'guest' stocks to their watch list and go to where the day's action is and join 'event' traders. Stocks to watch during the day include the biggest movers on the day (both risers and fallers), those experiencing high volume and constant gainers (popular with momentum players).
14.30	**US markets open** The US markets usually open at 14.30 UK time, although at certain times of the year, due to daylight saving, it may be an hour earlier or later. As the futures contracts on the US markets trade throughout morning trading in the UK, traders will always have a good idea where the US markets are due to open, subject to the release of economic figures at 13.30 UK time.
16.30–16.35	**Post-market auction** There can often be opportunities in the closing auction, particularly on the last business day of the month or when there are index constituent changes. The general strategy is to take the other side of a large 'at-market' order that is forcing the uncrossing price away from the day's trading range, in the anticipation that the stock will revert to the previous ('normal') level the following day.
17.30	**FTSE 100 Index Futures close**
18.30	**Regulatory News Services close** A number of key announcements can come out after the market close and although most newspapers will pick up any significant stories, it is worth scanning through the day's late announcements before the start of trading the following day.

Source: *The UK Trader's Bible* by Dominic Connolly.

FTSE 100 – 1984

The FTSE 100 was started on 3 January 1984 with a base level of 1000. The table below shows the original constituents. Of the initial 100 companies only 18 remain in the index today (indicated in bold, and with their new names in brackets) – a sign of the great changes in UK PLC in 32 years.

Allied – Lyons	Fisons	RMC Group
Associated British Foods	General Accident Fire & Life	Racal Electronics
Associated Dairies Group	General Electric	Rank Organisation
Barclays Bank [Barclays]	Glaxo Holdings	**Reckitt & Colman [Reckitt Benckiser Group]**
Barratt Developments	Globe Investment Trust	
Bass	Grand Metropolitan	Redland
BAT Industries	**Great Universal Stores [Experian]**	**Reed International [Reed Elsevier]**
Beecham Group	Guardian Royal Exchange	**Rio Tinto – Zinc Corporation [Rio Tinto]**
Berisford (S. & W.)	Guest Keen & Nettlefolds	Rowntree Mackintosh
BICC	Hambro Life Assurance	**Royal Bank of Scotland Group**
Blue Circle Industries	Hammerson Prop.Inv. & Dev. 'A'	Royal Insurance
BOC Group	Hanson Trust Harrisons & Crossfield	**Sainsbury (J.)**
Boots Co.	Hawker Siddeley Group	Scottish & Newcastle Breweries
Bowater Corporation	House of Fraser	Sears Holdings
BPB Industries	Imperial Chemical Industries	Sedgwick Group
British & Commonwealth	Imperial Cont. Gas Association	**Shell Trans. & Trad. Co. [Royal Dutch Shell]**
British Aerospace	Imperial Group	
British Elect. Traction Co.	Johnson Matthey	Smith & Nephew Associated Co's.
British Home Stores	Ladbroke Group	Standard Chartered Bank
British Petroleum [BP]	**Land Securities**	Standard Telephones & Cables
Britoil	**Legal & General Group**	Sun Alliance & London Insurance
BTR	**Lloyds Bank [Lloyds Banking Group]**	Sun Life Assurance Society
Burton Group	Lonrho	THORN EMI
Cable & Wireless	MEPC	Tarmac
Cadbury Schweppes	MFI Furniture Group	**Tesco**
Commercial Union Assurance [Aviva]	**Marks & Spencer**	Trafalgar House
Consolidated Gold Fields	Midland Bank	Trusthouse Forte
Courtaulds	National Westminster Bank	Ultramar
Dalgety Distillers Co.	Northern Foods	**Unilever**
CJ Rothschild	P & O Steam Navigation Co.	United Biscuits
Edinburgh Investment Trust	**Pearson (S.) & Son [Pearson]**	Whitbread & Co. 'A'
English China Clays	Pilkington Brothers	Wimpey (George)
Exco International	Plessey Co.	
Ferranti	**Prudential Corporation [Prudential]**	

The following table compares the market capitalisations of the top five largest companies in the index in 1984 and today.

	Rank (1984)	Capital (£m)	Rank (2016)	Capital (£m)
1	British Petroleum Co.	7,401	Royal Dutch Shell	151,790
2	Shell Trans. & Trad. Co.	6,365	HSBC Holdings	116,776
3	General Electric Co.	4,915	British American Tobacco	89,413
4	Imperial Chemical Industries	3,917	BP	80,259
5	Marks & Spencer	2,829	GlaxoSmithKline	79,387

Oil is still there today, but industrial, chemical and retail have been replaced by bank, consumer goods and pharmaceutical.

In 1984, the total market capitalisation of the index was £100 billion; in 2016 the total market capitalisation is £1,906 billion. It's interesting to note that Shell's market cap. today is 52% larger than the whole FTSE 100 in 1984.

FT 30 INDEX 1935 – WHERE ARE THEY NOW?

The FT 30 index was started by the *Financial Times* on 1 July 1935. Today the most widely followed index is the FTSE 100, but for many years the FT 30 (originally called the FT Ordinaries) was the measure everyone knew. The table below lists the original companies in the FT 30 index in 1935 – a time when brokers wore bowler hats and share certificates were printed on something called paper. It's interesting to see what became of the stalwarts of UK PLC from over 70 years ago.

Company	Notes
Associated Portland Cement	The name was changed to Blue Circle Industries in 1978, and then left the index in 2001 when it was bought by Lafarge.
Austin Motor	Left the index in 1947. In 1952 Austin merged with rival Morris Motors Limited to form The British Motor Corporation Limited (BMC). In 1966 BMC bought Jaguar and two years later merged with Leyland Motors Limited to form British Leyland Motor Corporation. In 1973 British Leyland produced the Austin-badged Allegro... (the story is too painful to continue).
Bass	Left the index in 1947. In 1967 merged with Charrington United Breweries to form Bass Charrington. In 2000 its brewing operations were sold to Interbrew (which was then instructed by the Competition Commission to dispose parts to Coors), while the hotel and pub holdings were renamed Six Continents. In 2003 Six Continents was split into a pubs business (Mitchells & Butlers) and a hotels and soft drinks business (InterContinental Hotels Group).
Bolsover Colliery	Left the index in 1947. The mines were acquired by the National Coal Board on nationalisation in 1947. Bolsover Colliery closed in 1993.
Callender's Cables & Construction	Left the index in 1947. Merged with British Insulated Cables in 1945 to form British Insulated Callender's Cables, which was renamed BICC Ltd in 1975. In 2000, having sold its cable operations, it renamed its contruction business Balfour Beatty.
Coats (J & P)	Left the index in 1959. Traded as Coats Patons Ltd after the takeover of Patons & Baldwins, then as Coats Viyella, finally as Coats plc. Finally taken over by Guinness Peat Group in 2004.
Courtaulds	Demerged its chemical and textile interests in the 1980s, with the former eventually being bought by Akzo Nobel and the latter by Sara Lee. Left the index in 1998.
Distillers	Purchased by Guinness in the infamous bid battle of 1986 when it left the index.
Dorman Long	Left the index in 1947. Joined British Steel following nationalisation in 1967.
Dunlop Rubber	Left the index in 1983 and was bought in 1985 by BTR (which became Invensys).
Electrical & Musical Industries	In 1971 changed its name to EMI and later that year merged with THORN Electrical Industries to form Thorn EMI but then de-merged in 1996. In 2007 EMI Group plc was taken over by Terra Firma Capital Partners but following financial difficulties ownership passed to Citigroup in 2011.
Fine Spinners and Doublers	Fell out of the index in 1938, and was later bought by Courtaulds in 1963.
General Electric	General Electric was re-named Marconi in 1999, suffered disastrous losses in the dot-com crash and was bought by Ericsson in 2006.
Guest, Keen & Nettlefolds	Guest, Keen is better known as GKN and is still in the FT 30 today.
Harrods	Left the index in 1959 when it was bought by House of Fraser, and then later by Mohamed Al Fayed.
Hawker Siddeley	Left the index in 1991, and was then bought in 1992 by BTR (which became Invensys).
Imperial Chemical Industries	Spun out of Zeneca in 1993, and the rump (called ICI) was sold to Akzo Nobel in 2007.
Imperial Tobacco	Still going strong.
International Tea Co Stores	Fell out of the index in 1947, was acquired by BAT Industries in 1972 and ended up as Somerfield in 1994.
London Brick	Replaced in the index by Hanson which bought it in 1984.
Murex	Left the index in 1967 due to "poor share performance". Acquired by BOC Group in 1967.
Patons & Baldwins	Left the index in 1960 when bought by J&P Coats.

Company	Notes
Pinchin Johnson & Associates	Left the index in 1960 when bought by Courtaulds.
Rolls-Royce	In 1971 RR was taken into state ownership, the motor car business was floated separately in 1973, and RR returned to the private sector in 1987.
Tate & Lyle	Still going strong, although its sugar refining and golden syrup business was sold to American Sugar Refining in 2010.
Turner & Newall	Left the index in 1982. The company was heavily involved with asbestos production, so it is not surprising that things ended badly. In 1998 the business was acquired by Federal-Mogul, which soon after filed for Chapter 11 protection as a result of asbestos claims.
United Steel	Left the index in 1951. The iron and steel works on nationalisation became part of British Steel Corporation (and now part of Tata Steel); while the mining interests passed to the National Coal Board (now closed).
Vickers	Left the index in 1986. Bought by Rolls-Royce in 1999.
Watney Combe & Reid	Left the index in 1972 when it was bought by Grand Metropolitan, which itself became part of Diageo.
Woolworth (FW)	Left the index in 1971. Bought by the forerunner of Kingfisher in 1982, and then de-merged and re-listed in 2001. But the remaining Woolworths stores all closed by January 2009.

Of the 30 companies only four exist today as listed companies: GKN, Imperial Tobacco, Rolls-Royce and Tate & Lyle (all of which are in the FTSE 100). And only GKN and Tate & Lyle are in today's FT 30.

The star performer from the original line-up has been Imperial Tobacco.

It's interesting to note the complete lack of representation of the four sectors that dominate the UK market today – no banks, telecom, oil or drug companies.

Index performance

Since 1935, the FT 30 has risen 2748%; by comparison the FTSE All-Share over the same period has risen 10,972%. The following chart plots the year-end values of the FT 30 against the FTSE All-Share (the latter has been rebased to start at the same value as the FT 30).

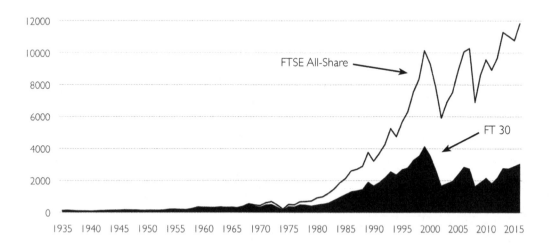

One of the reasons for the very large difference in performance is that the FT 30 is a price-weighted index (as are the Dow Jones Industrial Average and Nikkei 225), whereas most indices today (including the FTSE All-Share and FTSE 100) are weighted by market-capitalisation. When the FTSE 100 was introduced in 1984, if it had been price-weighted and performed in line with the FT 30, today it would have a value around 3924.

COMPANY OLD NAMES

The following table shows a selection of companies listed on the LSE with their original names.

Note: Simple changes such as Reckitt Benckiser to Reckitt Benckiser Group have not been included.

Current name	TIDM	Previous name
1Spatial Holdings	SPA	Avisen
21st Century Technology	C21	TG21
365 Agile Group	365	Iafyds
4imprint Group	FOUR	Bemrose Corporation
7Digital Group	7DIG	UBC Media Group
88 Energy Ltd	88E	Tangiers Petroleum Ltd
Acacia Mining	ACA	African Barrick Gold Ltd
Accesso Technology Group	ACSO	Lo-Q
Active Energy Group	AEG	Cinpart
Advanced Oncotherapy	AVO	CareCapital Group
Aeorema Communications	AEO	Cheerful Scout
Afarak Group	AFRK	Ruukki Group
AGA Rangemaster Group	AGA	AGA Foodservice Group
Agriterra Ltd	AGTA	White Nile Ltd
Airea	AIEA	Sirdar
Alecto Energy	ALO	Cue Energy
Alliance Pharma	APH	Peerless Technology Group
Alpha Returns Group	ARGP	Shidu Group
Altitude Group	ALT	Dowlis Corporate Solutions
Amara Mining	AMA	Cluff Gold
Ambrian	AMBR	East West Resources
Amec Foster Wheeler	AMFW	AMEC
Amedeo Resources	AMED	Creon Corporation
Amerisur Resources	AMER	Chaco Resources
Andes Energia	AEN	Ragusa Capital
Anpario	ANP	Kiotech International
APC Technology Group	APC	Advanced Power Components
APR Energy	APR	Horizon Acquisition Co
Arbuthnot Banking Group	ARBB	Secure Trust Banking Group
Arcontech Group	ARC	Knowledge Technology Solutions
Armadale Capital	ACP	Watermark Global
Armstrong Ventures	AVP	iPoint Media
Artilium	ARTA	Future Internet Technologies
Asiamet Resources Ltd	ARS	Kalimantan Gold Corporation Ltd
ASOS	ASC	asSeenonScreen Holdings
AssetCo	ASTO	Asfare Group
Atlantic Coal	ATC	Summit Resources
Atlas Development & Support Services Ltd	ADSS	Africa Oilfield Logistics Ltd
AudioBoom Group	BOOM	One Delta
Aurasian Minerals	AUM	Triple Plate Junction
Avacta Group	AVCT	Readybuy
Avesco Group	AVS	InvestinMedia
Aveva Group	AVV	Cadcentre Group
Avingtrans	AVG	Usher (Frank) Holdings
Aviva	AV.	CGNU

Current name	TIDM	Previous name
Bahamas Petroleum Company	BPC	BPC
Baron Oil	BOIL	Gold Oil
BCA Marketplace	BCA	Haversham Holdings
BCB Holdings Ltd	BCB	BB Holdings Ltd
Belgravium Technologies	BVM	Eadie Holdings
Berendsen	BRSN	Davis Service Group (The)
Bezant Resources	BZT	Tanzania Gold
BHP Billiton	BLT	Billiton
Billington Holdings	BILN	Amco Corporation
Biome Technologies	BIOM	Stanelco
BMR Mining	BMR	Berkeley Mineral Resources
Booker Group	BOK	Blueheath Holdings
Boxhill Technologies	BOX	Weather Lottery (The)
BP	BP.	BP Amoco
Breedon Aggregates Ltd	BREE	Marwyn Materials Ltd
BSD Crown Ltd	BSD	Emblaze Ltd
BT Group	BT.A	British Telecommunications
Cable & Wireless Communications	CWC	Cable and Wireless
Camco Clean Energy Ltd	CCE	Camco International Ltd
Capital Management and Investment	CMIP	e-xentric
Carnival	CCL	P & O Princess Cruises
Castle Street Investments	CSI	Cupid
Castleton Technology	CTP	Redstone
Catalyst Media Group	CMX	Newsplayer Group
Centamin	CEY	Centamin Egypt Ltd
CEPS	CEPS	Dinkie Heel
Chamberlin	CMH	Chamberlin & Hill
China Nonferrous Gold Ltd	CNG	Kryso Resources Corp Ltd
Clarkson	CKN	Clarkson (Horace)
Clear Leisure	CLP	Brainspark
Cloudbuy	CBUY	@UK
Coal of Africa Ltd	CZA	GVM Metals Ltd
Coats Group	COA	Guinness Peat Group
Collagen Solutions	COS	Healthcare Investment Opportunities
Compass Group	CPG	Granada Compass
Coms	COMS	Azman
Concha	CHA	Hot Tuna (International)
Connect Group	CNCT	Smiths News
Conroy Gold And Natural Resources	CGNR	Conroy Diamonds & Gold
Consort Medical	CSRT	Bespak
Corero	CNS	Mondas
Craven House Capital	CRV	AIM Investments
Crawshaw Group	CRAW	Felix Group
Crimson Tide	TIDE	Cohen (A) & Co
Darty	DRTY	Kesa Electricals
DCD Media	DCD	Digital Classics

Current name	TIDM	Previous name
Dialight	DIA	Roxboro Group (The)
Distil	DIS	Blavod Wines and Spirits
Dixons Carphone	DC.	Carphone Warehouse
Dods (Group)	DODS	Huveaux
Doriemus	DOR	TEP Exchange Group
DS Smith	SMDS	Smith (David S) (Holdings)
Eastbridge Investments	EBIV	China Wonder Ltd
Ebiquity	EBQ	Thomson Intermedia
Eckoh	ECK	Eckoh Technologies
Eco Animal Health Group	EAH	Lawrence
ECR Minerals	ECR	Electrum Resources
Edenville Energy	EDL	TV Commerce Holdings
EKF Diagnostics Holdings	EKF	International Brand Licensing
Elecosoft	ELCO	Eleco
Elektron	EKT	Bulgin
EMED Mining Public Ltd	EMED	Eastern Mediterranean Resources Public Ltd
Emerging Markets Minerals	EMM	LP Hill
Environmental Recycling Technologies	ENRT	3DM Worldwide
Essentra	ESNT	Filtrona
European Wealth Group Ltd	EWG	EW Group Ltd
Evocutis	EVO	Syntopix Group
Fairpoint Group	FRP	Debt Free Direct Group
Fastjet	FJET	Rubicon Diversified Investments
Fastnet Oil & Gas	FAST	Sterling Green Group
Fidessa Group	FDSA	royalblue Group
Finnaust Mining	FAM	Centurion Resources
Finsbury Food Group	FIF	Megalomedia
First Property Group	FPO	Hansom Group
Fitbug Holdings	FITB	ADDleisure
Flowgroup	FLOW	Energetix Group
Flying Brands Ltd	FBDU	Flying Flowers Ltd
Formation Group	FRM	Proactive Sports Group
Fulcrum Utility Services Ltd	FCRM	Marwyn Capital I Ltd
G4S	GFS	Group 4 Securicor
Galliford Try	GFRD	Galliford
Gama Aviation	GMAA	Hangar 8
Gaming Realms	GMR	Pursuit Dynamics
GB Group	GBG	TelMe Group
GCM Resources	GCM	Global Coal Management
Gemfields	GEM	Gemfields Resources
Genel Energy	GENL	Vallares
GlaxoSmithKline	GSK	Glaxo Wellcome
Glencore	GLEN	Glencore International
Goldbridges Global Resources	GBGR	Hambledon Mining
Grafenia	GRA	Printing.com
Gusbourne	GUS	Shellproof Ltd
Guscio	GUSC	Talent Group
Hague and London Oil	HNL	Wessex Exploration
Harworth Group	HWG	Coalfield Resources
Hayward Tyler Group	HAYT	Specialist Energy Group
Helios Underwriting	HUW	Hampden Underwriting
Henderson Group	HGG	HHG
Hermes Pacific Investments	HPAC	Indian Restaurants Group

Current name	TIDM	Previous name
Highway Capital	HWC	Superframe Group
Homeserve	HSV	South Staffordshire Group
Howden Joinery Group	HWDN	Galiform
Hunter Resources	HUN	Gem Biofuels
Hvivo	HVO	Retroscreen Virology Group
Hydrodec Group	HYR	Vert-Eco Group
ICAP	IAP	Garban-Intercapital
IDOX	IDOX	i-documentsystems Group
Igas Energy	IGAS	Island Gas Resources
ImmuPharma	IMM	General Industries
Impact Holdings (UK)	IHUK	Nanotech Energy
IMPAX Asset Management Group	IPX	Impax Group
Impellam Group	IPEL	Carlisle Group Ltd
Infinity Energy SA	INFT	Global Brands S.A.
Informa	INF	T&F Informa
Infrastrata	INFA	Portland Gas
Inspiration Healthcare Group	IHC	Inditherm
Inspired Capital	INSC	Renovo Group
Inspirit Energy Holdings	INSP	KleenAir Systems International
Interbulk Group	INB	Interbulk Investments
InterContinental Hotels Group	IHG	Six Continents
International Consolidated Airlines Group SA	IAG	British Airways
International Mining & Infrastructure Corp	IMIC	India Star Energy
Interserve	IRV	Tilbury Douglas
IP Group	IPO	IP2IPO Group
IPPlus	IPP	County Contact Centres
Ironveld	IRON	Mercury Recycling Group
Ixico	IXI	Phytopharm
Jaywing	JWNG	Digital Marketing Group
JD Sports Fashion	JD.	John David Sports Group
Journey Group	JNY	Watermark Group
Judges Scientific	JDG	Judges Capital
K3 Business Technology Group	KBT	RAP Group
KCOM Group	KCOM	Kingston Communications (Hull)
Kellan Group	KLN	Berkeley Scott Group
Kemin Resources	KEM	GMA Resources
Kennedy Ventures	KENV	Managed Support Services
Ladbrokes	LAD	Hilton Group
Learning Technologies Group	LTG	In-Deed Online
LightwaveRF	LWRF	JSJS Designs
Lloyds Banking Group	LLOY	Lloyds TSB Group
M.P. Evans Group	MPE	Rowe Evans Investments
Management Consulting Group	MMC	Proudfoot Consulting
Manx Financial Group	MFX	Conister Financial Group
Marechale Capital	MAC	St Helen's Capital
Marlowe Holdings Ltd	MRL	Shellshock Ltd
Marston's	MARS	Wolverhampton & Dudley Breweries
MBL Group	MUBL	Air Music & Media Group
Metal Tiger	MTR	Brady Exploration

Current name	TIDM	Previous name
Mineral & Financial Investment Ltd	MAFL	Athol Gold Ltd
Mi-Pay Group	MPAY	Aimshell Acquisitions
Mirada	MIRA	YooMedia
Miton Group	MGR	MAM Funds
Mobile Tornado Group	MBT	TMT Group
Morgan Advanced Materials	MGAM	Morgan Crucible Company (The)
Mwana Africa	MWA	African Gold
MX Oil	MXO	Astar Minerals
MXC Capital	MXCP	2ergo Group
Mytrah Energy Ltd	MYT	Caparo Energy Ltd
Nakama Group	NAK	Highams Systems Services Group
Nanoco Group	NANO	Evolutec Group
National Grid	NG.	National Grid Transco
Nature Group	NGR	Nature Technology Solutions Ltd
NetPlay TV	NPT	Stream Group
Next Fifteen Communications Group	NFC	OneMonday Group
Norman Broadbent	NBB	Constellation Corporation
Nostra Terra Oil & Gas Company	NTOG	LHP Investments
Novae Group	NVA	SVB Holdings
Nyota Minerals Ltd	NYO	Dwyka Diamonds
Omega Diagnostics Group	ODX	Quintessentially English
OpSec Security Group	OSG	Applied Optical Technologies
OptiBiotix Health	OPTI	Ducat Ventures
Optimal Payments	OPAY	NEOVIA FINANCIAL ORD 0.01P
Orogen Gold	ORE	MEDAVINCI ORD 0.1P
Orosur Mining Inc	OMI	Uruguay Mineral Exploration Inc
Ortac Resources Ltd	OTC	Templar Minerals Ltd
Oxaco	OXA	Oxford Advanced Surfaces Group
Paddy Power	PAP	Power Leisure
Palace Capital	PCA	Leo Insurance Services
Panmure Gordon & Co	PMR	Durlacher Corporation
Parallel Media Group	PAA	World Sport Group
Parkmead Group (The)	PMG	Interregnum
Patagonia Gold	PGD	HPD Exploration
Paternoster Resources	PRS	Viridas
Petards Group	PEG	Screen
Petroceltic International	PCI	Ennex International
Petropavlovsk	POG	Peter Hambro Mining
PhotonStar Led Group	PSL	Enfis Group
Pinnacle Telecom Group	PINN	Glen Group
Pires Investments	PIRI	Oak Holdings
Polemos	PLMO	PLUS Markets Group
Porta Communications	PTCM	TSE Group
Power Capital Global Ltd	PCGB	Sportswinbet Ltd
Powerhouse Energy Group	PHE	Bidtimes
Premaitha Health	NIPT	ViaLogy
President Energy	PPC	Meridian Petroleum
Prime Active Capital	PACC	Oakhill Group
Pro Global Insurance Solutions	PROG	Tawa
Progility	PGY	ILX Group

Current name	TIDM	Previous name
Progressive Digital Media Group	PRO	TMN Group
Provexis	PXS	Nutrinnovator Holdings
Publishing Technology	PTO	Ingenta
PZ Cussons	PZC	Paterson Zochonis
Quadrise Fuels International	QFI	Zareba
Quoram	QRM	Bluebird Energy
Rare Earth Minerals	REM	Zest Group
Reach4entertainment Enterprises	R4E	Pivot Entertainment Group
React Group	REAT	Verdes Management
red24	REDT	ARC Risk Management Group
Redde	REDD	Helphire Group
Redhall Group	RHL	Booth Industries Group
Regenersis	RGS	Fonebak
RELX	REL	Reed Elsevier
Renew Holdings	RNWH	Montpellier Group
Restaurant Group (The)	RTN	City Centre Restaurants
Restore	RST	Mavinwood
Richland Resources Ltd	RLD	Tanzanite One Ltd
Richoux Group	RIC	Gourmet Holdings
Rose Petroleum	ROSE	Vane Minerals
Royal Dutch Shell	RDSB	Shell Transport and Trading Co
Royal Dutch Shell	RDSA	Shell Transport and Trading Co
RSA Insurance Group	RSA	Royal & Sun Alliance Insurance Group
RTC Group	RTC	ATA Group
RWS Holdings	RWS	Health Media Group
Sable Mining Ltd	SBLM	BioEnergy Africa Ltd
SABMiller	SAB	South African Breweries
Satellite Solutions Worldwide Group	SAT	Cleeve Capital
Savannah Resources	SAV	African Mining & Exploration
Science Group	SAG	Sagentia Group
SciSys	SSY	CODASciSys
Servoca	SVCA	Multi Group
Severfield	SFR	Severfield-Rowen
Sierra Rutile Ltd	SRX	Titanium Resources Group Ltd
Sigma Capital Group	SGM	Sigma Technology Group
Signet Jewelers Ltd	SIG	Signet Group
Silence Therapeutics	SLN	SR Pharma
Sirius Petroleum	SRSP	Global Gaming Technologies
Sky	SKY	British Sky Broadcasting Group
Smiths Group	SMIN	Smiths Industries
Solid State	SOLI	Solid State Supplies
Solo Oil	SOLO	Immersion Technologies International
Source BioScience	SBS	Medical Solutions
Spectris	SXS	Fairey Group
Speedy Hire	SDY	Allen
Sportech	SPO	Rodime
Stallion Resources	SPSM	Sports Star Media
Stanley Gibbons Group (The) Ltd	SGI	Communitie.com Ltd

Current name	TIDM	Previous name	Current name	TIDM	Previous name
Starvest	SVE	Web Shareshop (Holdings)	UBM	UBM	United Business Media
Stellar Resources	STG	CSS Stellar	UK Mail Group	UKM	Business Post Group
Sterling Energy	SEY	LEPCO	UK Oil & Gas Investments	UKOG	Sarantel Group
Stobart Group Ltd	STOB	Westbury Property Fund (The) Ltd	UMC Energy	UEP	Uranium Mining Corporation
Stratmin Global Resources	STGR	Woodburne Square AG	Urban & Civic	UANC	Terrace Hill Group
STV Group	STVG	SMG	UTV Media	UTV	UTV
Summit Therapeutics	SUMM	Summit Corporation	ValiRx	VAL	Azure Holdings
Sweett Group	CSG	Cyril Sweett Group	Vast Resources	VAST	African Consolidated Resources
Symphony Environmental Technologies	SYM	Symphony Plastic Technologies	Vela Technologies	VELA	Asia Digital Holdings
Synectics	SNX	Quadnetics Group	Velocys	VLS	Oxford Catalysts Group
Synety Group	SNTY	Zenergy Power	Vernalis	VER	British Biotech
Synthomer	SYNT	Yule Catto & Co	Verona Pharma	VRP	Isis Resources
Tanfield Group	TAN	comeleon	Vesuvius	VSVS	Cookson Group
Tangent Communications	TNG	Documedia Solutions	Vianet Group	VNET	Brulines (Holdings)
Tavistock Investments	TAVI	Social Go	Vodafone Group	VOD	Vodafone Airtouch
Taylor Wimpey	TW.	Taylor Woodrow	Vp	VP.	Vibroplant
Teathers Financial	TEA	Sperati (C.A.) (Special Agency)	W Resources	WRES	Caspian Holdings
Tengri Resources	TEN	Commoditrade Inc	Walker Crips Group	WCW	Walker, Crips, Weddle, Beck
Tissue Regenix Group	TRX	Oxeco	Water Intelligence	WATR	Qonnectis
TomCo Energy	TOM	Netcentric Systems	Waterman Group	WTM	Waterman Partnership Holdings
Toumaz Holdings Ltd	TMZ	Nanoscience Inc			
TP Group	TPG	Corac Group	Webis Holdings	WEB	betinternet.com
Tricor	TRIC	PNC Telecom	West African Minerals Corporation	WAFM	Emerging Metals Ltd
Trinity Exploration and Production	TRIN	Bayfield Energy Holdings	Xtract Resources	XTR	Resmex
Tri-Star Resources	TSTR	Canisp	Yolo Leisure and Technology	YOLO	Pentagon Protection
Tullett Prebon	TLPR	Collins Stewart Tullett	Zoltav Resources Inc	ZOL	Crosby Asset Management Inc
Turbo Power Systems Inc	TPS	Turbo Genset Inc			
Tyman	TYMN	Lupus Capital	Zoo Digital Group	ZOO	Kazoo3D

Notes

Obviously, there are many reasons why companies change their names, but a quick scan of the above table reveals a few themes. Firstly, a great many companies have taken to adding Group to their names, while a few have moved to the next stage by removing the word. The move to acronyms is always popular (e.g. British Telecommunications to BT Group), but in some cases the move is reversed (e.g. HHG to Henderson Group).

Some companies are unwinding their dot-com names (e.g. Printing.com to Grafenia), while others are just escaping silly names (e.g. Lo-Q to Accesso Technology Group, @UK to Cloudbuy).

Some companies seem to believe that appearing early in an alphabetically-ordered list is important and so have changed their names to a nonsensical word beginning with an a (e.g. CGNU to Aviva, Future Internet Technologies to Artilium).

When companies merge, often the new company name is an awkward amalgam of the old names, but these are usually unwound after a face-saving period of a few years (e.g. BP Amoco to BP, Lloyds TSB Group to Lloyds Banking Group, Granada Compass to Compass Group).

Quite a few companies seem to be trying to jump on the green bandwagon by squeezing an environmentally-friendly word into a new name (e.g. Camco International Ltd to Camco Clean Energy Ltd, 3DM Worldwide to Environmental Recycling Technologies, and Symphony Plastic Technologies to Symphony Environmental Technologies – nice one!).

In some cases one feels the directors must have been bored one afternoon and changed one silly name for another just for the hell of it (e.g. Zenergy Power to Synety Group – wasn't Synety Group one of Simon Cowell's girlfriends?). In other cases, companies went from wacky straight to catatonically boring and instantly forgettable (e.g. e-xentric to Capital Management and Investment).

Sometimes country names can become an awkward appendage and so they have to go (e.g. Centamin Egypt Ltd to Centamin, South African Breweries to SABMiller).

And, finally, there are just the mistakes (e.g. British Airways to International Consolidated Airlines Group, and Paterson Zochonis to PZ Cussons).

Which brings us to Royal Mail, which (briefly) changed its name to…? Anyone?*

* Consignia.

Lightning Source UK Ltd.
Milton Keynes UK
UKOW04n2017221216

290657UK00007B/44/P